A Hudson Valley Reckoning

A HUDSON VALLEY RECKONING

Discovering the Forgotten History of Slaveholding in My Dutch American Family

DEBRA BRUNO

WITH AN AFTERWORD BY ELEANOR C. MIRE

THREE HILLS

AN IMPRINT OF CORNELL UNIVERSITY PRESS

ITHACA AND LONDON

Afterword by Eleanor C. Mire, copyright © 2024 by Cornell University
All rights reserved. Except for brief quotations in a review, this book, or
parts thereof, must not be reproduced in any form without permission in
writing from the publisher. For information, address Cornell University
Press, Sage House, 512 East State Street, Ithaca, New York 14850. Visit
our website at cornellpress.cornell.edu.

First published 2024 by Cornell University Press

Printed in the United States of America

Library of Congress Cataloging-in-Publication Data

Names: Bruno, Debra (Debra Ann), author. | Mire, Eleanor C., writer of
    afterword.
Title: A Hudson Valley reckoning : discovering the forgotten history of
    slaveholding in my Dutch American family / Debra Bruno, with an
    afterword by Eleanor C. Mire.
Description: Ithaca [New York] : Three Hills, an imprint of Cornell
    University Press, 2024. | Includes bibliographical references and index.
Identifiers: LCCN 2024003294 (print) | LCCN 2024003295 (ebook) |
    ISBN 9781501776564 (hardcover) | ISBN 9781501777226 (pdf) |
    ISBN 9781501777233 (epub)
Subjects: LCSH: Enslaved persons—Hudson River Valley (N.Y. and
    N.J.)—History. | Slaveholders—Hudson River Valley (N.Y. and
    N.J.)—History. | Dutch Americans—Hudson River Valley (N.Y. and
    N.J.)—History. | African Americans—Hudson River Valley (N.Y. and
    N.J.)—History. | Coxsackie (N.Y.)—History.
Classification: LCC F118 .B78 2024 (print) | LCC F118 (ebook) |
    DDC 306.3/6209747277—dc23/eng/20240313
LC record available at https://lccn.loc.gov/2024003294
LC ebook record available at https://lccn.loc.gov/2024003295

For Mary Vanderzee, the matriarch,
and Bob, my everything

CONTENTS

Historical Figures

I have tried here to highlight some of the important people in what is a far-reaching network of intermarried families, friendships, and associations. The names in this list are shown in the order of their significance to the story and, if possible, by chronological order. I have tried to keep family members together as well.

Cesar Egberts: the father of Mary Vanderzee, married to Rebecca Dunbar. Formerly enslaved, he bought his freedom in 1817.

Rebecca Dunbar: the mother of Mary Vanderzee. Some records noted she had eleven children.

Mary Vanderzee: (1802–1906) the matriarch of the Vanderzee family, mother to Sarah, Thomas, Cato, Julia Ann, Caesar, and Anthony. Stepmother to Peter, William, and John. She lived to age 105.

John Van Bergen: the first husband of Mary Vanderzee, father of Caesar and Julia Van Bergen. Mary and John Van Bergen married in 1825.

John Vanderzee: the second husband of Mary Vanderzee. With his first wife, Sarah Kniffen, he had Peter, William, and John. With Mary, he had Anthony. Mary's sons Thomas, Cato, and Caesar took the Vanderzee name. He died in 1860.

Sarah Vanderzee: the daughter of Mary Vanderzee, married to Thomas Van Allen.

Thomas Vanderzee: the son of Mary Vanderzee, boatman on the Hudson River and patriarch of the Kingston Vanderzees: Sylvester, Thomas, William Franklin, Sarah Louisa, Charlotte, Ella May, Melissa Jane, Victoria, and Martha.

Cato Vanderzee: the son of Mary Vanderzee, and a Civil War soldier and musician who was at Appomattox to see General Robert E. Lee resign.

Caesar Van Bergen: the son of Mary Vanderzee who changed his name to Caesar Vanderzee.

Julia Ann Van Bergen: the daughter of Mary Vanderzee and wife of Peter Vanderzee. Mother of Anthony and Edward Vanderzee, who died young, and Mary Jane (Janey) Vanderzee.

Peter Vanderzee: son of John Vanderzee, stepson of Mary Vanderzee, married to Julia Ann Van Bergen. A boatman on the Hudson who attended the 1855 Colored Men's Convention, where he heard Frederick Douglass speak.

Mary Jane Vanderzee: daughter of Peter Vanderzee and Julia Van Bergen, granddaughter of Mary Vanderzee. Known as Janey, she never married.

William Vanderzee: stepson of Mary Vanderzee who moved west to Kansas and Nebraska. His son William married Matilda Adams, the niece of Frederick Douglass.

Nancy Jackson: the former slave of Casper Collier who sought legal redress for her daughter Sarah.

Ezra Bronk: The Civil War Colored Troops soldier who is buried in the Black section of the Bronk cemetery. He was at Appomattox with the Eighth USCT.

Storm Vanderzee: My nine times great-grandfather and the origina-
tor of the Vanderzee family name; originally named Bradt, he was
born in a storm on a ship in 1636.

Claus Van Petten: the earliest ancestor I found who enslaved people.

Isaac Collier: my five times great-grandfather, the first ancestor I discovered who bequeathed his enslaved in his 1796 will. My maternal grandmother's maiden name was Collier.

Casper Collier: my four times great-grandfather, the former enslaver
of Nancy Jackson. He was married to Anna Bronk.

Martin Van Bergen: the owner of Van Bergen Overmantel house, who
bequeathed seven slaves to his descendants in his 1770 will. His
daughter Anna Maria married Johannes Schuneman, the Dutch
pastor who collected signatures for the Coxsackie Declaration.

Gerrit Van Bergen: the brother of Martin, also depicted in the Overmantel. He bequeathed ten slaves to his descendants in his 1758 will.
His daughter married David Abeel, whose home was attacked in
1780 by Loyalists and Native Americans.

Peter Van Bergen: the younger brother of Martin and Gerrit, who
moved to Coxsackie. He died in 1778.

Thomas Houghtaling: Brother of Conraedt and Susannah Houghtaling Bronk. He was also the father of Hester Houghtaling, who
married Peter Anthony Van Bergen, grandson of Peter Van Bergen.
He hosted the Scottish doctor Alexander Coventry.

Conraedt Houghtaling: Brother of Thomas and Susannah, and the
slaveholder where Mary Vanderzee spent her earliest years and
had her first children. Also enslaver of Cesar Egberts and Rebecca
Dunbar.

Susannah Houghtaling Bronk: Sister to Thomas and Conraedt,
widow of Jan Bronk, stepmother to Leonard Bronk. She freed her
slaves in her will and gave most of her property to her slaves. She
had no children.

A Note about Dutch Names

Scholars have noted that early Dutch names were not as fixed as today's names, and people could be identified by their country of origin, jobs, or fathers' names. To add to the confusion, many families modified spellings over time, and semiliterate recordkeepers could mangle spellings. Capitalization was also inconsistent, and "Van" and "van" were often interchangeable. Some branches of the Van Valkenburg family used the spelling Van Valkenburgh. Houghtaling could be Hoogteeling, Hoeghtelen, Hogtaling, or Hotaling. Van Bergen could be VanBarGin, Vanbargin, or Vanbargen. Collier could be Colyer, Kallier, or Caljer. Even first names changed over time: Catryntie, Catrina, or Catrine became Catherine; Antje became Anna. I have tried to standardize the spellings as much as possible.

A Hudson Valley Reckoning

Introduction

The Reluctant Archeologist

It's so pretty, my hometown. Old houses line up along streets like friendly spectators shoulder to shoulder at a parade. The village is built on rolling hills leading all the way down to the Hudson River, which flows in a wide band at the village's feet. In the summer, flowers in baskets cascade from telephone poles, alternating with banners showing the boyish faces of hometown veterans, the Dutch and Italian sons who fought for our country in World War II, Korea, Vietnam, and Iraq.

If you drive north from Athens toward Coxsackie on Route 385, you come to an area known as the Flats, where the land opens up to golden fields. On the right, the Hudson River peeks through the trees, choppy with waves some days as the tide's currents push the river north to Albany and south to New York City, and smooth as a mirror on other days, as the wind and tides slow for an hour or two. On the left, the Catskill Mountains shimmer blue-gray in the distance, a sight so romantic and grand it drew a school of painters to the area in the nineteenth century.

That's the bucolic part.

Athens and Coxsackie have their dismal sides too, seedy and insular. Ramshackle houses with peeling paint and plastic flowers in the window boxes sit next to garages that seem to breed junk cars. Homes with weeds sprouting out of the gutters next to sheds covered up with cardboard and plywood—these are the manifestations of year after year of poverty and few good jobs.

In the nineteenth and early twentieth centuries, Italian, Irish, and German immigrants passed through Ellis Island and up the Hudson seeking work. They took dirty, bone-breaking jobs in the brickyards, the icehouses, the trains, the mushroom farms, and the cement plants.

One of the Italian immigrants was my grandfather, Pasquale Bruno, who made his way from Calabria in Italy's south to Athens around 1919 when he was still a teenager. When he married my grandmother, Mary Del Vecchio, the couple moved into a modest house on Franklin Street, where they raised their four boys.

My mother, a slender, raven-haired kindergarten teacher named Arlene Van Valkenburg, married into this family. The Brunos welcomed her unreservedly, even though she was certainly not Italian or Catholic. Even more surprisingly, the Dutch side loved my father with an equal devotion. Orrin and Edna Van Valkenburg never balked at their daughter marrying a Catholic Italian, a boy from the red-sauce side of the village. It helped that Charlie Bruno was both handsome and smart—valedictorian of the Coxsackie-Athens High School Class of 1951, a star athlete with a dazzling smile and a scholarship to Siena College. Athens was a small town then, and it remains small today, with fewer than four thousand people, thirty miles south of the state capitol in Albany and 120 miles north of Manhattan. We were close and a world away.

My parents wasted no time in starting a family, and I was born ten months after their rainy April wedding, followed in the next five years by three more siblings. Life centered on two immovable forces: the church and food. Both of them were Italian-centric.

Every Sunday began with Mass at Saint Patrick's Catholic Church, and every Sunday Uncle Frank Del Vecchio bellowed out the hymns two beats behind the rest of the congregation. After picking up the *New York Daily News* at the tiny grocery, our family headed to Nana and Pop pop's house, where a long table would fit a dozen or more Brunos, and we'd eat the cavatelli, meatballs, and eggplant that Nana had been cooking all week.

Nana's kitchen smelled like ripe green peppers and the fennel seeds she mixed into her sausage. Christmas and Easter were expanded, joyous versions of that weekly Sunday meal: feasts of ravioli filled with cheese and meat, sausage and peppers, braciole, bowls of extra sauce, fresh bread.

I always felt sorry for everyone else, stuck with turkey or ham on Christmas and Easter.

Holidays like Thanksgiving—the patriotic celebrations—belonged to my Dutch family. We descend from Lambert Van Valkenburg, who emigrated to New Netherland in 1644 and first settled in New Amsterdam, today's Manhattan.[1] Lambert was restless, so he sold his fifty acres of land, his first property in the New World, to an ancestor of the Roosevelts. His Manhattan property included the blocks where the Empire State Building sits today. Lambert decamped to Fort Orange, what is today Albany. For years, that was my rather tone-deaf cocktail party line: my eight times great-grandfather had made the worst land deal after the Native Americans supposedly sold Manhattan to Peter Minuit.

My knowledge stopped about there. It was enough for me to think of my Dutch ancestors as farmers, country people who talked about backhoes and berry bushes, lemon meringue pie and games of bridge. Every Sunday while we were at Saint Patrick's, my mother and grandmother would sit in the seventh row of the First Reformed Church in Athens, established in 1825 and situated on a hill overlooking the village.

Like many kids, I grew up barely conscious of this heritage. Kids live the life that is before them. My world was playing hopscotch on slate sidewalks and walking home from school by myself. It was the smell of pine needles underfoot and hot dogs on charcoal grills at Lake Taghkanic. What mattered to me was watching Tom and Jerry on Saturday mornings, seeing how long I could hold my breath underwater at the Athens pool, and, later, comparing baby-oil tans with my friends by placing our arms side by side.

If I thought about my family history at all, it was with pride that I was practically a symbol of all that is uniquely American. Think of it: My ancestry represents the great melting pot, a mixture of old families and just-off-the-boat immigrants.

But as I got older, I started to wonder more about the Dutch. My family has lived in the Hudson Valley since the 1600s, and my history is intricately intertwined with people who have known me, my parents, my grandparents, my great-grandparents, and their cousins and best friends and classmates practically forever. Of course, I realized that if my Dutch family had been in this country for so long—for longer than it's been a country, after all—there must be something interesting. Maybe a connection to a president, say, Martin Van Buren or one of the Roosevelts. Maybe some digging would get me a membership in the Daughters of the American Revolution and my pedigree would mean I'd suddenly be belting "God Bless America" like Kate Smith. Like many people, I tucked the idea of genealogy research into a list for the days when I was retired or recovering from a hip replacement.

Then a historian friend got my attention. "If you have Dutch ancestors in the Hudson Valley, they were probably slave owners," she told me.

Slavery in the North? This was news to me. My first reaction was defensive. Not my family, I said. "You have to understand—they were poor farmers. They couldn't afford slaves." I was imagining the enormous plantations of the South, hundreds of people forced to work in cotton fields.

"Keep looking," she said.

I had been picturing an ancestor in the fife and drum corps or maybe even a Civil War officer fighting for the Union army. Then I got different visuals. And they weren't so good. It would have been easy to shrug and get on with my life. In fact, not long after that conversation, I did execute a successful delaying tactic by moving with my journalist husband to Beijing for three years. There, I prowled the ancient city's hutongs and learned how to row a dragon boat. Genealogical work would have to wait a bit longer.

Maybe the truth is that I didn't want to know. After we came home from China, I managed to find enough freelance writing, busy work that meant I always felt just a little too distracted to dig into genealogy. The thought nagged at me enough, though, that after a few years of writing about law firms and drum circles and Portuguese egg tarts, I broke down and paid for a subscription to Ancestry, the site where amateur genealogists can find digital records of tombstones, newspaper articles, census reports, photographs, and last wills and testaments.

It was almost too easy.

I started with the Van Valkenburgs and stuck to my mother's patrilineal line. Orrin to Omar to Amasa to Jacob to Lambert to Jacobus to Lambert to Jacobus, and, well, you get the idea. Nothing much stood out. In fact, my branch of Van Valkenburgs seemed to be populated with subsistence farmers, hardly able to feed their growing families high up in the Catskill Mountains, often dying young. Rip Van Winkle without the homespun charm.

Then I shifted to the Colliers, as my grandmother was born Edna Elizabeth Collier. The spelling of the name shifted over the centuries, from Kalior to Kalyer to Calyer to Collier, and historians debated whether the family had originated in the regions that today are Sweden or Germany or the Netherlands. One, two, three, four, five generations I went back, looking at census records, baptisms, marriages, last wills and testaments.

Finally, I found a will from 1796. Isaac Collier,[2] my five times great-grandfather, must have known that at seventy he was nearing the end of his life. Maybe he was sick. He had eight surviving children plus grandchildren scattered around Coxsackie, and he wanted to make sure they were cared for. His wife, Sara Van Vechten Collier, had died seven years earlier.

Figure 1. The opening pages of the 1796 will of Isaac Collier, my five-times great-grandfather, in which he bequeathed his slaves to his children and grandchildren. Photo courtesy Ancestry.com.

He wasn't sick enough to shrink from writing a will that left nothing to chance: he distributed land, horses, feather beds, and wagons to his sons, daughters, and various grandchildren. Isaac was careful to delineate where his property lines went and who got the farm implements. He was also, like so many of those early Dutch, focused on the divine: "whenever it shall please the Almighty to take me to him," he wrote.

I scrolled through the pages, enlarging the whispery writing, preserved on the computer screen. The will goes on for four pages and more than seventeen hundred words. Then I froze. I blinked. I enlarged the writing even more.

There it was. Shit. Detailed like inventory along with his property lines and cows were slaves.

In a matter-of-fact way he distributed a male named Sansom to his daughter Hannah, a boy named Will to his son Joel, and a "negro wench" named Marie to his granddaughter Christinetie Spoor. "The remains of my negro slaves male and female," he wrote with an insouciance that made me shudder, should be "equally divided, share and share alike."

I found Isaac Collier's name on the first federal census, six years earlier.[3] There, he listed five enslaved people. It's possible he acquired a few more in the waning years of his life. It's also wrenching that he would take such care with each acre, each horse, and each wagon, and yet lump the "remains" of his slaves to be divided in whatever way his heirs wanted.

There's something else about that moment that hit me in a second gut punch. This all happened right under my feet. This quiet drama took place on the land where I was born, learned to walk, learned to drive, and was married. My ancestors and the people they enslaved cultivated the very earth where I played jacks, kissed my first boy, and sang my high school anthem. It was in my blood and on my land.

I didn't stop with Isaac Collier. The more I looked, the more enslavers I found. Isaac Collier, after all, is only one of 128 five times great-grandparents I or anyone else have. Even if you deduct the Italians who mostly stayed in Italy, that's still sixty-four Dutch in the Hudson Valley, mixed in with the Huguenots from a bit farther south along the river. While it was harder to find records of enslavement in the seventeenth century, I found that in the eighteenth century, nearly every one of them was an enslaver, registered with a check mark on the far edge of the 1790 census, our new country's first official count. Ironically, a massive fire in 1911 at

Albany's New York State Capitol, which held its library, charred the records for much of the 1790 census. Many of the pages have a jagged black edge, as if the measure of sin created a hell-like combustion. In more than one census page, the column for slaves at the very edge was burned off.

Even with the lost edges, I kept finding Dutch names: Hallenbeck, Vandenburg, Van Loon, Houghtaling, Bronk. All of them listed the enslaved as property in their wills. I also found them in the 1800 census. In the 1810 census. As the tree fanned out, I was a reluctant archeologist, turning over rock after rock, finding something rotten and ugly beneath, and feeling both compelled and anxious about digging further.

I became obsessed. I spent hours online, falling down the rabbit hole of research. I wanted to know—but I also felt queasy each time I'd murmur to myself, "Here's another one" when I clicked on a digital will or found a census record. I couldn't stop talking about it, couldn't stop slipping this disturbing little fact into the repartee at dinner parties and casual sidewalk conversations.

Did you know northerners embraced slavery for almost two hundred years? I would ask. Did you know that the Dutch were a big part of slavery in the Hudson Valley? Can I tell you about my family? My need to tell people was starting to have the haunted tone of the Ancient Mariner or a Catholic at confession.

The truth is that few people I encountered knew the story of New York slavery. Not everyone wanted to hear it, either. "That's the past, and we should live in the present," people said. "It's like the Confederate monuments—it's history."

"At least New York ended slavery without a war," my husband said. Duly noted.

Some family members made jokes. "Does this mean we have to give out reparations?" one asked. Friends asked if slavery in the North was as brutal as slavery in the South.

Before this moment, I thought of New York as the home of abolitionists like John Brown and Lucretia Mott. I remembered hearing that the old homes in Athens held hiding places for the Underground Railroad. I thought we were the good guys.

I was beginning to realize, though, that the true history and the imagined narrative are very different. Even though my towns today are very rural and mostly white, there were more than a few Black people in

Athens, Coxsackie, and Catskill three hundred years ago. They were the slaves who lived in the cellars and attics and lean-tos propped up against their owners' homes.

At the same time, I had to confront what this new knowledge meant for me. I had to understand why it seemed to me that this truth was obscured or tucked behind a curtain like a ghost. I could find out, without much effort, that the same Isaac Collier who wrote his will had also signed an early revolutionary document called the Coxsackie Declaration.[4] I knew that Isaac's son, Casper Collier, served in the War of 1812.[5]

But what about Will and Marie and Sansom? On the first census, they were check marks. There was a glimpse of lives in the first names of the "wenches" and "Negro boys" bequeathed in wills. Other than that, I didn't know what happened to them, who was their family, or what became of their children. I wanted to find out.

I found a group that seemed to be thinking about descendants. Coming to the Table is an organization inspired by these lines from Dr. Martin Luther King Jr.'s 1963 speech: "I have a dream that one day on the red hills of Georgia the sons of former slaves and the sons of former slave owners will be able to sit together at the table of brotherhood." The Coming to the Table website shows a kumbaya-like multiracial group of people standing in a circle, holding hands. Maybe, I thought, I can find other people who are grappling with this ancestral burden.

I went to a meeting of Coming to the Table in Rockville, Maryland. The members turned out to be a welcoming collection of passionately earnest people, all wanting to talk about racism, social justice, reparations, and how to make the world a better place. Each person passed a Native American talking stick to the next one when it was that person's turn to speak. Our task was to ask ourselves whether any of our actions were racist. The whole thing made me squirm, which I'm sure was the point. Sure, I could be more openly anti-racist. But I wanted to ask a question about their motivations for joining the group: how many were descendants of enslavers or enslaved people? The Black members were, but no white person there that day had a direct family line to enslavers the way I had. I was disappointed. The vision of CTTT, in its own words, is to create "a just and truthful society that acknowledges and seeks to heal from the racial wounds of the past, from slavery and the many forms of racism it spawned."[6]

I'm all for healing. But first, I needed to find out just what part of my own history is founded in these racial wounds. We can't heal until we examine the wounds. And we can't examine the wounds without opening them to the light.

Cathy Roberts, at the time a cofacilitator of the local chapter, told me about another group that might be a better fit. "I've Traced My Enslaved Ancestors and Their Owners" is a Facebook community with a cumbersome name and strict rules prohibiting debates on racial justice or current issues. It's a group about "genealogy and having fun," the site proclaims, and everyone is welcome—if they follow those rules and stick to the genealogy. The organizers worried that if the online conversation drifted from that topic, its purpose would change.

With more than sixteen thousand members, "I've Traced" hosts a lively conversation among people looking for ancestors, sharing names and stories, and building on snippets of data: death certificates, emancipation records, and DNA tests that link them with extended family and sometimes their white enslavers. Most of the chatter involves the South, with members able to track plantation ledgers going back to the nineteenth century, but rarely before that. Falling into the second category of genealogists—the "owners"—I realized that I needed to tread carefully. But I also needed to see who was out there. I thought there could be an article in it.

I took a chance—any northerners here? "Hello all, thank you for adding me to this group," I wrote. "I'm interested in northern slavery, particularly upstate New York, where my Dutch ancestors enslaved people. I'm a journalist working on a story about this and would love to chat with any people who know they descend from enslaved people in the Hudson Valley or Albany, New York area."

Within twenty-four hours, a text popped up. "I have ancestors who were enslaved in Coxsackie/New Baltimore," wrote a woman named Eleanor Mire.

I took a deep breath. I hadn't mentioned a specific town, but she had pinpointed my home turf. Eleanor wrote, "My [great-great-great-]grandmother Mary Vanderzee . . . was enslaved by the Houghtalings in Coxsackie. She apparently had her first child at approximately 13 years old, while enslaved, and 3 more within the next few years until she was manumitted under the law of emancipation." The wife of her cousin had been fascinated by their family history and had spent years digging into records to find these details. She had passed dozens of pages on to Eleanor, a woman who loved history, especially history that involved her own family.

I'm one of those people who believe that some important moments fall into your lap at the perfect time like a gift. This was one of those moments. Eleanor had no idea who I was. But I realized immediately that we were connected in degrees far deeper than the simple geography of two people sharing a history through these few small villages on the shore of the Hudson.

I immediately jumped at the name Houghtaling. I have Houghtalings in my family tree. My tree branches out from Catrina Houghtaling (born in 1680), the daughter of Mattias Houghtaling, one of the first Coxsackie settlers.[7] That means my ancestors enslaved hers.

There was something else, too. Eleanor's great-great-grandfather, Thomas Vanderzee, was probably the result of a union between a teen-aged Mary and a white man. It could have been someone in the Houghtaling family. Mary Vanderzee gave birth to three (and maybe four) children when she was still a child herself. Eleanor's DNA results link her to Houghtaling names, and, in the words of Eleanor's grandmother, Thomas had "blond hair and blue eyes."

Eleanor and I are "linked descendants," people whose history goes back through both blood and ownership. After we connected, Eleanor and I spent weeks messaging back and forth online. I had found someone else who cared as much as I did about slavery in the Hudson Valley, especially the kind that tied our families together in a permanent link. In the beginning of my research, I wasn't sure where the investigation would lead us, but I knew we were both willing to try to figure it out.

1

FIFTY BEAVER SKINS

I wonder if they had any idea what they were getting into.

The thirty-eight passengers on the *Rensselaerswyck* were far from the first settlers to venture from the Netherlands to the Americas in the fall of 1636.[1] By then, fifty-two ships, many of them owned by the Dutch West India Company, had already made it to New Amsterdam.

Ship number 53 set off from Holland in September. But stormy weather kept the *Rensselaerswyck* from traveling far, and the ship lingered for months off the coast of Europe, once ending up off course and drifting for seventeen days along the coastline of Spain. It was during those seasick, choppy months that a baby was born to Albert Andriessen Bradt and Annetje Barents. The couple decided to give the infant a first name befitting his birth: Storm.

The months of tedious inaction were hard on everyone. As the *Rensselaerswyck* waited out the bad weather, the ship's hands killed time on shore. Then came the almost inevitable, a moment probably fueled by alcohol, irritation, and gloomy skies: the ship's blacksmith, Cornelis

Thomasz, and his assistant, Hans van Sevenhuysen, got into a fight as they were drinking in a bar in England's harbor city of Ilfracombe. Van Sevenhuysen stabbed his boss to death and was thrown in an English jail.

Three months after it had tried to begin that voyage across the churning Atlantic—with one birth, one death, and one incarceration—the *Rensselaerswyck* finally set sail for the New World on January 9, 1637. It took the ship another two months to cross the ocean, enough time for two more babies to be born. The ship had evaded pirates and pushed through many days of fierce storms with mountain-sized waves threatening to topple the vessel, alternating with quiet weeks in which the wind refused to push them along. Finally, the *Rensselaerswyck* landed in New Amsterdam on March 4. Even then, the journey wasn't over. The ship was stuck at the mouth of the Hudson yet another month, waiting for the thick river ice to break up.

Once the ice cleared, it took another twelve days for the ship to sail the 140 miles up the Hudson. It briefly stopped opposite Coxsackie, which was when another of my ancestors, Martin Gerritson Van Bergen, hopped a ride north. Finally, on April 7, the ship landed at its destination: the colonial estate of Rensselaerswyck, today's Albany. That's where Albert, Annetje, two other children who had made the trip with their parents, and baby Storm disembarked.

The passengers had been biding their time on this leaky vessel with primitive toilets, probably wearing the clothing they set out in, eating hardtack, moldy bread, and pickled goat meat for more than six months. Their nerves must have been raw from the mixture of tedium and terror, not to mention the sound of the wails of three crying newborns on a small vessel.

For many of these earliest settlers, that long journey paid off. They would go on to establish themselves in this frontier world, becoming the wealthy landowners of New Netherland and—if they lived long enough—setting themselves up for generations of prosperity.

Baby Storm, a new child for a new world, was the perfect symbol of their moxie. The settlers adopted family names, eventually abandoning the ancient practice of taking patronymic names based on one's father. In the old form, Albert Andriessen's name would mean he was Albert, son of Andries. In the New World, the Dutch families often took family names from their hometowns: Van Valkenburgh was a man from the town of Valkenburgh, for instance. But Storm seemed to have decided he would fashion a completely new family name for himself, something to fit his first name. The baby who was born on the *Rensselaerswyck* became Storm Vanderzee. *Vanderzee*—Dutch for "from the sea."

How romantic, how evocative. I loved the story when I first came across it in my reading, even more so when I worked out that Storm Vanderzee was my ninth great-grandfather. Storm's father, Albert Bradt, was my tenth great-grandfather. After I met Eleanor, I realized that we had yet another thread of connection, and that this made-up name of Vanderzee was even more resonant for her family. I wouldn't realize until later what that all meant.

Storm and the rest of the colonists would need his brand of moxie for this land of extremes, with winters more bitter and summers more scorching than the moderate European climate they knew. The place might have been called New Netherland, but it was a brighter, harsher version of the cultivated and mannered land the Dutch settlers left behind. Yes, the earth was fertile, but New Netherland was also filled with hungry wolves, often impenetrable forests, and Algonquian and Iroquois people who, with good reason, didn't always appreciate the interlopers. Those who ventured past the clusters of houses set up inside stockades for the fur trade were risking attacks, bitter winters, and starvation. On the far western front of Schenectady, the homes were simple huts, built of pine boards filled in with straw thatching. Only the homes' stone chimneys were sealed with masonry.[2]

It's easy to see why not every European settler wanted to linger. Many saw New Netherland as a place where they could make a quick fortune in beaver pelts, peddling those water-repellent, thick furs that Europeans made into hats, coats, and muffs, and then returning to Amsterdam as prosperous men. Beavers, which had been trapped to near extinction in Europe, were abundant in the streams and forests of New Netherland. The pelts were so common—and coinage so rare—that beaver served as the currency of the time. The New Netherland settlers wasted no time trapping as many beavers as they could as well as buying them from the Mohawk tribesmen nearby. In one peak period between June and September 1657, Beverwyck (or "beaver district," of course), a fur-trading settlement, had shipped thirty-seven thousand beaver pelts down the river to New Amsterdam.[3]

For the farmers, fur trappers, and traders who did choose to stay, another problem added to their travails: too few people. There wasn't enough manpower to farm the farms, build the forts, and work the boats that shipped the beaver pelts out. Importing servants from Europe had only limited success. Life in the Old World for many was comfortable enough. Risking a cross-Atlantic voyage to the unknowns of a new world was a huge risk—unless you had nothing to lose. The young men who were willing to take that risk tended to be orphans, later-born children of families with too many mouths to feed, or those who imagined a fur-based fortune.

The Dutch West India Company, established by merchants and investors to trade from Africa to the Americas, ran New Netherland as a crucial arm of its trade empire. It came up with a deal. The youngsters would serve as indentured servants for four to seven years, to pay off the cost of their transport, and then be free to do what they wanted.

That strategy only worked up to a point. The young servants who were convinced to come, many of them barely past childhood, were dying. Harsh work conditions, scurvy, yellow fever, dysentery, and infection meant that the death rate for indentured servants was high even for the seventeenth century, and many died before they could serve out their indenture. The young men also soon realized that they could run off from their servitude and do better for themselves in this land of possibility. Others jumped on a ship back to the known world as soon as they could.

One orphan who stuck it out was an ancestor of mine. In 1655 sixteen-year-old Mathys Coenratsen Houghtaling—my eight times great-grandfather—left an almshouse in Amsterdam to take his chance in New Netherland. Houghtaling lived up and down the Hudson Valley and eventually bought a plot of land from the Mohawk Indians in a place called Kockxhachkingh, today's Coxsackie. He survived into his sixties and fathered six children. This orphan from Holland built a legacy that to this day shows up in my hometown on road names, farmhouses, and old maps, and in descendants named Houghtaling. He also left an imprint of slavery, an influence that was far harder to detect on the landscape of the Hudson Valley in the twenty-first century. But even servants like Mathys Houghtaling didn't do enough to fill in the labor gaps. If New Netherland was going to survive, it needed more people than the almshouses of the European lowlands could supply.

This is where Petrus Stuyvesant came in. Born in Friesland around 1610, Stuyvesant found work with the Dutch West India Company rather than follow his father's calling as a minister. He was a colorful character: after a Caribbean battle when he was hit by a cannonball and lost his leg to an infection, he spent the rest of his life hobbling (almost certainly painfully) on a wooden prosthesis. It didn't help his mood: he was known as stubborn and tyrannical.

Stuyvesant spent much of his early adult years running the affairs of the Caribbean island of Curaçao. By 1643 the planters on Curaçao had realized that the island was too arid to grow much tobacco or sugar cane.[4] But help was needed to harvest the valuable salt in salt flats, and other nearby islands were having better luck with their sugar cane production. Harvesting and milling of sugar cane was a labor-intensive, brutal process. The indigenous population—the Arawak—had already been slaughtered or deported as slaves to other islands. The planters soon realized that the most direct way to procure labor was to capture and enslave people from Africa and bring them to the West Indies, and replace them with new slaves when they died.

In the 1600s starvation was a constant danger. With almost no arable land and a growing population of slaves waiting, often for months, in warehouses near the port to be shipped elsewhere in the Caribbean, food often had to be imported.[5] Whites were given first dibs at whatever meager sustenance was brought to the island, and the enslaved—already weakened by their Middle Passage transport—were last in line.

In 1643 Stuyvesant wrote to the managers of the West India Company that they were running low on provisions, even if they gave their Blacks only "flour, beans and fish."[6] The goal, planters admitted, was to give their enslaved enough to eat so that they would have the strength to work, but not so much that the whites would be forced to sacrifice their own well-being. Diseased horses and cattle, sea turtles, corn, and plantains made up the diet of the enslaved. In addition, most enslaved wore very little clothing: loincloths for the men, simple smocks for the women, and not a stitch of clothing for the children until they hit puberty, if they lived that long. Few slaves had shoes or hats.

Stuyvesant, meanwhile, was finding that looming starvation was just one problem for the white colonizers. Ever present was the hint of insurrection or escape. He reported to his bosses in 1643 that some slaves were found building a raft on the east side of Curaçao when no one was watching. Whatever the slaves were up to, it was clearly not designed to add to the bottom line. Maybe they were thinking of a shot at freedom: the island is only about forty miles from the coast of South America, where they might have had a better chance of escaping into the wilderness. Stuyvesant decided to be both generous—at least in his estimation—and practical: he wouldn't order the slaves' execution, "which they well deserved," he wrote. It would be "most profitable for the Company, after whipping them severely, to send them off to St. Cruis [today's Saint Croix in the Virgin Islands] or other Caribbean islands to be traded for provisions."[7]

Matthias Beck, who later took over Curaçao for Stuyvesant, was also filled with complaints about his responsibilities for these enslaved workers. In 1657 he wrote that one shipment of moldy beans and peas were in "such a state that they are more suitable to be fed to beasts than humans; I dared not give them to the Negroes for fear of causing a sickness among them."[8] Beck was also annoyed because he was dealing with some slaves who could not work and yet had the audacity to want to eat as much as those who toiled in the fields.

In 1647 Stuyvesant had moved on to become director-general of New Netherland. It was there that he realized a solution to the northern colony's labor shortage: a trade deal between Curaçao and New Netherland. In return for sending necessities like lumber and food to the Caribbean, New Netherland would receive enslaved workers to help build up the northern workforce, from New Amsterdam at the mouth of the river to Beverwyck, today's Albany, and the farms and mills along the river in between.

To make that happen, Stuyvesant had to smooth the process on his end. The settlers had no qualms about buying enslaved Africans. But they did encounter a more practical obstacle: capital. Slaves were an expensive investment. In 1661 Stuyvesant decreed that the northerners could buy slaves with whatever provisions they had on hand: meat, grain, peas, tobacco. They could also pay on an installment plan, which was useful because few Dutch had enough of any ready commodity to pay the price of a human being.

At first the Caribbean planters were less than thrilled with the idea of sending off their valuable free labor, even with all the problems they caused. Their solution was to ship people who were too old or sick to be of much use in the West Indies. Stuyvesant complained in 1664 that of the three hundred slaves sent north on the slave ship *Gideon*, eighty-nine were over the age of thirty-six—the cusp of old age at a time when the enslaved, especially in the Caribbean, were underfed, overworked, and abused.[9]

Sometimes the Caribbean administrators would hold slaves back because there wasn't enough warm clothing; these enslaved Africans would freeze to death on the weeks-long ship journey or once they landed in the frigid North. As he sent two slave boys and a girl north, Beck wrote, "We outfitted them as much as possible against the cold."[10] The New Netherlanders would have to wait for more enslaved until there was warmer clothing.

The numbers of slaves brought to New Netherland was accordingly small at first. A dozen here, a couple hundred there—records cannot pinpoint the precise number. But even though the early traffic in human property was limited, especially in comparison to later numbers, the introduction of slavery in New Netherland had begun. This moment signals a turning point for the North: a northern colony that accepted the ownership of other humans had planted a seed and set it on a path that wouldn't alter for another two hundred years.

By the time that Stuyvesant was expanding his slave-import system, England surrounded New Amsterdam with four warships and took control of the colony. The Netherlands' fifty-year reign over this new territory ended. A change of government didn't mean much initially when the English began ruling in 1664. As the colony became anglicized, Dutch place-names died out: New Amsterdam became New York City, Beverwyck became Albany, and the North River turned into the Hudson. Of course many other Dutch names did linger, especially Stuyvesant. New York today has Stuyvesant Town, Street, Square, and High School in Manhattan, Bedford-Stuyvesant in Brooklyn, Stuyvesant Place on Staten Island, and Stuyvesant as well as Stuyvesant Falls in the Hudson Valley.

As for attitudes toward slavery, not only were the colony's slave owners allowed to keep their slaves, but the English also instituted a system of slavery that was far more restrictive, formalized, and race-based than slavery under the Dutch. In the first five volumes of the *Laws of the Colony of New York*, at least thirty-three laws governed all aspects of slavery, from what kind of punishment was doled out to a slave who struck a Christian, to how much a slaveholder was personally responsible for wrongdoing by his slave.[11] The iron hand was just fine for the conservative Dutch farmers along the Hudson. More and more colonists bought slaves and increased their wealth with all that free labor.

This is where we find a Dutch immigrant named Claes Van Petten. The nineteen-year-old had arrived in the colony around 1664, just as the English became rulers of the land, and almost immediately leased a farm in Schenectady, along with six horses, ten cows, and eight pigs, plus enough acreage to farm wheat, oats, and peas.[12] He also dabbled in shipping wheat on a schooner down the Hudson.

By the age of twenty-seven, he could afford to pay 330 beaver pelts to buy his own farm with a partner, a swampy estate called Papscanee along the Hudson River south of Albany. A few years after that, he married into one of the biggest established families in the region: the Bradts, descendants of the two brothers and their wives who were passengers on the *Rensselaerswyck*, the 1636 boat. His new wife, Aeffie Arentse Bradt, born after her father Arent landed in New Netherland, was Storm Vanderzee's first cousin.

Next, he needed labor to work his farm. On May 27, 1682, Van Petten bought "a certain negro called Jan" from another farmer for fifty beaver pelts.[13] The deal allowed him a gradual payment plan much like the one Stuyvesant had instituted twenty years earlier: if he couldn't procure enough beavers, he would make up the difference with winter wheat or peas, his bill of sale noted. It would take Van Petten the next few years to pay for Jan. Van Petten must have been making himself into a big man around the stockade at this point. His name showed up in court documents: serving on a jury in cases brought before the regional council or finding himself the occasional defendant when his farm's fencing didn't keep the animals in where they belonged. His farmland today is the Papscanee Island Nature Preserve, recently given back to the Stockbridge-Munsee Native American tribe that originally lived on the land.[14] It's thirty miles north of Athens, my hometown.

Van Petten was my eight times great-grandfather. He was also the earliest ancestor I could find on record buying a slave. And, like so many of my ancestors, my family-tree connections link me with him in more ways than one. His wife Aeffie Arentse Bradt, Storm's cousin, was the daughter of Arent Bradt, also my nine times great-grandfather and the other brother who had arrived on that ship in 1637.

I dug deeper, reading through *Minutes of the Court of Fort Orange and Beverwyck* from 1657 to 1660, and then *Minutes of the Court of Albany, Rensselaerswyck and Schenectady* from 1668 up to 1685.[15] I found a tally of the names of all the settlers of Rensselaerswyck from 1630 to 1658. It listed the jobs of those *Rensselaerswyck* boat passengers: tobacco planters, shoemakers, farmhands, roof thatchers, carpenters, brewers, and hog dealers.[16]

With a quick search of wills on sites like Ancestry, I could find, without much trouble, that generation after generation of Van Pettens and Vanderzees bequeathed their enslaved to their descendants. I wondered about the families closer to where I grew up, so I started looking into more of the names in my family tree: Cathlyntje Van Petten, Claes and Aeffie's daughter, married Teunis Dirckse Van Vechten, the scion of a large, slave-owning family in Catskill. The Bronck family was busy settling Coxsackie. Pieter Bronck built his first stone house on his new land in 1663. In nearby Loonenburg, today's Athens, Jan Van Loon was setting up his estate. They all owned slaves. And they too were all my kin.

As I spent more time reading into these histories, I saw, again and again, that the chronicles of births and baptisms and marriages and deaths, the participation in the American Revolution, the War of 1812, the establishment of this country, dodged a topic that was beginning to loom large in my mind: What happened to their enslaved? Did Jan, the enslaved man bought by Claes Van Petten, ever take a family name? Or did he live and die as Jan? I wondered how I could even begin to find this man with a common Dutch first name and no given family name.

I found a partial answer to that question, in a labyrinthine story of theft in 1679.[17] Barent, an enslaved man owned by Gideon Schaets, a dominie, or minister, of the Dutch Reformed Church in Albany, and an enslaved man named Claes Croes, owned by Gert Banker, were hauled before the Court of Albany, Rensselaerville, and Schenectady. The two men had been found with money, a silver thimble, and some pieces of broken silver. They blamed it all on another enslaved man named Jacob, owned by Sweer Teunissen Van Velsen, who had bought Jacob for 100 beaver pelts just a year earlier.

Jacob, however, was nowhere to be found. The other two men gave a series of muddled, changing answers: they found the treasure on the street, they said that Jacob told them the money was a gift from an unknown maid. Finally, they admitted that Jacob had asked them to help him find a way to make the silver into buttons for their breeches.

Over the next few days of the trial, one thing became clear. The men, the court said, had "greatly departed from the truth." A jury of twelve men found the two guilty of theft and sentenced them both to be whipped. Taken the next day to the whipping post, Claes got twenty lashes on his bare back from the public executioner. Barent received thirty and an even harsher sanction: "to be branded on his right cheek as an example to other rogues." Gideon Schaets, Barent's enslaver, asked the court if Barent could be branded on his back instead of his cheek. Maybe the Dutch Reformed minister wanted to appear more merciful, or maybe he wanted to avoid the embarrassment of owning a slave who had been branded as a thief for everyone to see.

The court also tried a white woman named Maritie Daeme, whom the slaves had asked to help make the silver into buttons. Daeme was found guilty too, but her punishment was just a fine of 100 guilders plus the costs of the trial. A month later, Jacob turned up in New York City, where he was taken into custody and hauled back to the court at Albany. His owner, Van Velsen, asked the court "to punish him as speedily as possible in order that he may have him home, as he needs him very much." Clearly, Van Velsen was imagining that Jacob would not be so incapacitated by his whipping that he would be unable to help harvest the wheat.

But Jacob was in bigger trouble than his friends. Not only did he run off, but he also stole a horse to help him get farther in his escape. Jacob told the court he ran away out of fear. Finally, he admitted he stole the horse too. Jacob's sentence was thirty-eight lashes on his bare back.

These are the kinds of punishments that can kill a man. And while it's true that the enslaved faced harsher discipline than other members of the community, seventeenth-century standards were already severe by any modern sense of what is cruel and unusual: fines, whippings, being held in a pillory, and being banished were part of the normal system for every member of a community. Anyone could be punished for engaging in unauthorized trade with the Native population, for telling lies about their neighbors, for violating the Sabbath by shouting, chopping wood, or drinking in a pub, and especially for adultery.

At the same time, most people operated under a frontier mindset. What escaped notice often also escaped punishment. Just as the indentured

Dutch from the orphanages of Amsterdam often took to their heels once they found themselves in the North American wilderness, these earliest enslaved Africans pushed as many boundaries as they thought they could, by pilfering small items, wandering to visit friends or family, or taking an extra day or two on a holiday.

Even though the stakes were higher for the enslaved, fear of punishment didn't stop Jacob, Claes, and Barent from imagining they could walk around town sporting breeches adorned with silver buttons. Maybe, I thought, well-dressed enslaved men were proof that the enslaved in this early society lived a more nuanced, intimate version of enslavement. Maybe they had more control over their destinies than I imagined. For much of the seventeenth century, when the colony was still New Netherland, even the basic facts of enslavement as Americans understand it were different: the enslaved could sometimes earn enough money to buy their freedom, they could negotiate levels of independence that might only demand that they return from time to time to work for their former enslavers, they occasionally married in the Dutch Reformed Church, and sometimes they carried weapons to protect the communities from attacks by Native tribes. Some enslaved even were given the chance to find themselves a new owner when they were at odds with the previous one. In most cases they lived within the homes of their enslavers, which implies a level of intimacy, even if the enslaved lived in the dank cellars or tiny attics of those homes.

As I continued my research, I began to develop an image of that more moderate, negotiable slavery. Maybe for Claes Van Petten, the purchase of Jan was simply a matter of practicality, just another bookkeeping mark in his ledger. Plough—check. Milk cow—check. Enslaved man—check. Maybe Claes treated Jan more like an indentured servant than, say, a head of cattle, and maybe Jan got the chance to negotiate his living conditions with the family who owned him.

But I kept looking, and I started to find more proof that seventeenth-century New Netherland enslaved workers were not just farmhands who might have a cup of warm cider around their owners' winter fireplace. Wrongdoing, whether it was theft, arson, escape, or telling lies about their whereabouts, could land a slave in jail, bring him dozens of whippings, or a earn him a branding. One of the most severe—and insulting—sentences for whites who broke the law was to be attached to a chain gang of the enslaved and forced to work alongside them. For the worst crimes, the enslaved got the most inhumane measures: being hung, drawn and quartered, or burned at the stake. Arson meant almost certain and cruel death. For example, in 1685 Cuffy, a man owned by a large slaveholder named Lewis Morris, was executed for arson.[18] His body was buried and then, for good measure, dug up and hung in chains as an example to others.

Even the stories that seemed to have nothing to do with slavery turned out to expose a harsh reality. As the burgeoning communities vied for control of the beaver business, tensions grew between the British and the French, who were allied with many of the Mohawk and Algonquian tribes. By 1690 the Native tribes, the French, and the colonists in Schenectady were in a state of near war, which came to a climax on the frigid evening of February 8. Some stories of the night said that only two snowmen guarded the open gates of the Schenectady stockade. French, Mohawk, and Algonquian fighters walked through one gate, slaughtering sixty people, including eleven enslaved, and taking twenty-seven men and boys hostage, whites and enslaved. More than sixty houses were burned.

As the attackers set fires from house to house and men, women, and children ran out of their burning houses in their nightclothes, most were scalped and killed on the spot. Babies were dashed against walls. More than a foot of snow fell that night, so those who survived the massacre and were taken hostage risked dying of exposure on the trek back north to Canada. Two of Aeffie Bradt Van Petten's siblings—Andries Bradt and Cornelia Bradt Putnam—were murdered. Cornelia was scalped. Another was a son of Gideon Schaets, the minister whose enslaved man had been caught up in the trial for theft.

Also killed was Sweer Teunise Van Velsen, the man whose enslaved man, Jacob, got thirty-eight lashes for stealing silver. Van Velsen, his wife, and his four unnamed slaves show up on the list of those who were killed that night. If Jacob was still enslaved by Van Velsen eleven years after that trial, this is a bitter end for the man who pictured himself sporting those silver breech buttons. As I read through the list of those killed, I saw that almost all the enslaved were identified not by name but by owner. Even in death, their story was hidden behind the veil of slavery. The lives of murdered slaves were further erased, further removed from history's ledger. The Schenectady massacre of 1690, which seemed at first to have almost nothing to do with slavery as the brutality of frontier life spread its cruelty equally among free and enslaved, turned out to employ double standards even there.[19]

One man did escape the slaughter. According to a story passed down for generations, Claes Van Petten had already been kicked out of the Schenectady stockade for doing illegal business with Mohawk tribes. The rumor took it one more step: they said his Mohawk trading partners had warned Van Petten to stay away from the stockade on the night of the massacre. Whether that rumor is true or not, or whether it was a matter of chance or planning, I know that Van Petten caught a lucky break. He could have been slaughtered. Enslaving humans, in his case, had no cosmic revenge.

Then I came upon a story that seemed to show just the opposite: revenge in its cruelest form. As I was reading through court documents, I noted a small entry from July 1682, just two months after Van Petten bought Jan. It appears in brief form in the court records, with almost no context: a slave owned by a man named Jacob Casperse slit the throats of Jacob's two children along with Jacob's father-in-law.[20] We never learn the name of the enslaved man, even one both angry and desperate enough to sneak in while they were asleep and do something that he had to know, if he were caught, would result in torture and his own horrible death.

One month later, the man's body was found along the Mohawk River west of Albany. It's not clear how he died—suicide, a fall, an attack? Eager for some sort of demonstration, the authorities decreed that a few slaves should be commandeered to retrieve the body to be "hung as an example to others."[21] If they couldn't punish the murderous slave in life, they would at least use his hanging corpse as a warning.

Since I had so little information about the enslaved man, I wondered what I could learn of the enslaver himself. Jacob Casperse is a mysterious, shortened name. In Dutch it would mean Jacob, son of Casper. What was his family name? He apparently hadn't adopted the practice of taking on a surname based on place of origin or occupation. Many of the earliest settlers of New Netherland didn't do that until later generations.

I dug a little more. "Jacob Casperse" showed up quickly on several genealogy sites and in articles.[22] There was my answer: his family name was Hallenbeck. He once lived in Loonenburg, my hometown of Athens. When his children were murdered, he was living at a farm along the Normans Kill creek that feeds into the Hudson, just south of Albany.

After that incident, he moved farther south to a farm along the Hudson River between Loonenburg and Coxsackie. He and his wife had eight more children.

Did he buy more enslaved people, or did that nightmarish experience put him off the practice of keeping people as property? I couldn't find further records on Jacob Casperse Hallenbeck's enslaved, but I found that it didn't deter the generations that came after him. Over the next hundred-plus years, the Hallenbecks listed slaves on their census records. Jacob's nephew, Casper Janse Hallenbeck, doled out at least five enslaved people in his 1756 will. "To my sons Jan Casper and William certain negro slaves: to my two daughters Mary wife of Johannes Klaw and Rachel wife of Jacob Hallenbeck, each a negro woman; granddaughter, daughter of Johannes Klaw a negro child; and the same to my grandson Casper, son of William Hallenbeck," he wrote.[23] Casper's son, also named Casper Janse Hallenbeck, left enslaved people to his family in his 1798 will: "a negro wench named Elizabeth, two cows, and four sheep."[24]

Jacob Casperse was my eighth great-grandfather. My great-grandmother was Huldah Hallenbeck. I confronted a new truth: an enslaved man had murdered some of my ancestors. It wasn't just a murder but a slaughter of the innocents in their sleep. Anyone who has gazed on the faces of sleeping babes couldn't help but shudder.

And yet I understand. This man felt he had no other choice. Maybe he was driven mad by his enslavement. In a larger sense, his act seemed to change nothing. The Hallenbecks' determination to continue to enslave people showed me that this Hudson Valley institution of slavery would not be deterred by one horrible incident in 1682. A slave murdering one's children was wrenching, but it didn't seem to lead the Hallenbeck family to make the soul-searching leap that maybe, possibly, chattel slavery was wrong, that it led to violence given and violence received. It was proof beyond any doubt I might have harbored that early slavery in New York was anything but purely transactional. Slavery was not just another way to get help down on the farm.

What petty transgressions appeared on the surface in so many of these records—running away, stealing a bit of silver, navigating life in a new colony—were hints of a deeper pool of hatred on both sides. They also were a sign that fears of insurrection or resistance, along with the belief that the enslaved were less than human, allowed these early Dutch to take

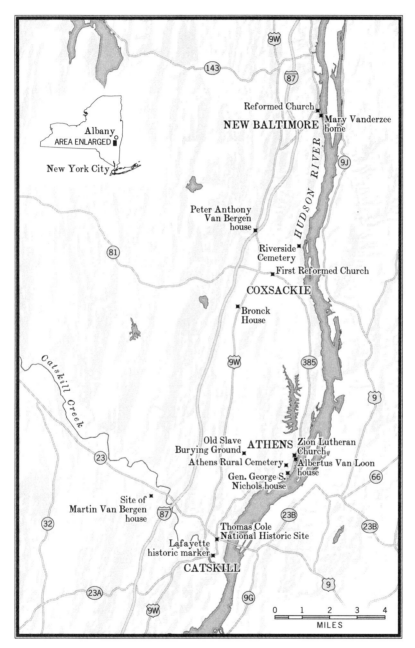

Figure 2. A close-up map of Greene County shows some of the sites of slavery.
Map by Glen Pawelski, Mapping Specialists, Ltd.

a sledgehammer to any misstep, real or perceived. And from time to time, it also allowed the enslaved to take a sledgehammer right back.

This all happened on my doorstep. It was 340 years ago, true. More and more, though, it also felt like something that took place just yesterday. The quiet streets of Athens, from the river to its old cemeteries on its overlooking hills, were hiding stories, far more stories than I might be able to uncover. I needed to understand why I hadn't known about any of this.

2

THE LOST HISTORY

It was 1972. From a stone-clad historic estate in Westchester County came the release of a new film called *The Mill at Philipsburg Manor*.[1] With chirpy music and smiling actors, the film was a proud tribute to the recently restored estate of the prosperous Philipse family.

"To the first settlers, America was mostly wilderness and water," the narrator intoned, cheerfully ignoring the Native populations who already roamed that wilderness and canoed those waterways. The camera zoomed in on the man in charge, a slightly chubby miller in a three-cornered hat. He was bagging sacks of wheat and supervising a staff of young men in loose muslin shirts as they flailed the wheat by hand, turned the millstone, and shoved boards into molds to create casks. They were clearly delighted to be working on this sunny day in someone's idea of life in the eighteenth century.

Over the backdrop of paddle wheels spinning under the cascading water, the narrator continued, "From the tumbling streams, power—to help build a civilization." The film, self-satisfied and optimistic, embraced that ongoing theme in our collective American story: from hard work comes wealth and happiness.

There was just one problem—every person in this film was white. Absent were the enslaved workers, even though an accurate dramatization of life at Philipsburg Manor should have shown dozens of the enslaved planting crops, threshing wheat, and hoisting sacks of grain. Generations of enslaved workers, from 1685 to 1750, lived, labored, and died at Philipsburg Manor. It was, in fact, a plantation with some of the largest concentrations of enslaved workers in the Hudson Valley. Without slaves, the family would not have accumulated its wealth or contributed to the collective American story that the film celebrates. In fact, Frederick Philipse, the family's patriarch, was a slave trader. Philipse owned ships that captured people from Madagascar and brought at least 350 of them to New York. The Philipse family never lived at the manor.

The Mill at Philipsburg Manor was the sort of soporific film that filled slow afternoons in my high school social studies classes. In 1972 I was fifteen, a student just a few hours north of this manor in Sleepy Hollow. I don't remember this film, but I saw many more just like it, anodyne portrayals of millstones and bonnets and happy settlers, American advancement much like the Carousel of Progress at New York's 1964 World's Fair. I was just seven years old when my parents brought me to the fair, but I remember being entranced by the carousel in the General Electric Pavilion. The world, along with our seats in the rotating theater, was always turning in the direction of progress. "There's a great, big, beautiful tomorrow," the animatronic man sang.

It would not have occurred to me to question whether the white men and women portraying the workers in the Philipsburg Manor film were hiding something. It's easy to miss a whitewashing when you don't realize there has been an erasure. The filmmakers at Philipsburg Manor knew very well that the manor's enslaved people worked the mill and the farm. A farm inventory from 1749, at the death of Frederick's son Adolph Philipse, listed twenty-three slaves along with silver spoons and flax spinning wheels.[2] After Adolph's death, the enslaved humans in the inventory were separated, sold, and scattered through the Hudson Valley and New York City. As Michael Lord, the former education director for Historic Hudson Valley, put it, the filmmakers in 1972 made a "conscious decision to negate" the presence of the enslaved.[3] Maybe that instinct to whitewash is the same reason slavery in New York was absent from the curriculum at Coxsackie-Athens High School. I would have noticed the part where my teachers started talking about slaves living, working, and dying in Athens and Coxsackie.

I loved learning about local history, such as the place I once thought of as a castle on a hill. As we sat in the back of our station wagon crossing the Hudson River from Catskill to Hudson on the Rip Van Winkle Bridge, we kids would look up at the outline of the mysterious building on the small mountain in front of us and yell, "There's the castle! There's the castle!" (My parents, understandably, were probably focused more on driving than on the shouts of four rambunctious kids asking endless questions.) Later I found out that the castle was a place called Olana, the Persian-styled home of the Hudson River School painter Frederic Church. I devoured every detail I could about Church and the other romantic painters of the nineteenth century, artists who could fill wall-sized landscapes with sweeping, pink-tinged clouds, glorious mountain summits, and peaceful rivers.

I also loved the stories about the icehouses of the Hudson. My Italian grandfather owned an icehouse on riverside land that he gave to my father when the ice business died out. There, my father built our home. I spent many a summer afternoon staring at the earth in my backyard, tracing the brick outlines of the building's foundation and imagining the chunks of ice hauled out of the river and stored in sawdust, right there, in a building the size of a football field.

Slavery would have captured my attention the way a children's poem once made me think of Native Americans. The first stanza reads:

Where we walk to school each day

Indian children used to play,

All about our native land,

Where the shops and houses stand.[4]

Of course, my imagination had its limits. I never asked the follow-up question: where were those same Indian children now? They weren't playing in my backyard. But I did love the romantic imagery it created. I loved imagining that different and exciting things happened right under my feet.

If I learned anything at all about slavery, I learned that our country's original sin belonged to the South. From time to time, I would hear that the older homes in my town held cellars for the Underground Railroad, places where fugitive slaves could hide and escape capture as they made their way to freedom in Canada. We northerners—the good guys—fought to preserve the Union and end slavery. We were the ones who set this country straight.

I started digging through local records to see if slavery was just hiding in plain sight. To celebrate America's bicentennial in 1976, the year after I graduated from high school, the New Baltimore Bicentennial Committee put together a book about the hamlet just north of Coxsackie.[5] The book was written by multiple authors. One chapter, written by Emma Lou Johnson Baldwin—"New Baltimore's Story in Verse"—captured the village's colonial history in rhyme, alliteration, and the same cheerful but clueless spirit I found in the Philipsburg Manor film. Baldwin, at least, acknowledged the truth:

> *Agriculture in Colonial days depended on hands to work in the fields,*
>
> *So the doughty Dutch burghers used sons and slaves to augment their yields.*
>
> *In a land where devotion to freedom was the patriot's zeal*
>
> *That our citizens owned slaves was an anomaly, but real;*
>
> *Since their descendants lived in New Baltimore to the end of their days,*
>
> *We citizens of New Baltimore should remember the part their history plays.*

I didn't read that book when it first came out in 1976. Even if I had, I wonder if I would have picked up on what the author described as an anomaly. It did make me wonder whether the truth was tucked inside the books I had read more carefully. I went back to my childhood favorite, Louisa May Alcott's *Little Women*. I read the book so many times I could recite entire paragraphs. Slavery is a shadow on the periphery, never mentioned directly, even though the first half of the novel is set during the Civil War, and even though the girls' father had gone off to serve as a chaplain in that war. I wondered about earlier literature, works that were the foundation of our literary heritage and essential in shaping our understanding of the Hudson Valley—and of America. I began with the man who created much of the mythology of my Hudson Valley: Washington Irving. I grew up surrounded by Irving's legacy, an imprint that lives on in kitsch and campgrounds. Besides the Rip Van Winkle Bridge, today there's the Rip Van Winkle Brewing Company, Rip Van Winkle Realty, the Rip Van Winkle Golf Trail, Lake Rip Van Winkle, the Rip Van Winkle Motor Lodge, and the Rip Van Winkle Campgrounds. A carved wooden Rip Van Winkle sits during the summer months like a wizened mummy at the head of Catskill's Main Street. It's not far from a store called Catskill Collectibles, with Rip Van Winkle beer steins and reproductions of Hudson River School paintings. There's Sleepy Hollow Lake, Sleepy Hollow Trail, and the Sleepy Hollow Camp. There's the Ichabod Crane Schoolhouse and the Ichabod Crane Central School District (mascot: the "Riders") in Kinderhook on the other side of the Hudson. Every antiques shop has at least one Rip Van Winkle plate or figurine or postcard. When we heard thunder on hot summer nights, we would say, "That's Rip Van Winkle and his friends bowling up in the mountains." When we carved jack-o'-lanterns on Halloween, we would think of the Headless Horseman in Irving's tale of Ichabod Crane.

But where was the evidence of slavery? I didn't remember reading anything about slavery in Irving's most famous stories. In "The Legend of Sleepy Hollow," one scene introduced a "negro boy" who showed up to deliver an invitation to Ichabod Crane.[6] Later, Black musicians played their fiddles for a party. If I noted that detail at all, I probably assumed they were free, not enslaved, servants of the Dutch. In fact, Irving described the Dutch as the inferior beings here, bumbling peasants, uncouth and conservative, so ridiculous that even the Black people laughed at them.

I looked for other Irving stories and found one I hadn't read before. In his 1824 story "The Devil and Tom Walker," slavery got a glancing reference.[7] Greedy Tom Walker sold his soul to the devil by agreeing to be a money lender. But he recoiled in horror at the devil's first suggestion. "He was bad enough in all conscience, but the devil himself could not tempt him to turn slave-trader." Even with that reference, I could easily imagine that the slave trading happened somewhere else, not in the North.

Irving, in fact, had no taste for looking directly at slavery or talking about emancipation. According to his biographer Brian Jay Jones, Irving was noticeably quiet about slavery and never an "outspoken abolition-ist."[8] Abolitionists, to Irving, were pugnacious figures, willing to take up unpopular causes and risk their reputation in the process. He was, Jones wrote, no James Fenimore Cooper.

Again, I didn't recall slavery being part of Cooper's oeuvre. James Feni-more Cooper's male-centered frontier themes never drew me the way the novels of Louisa May Alcott did. But since I went to college in Oneonta, I was familiar with the region, including the nearby village of Coopers-town, home of the Baseball Hall of Fame and dozens of grand eighteenth-and nineteenth-century homes.

I knew little about the Cooper family. James Fenimore Cooper's father, William Cooper, the founder of Cooperstown, embodied many of the con-tradictions of propertied men of the time. Even as he worked to develop the maple sugar industry in upstate New York, which, he thought, could compete with the sugar cane plantations in the West Indies and undermine West Indian slavery, William Cooper also enslaved people. To Cooper, publicly owning enslaved servants was an important part of his conspicu-ous consumption in the late eighteenth century. William Cooper was an uneducated man, peppering his letters with misspellings and struggling to feel respected by his contemporaries, New England–born Yankees who looked down on this frontier upstart.

As the eighteenth century drew to a close, Cooper was also likely aware of slavery's moral gray areas when he advertised to sell one of his enslaved women. In 1799 he posted in the *Otsego Herald*: "A YOUNG WENCH FOR SALE. She is a good Cook, and ready at all kinds of housework— None can exceed her if she is kept from Liquor." The advertisement then notes: "Inquire of the Printer."[9] It looked as though William Cooper didn't necessarily want his fellow townspeople to associate the name Coo-per with the man who was selling an enslaved woman, especially one with a fondness for the bottle. Conspicuous consumption had its downsides.

But was his son, the creator of *The Last of the Mohicans* and *Leather-stocking Tales*, an abolitionist? Hardly. James Fenimore Cooper may have slowly come around to a stand against slavery toward the end of his life, but he spent many of the years before that time advocating, like so many others, for its gradual end and rationalizing his own general acceptance of slavery.[10] One article he wrote in French in 1827 said, "For near two centuries that my family has been in America we have never held a slave;

but if called on to give my testimony on such a question, I should not hesi-
tate to say that, in my judgment, the American slave is better off, so far as
mere animal wants are concerned, than the lower order of the European
peasants."[11] Beyond the cringeworthy line about "animal wants," this is
a lie, plain and simple. Cooper's family did enslave people. Before he was
shipped off to Yale as a young college student, Cooper spent his first thirteen years in his father's home, surrounded by slaves.

One Cooper novel put slavery in the forefront. In his 1845 novel *Satanstoe*, a fictional autobiography of a family in eighteenth-century New
York, Cooper created a character named Jaap, sometimes called Jacob, the
enslaved man of hero Corny Littlepage. Jaap was a heroic figure, risking
his life to rescue Littlepage and fight attacks from the Huron. Cooper also
used *Satanstoe* to address slavery. To him, slavery was akin to a business
arrangement, one that both the enslaved and the enslaving sought out.
Everybody benefited. "Among the Dutch, in particular," Cooper wrote,
"the treatment of the negro was of the kindest character, a trusty field
slave often having quite as much to say on the subject of the tillage and the
crops, as the man who owned both the land he worked, and himself."[12]

Where had I read those words before? Cooper may have drawn those
lines about "kindest character" from his childhood, but I remembered
coming upon an earlier book that used nearly those same words: Anne
Grant's *Memoirs of an American Lady*. Grant, the daughter of a Scottish
officer, lived with her family in the colonies of America in the 1760s. From
her recollections come a vision of life around Albany, including slaves.
Her memoirs were published in 1808, toward the end of her life of eighty-
three years, as she was recalling and probably romanticizing the details of
her childhood.

In her analysis, "even the dark aspect of slavery was softened into
a smile." The relationship between "master" and "servant" was idyllic. "Let me not be detested as an advocate for slavery, when I say that
I think I have never seen people so happy in servitude as the domestics of
the Albanians," she wrote. Each family only had one or two slaves, and
"there were no field negroes," she explained. "They were baptized too,
and shared the same religious instruction with the children of the family;
and, for the first years, there was little or no difference with regard to food
or clothing between their children and those of their masters." In Grant's
description, slavery sounded like a rustic boarding school or sleepaway

camp—each "negro was indulged with his raccoon, his great squirrel or muskrat, or perhaps his beaver, which he tamed and attached to himself, by daily feeding and caressing him in the farm-yard."[13]

When a Black child turned three, "it was solemnly presented to a son or daughter, or other young relative of the family, who was of the same sex with the child so presented. The child to whom the young negro was given, immediately presented it with some piece of money and a pair of shoes; and from that day the strongest attachment subsisted between the domestic and the destined owner." She continued, "I have no where met with instances of friendship more tender and generous, than that which here subsisted between the slaves and their masters and mistresses." No need to worry about this three-year-old being torn from his mother, she assured her readers. "They were never sold without consulting their mother, who, if expert and sagacious, had a great deal to say in the family, and would not allow her child to go into any family with whose domestics she was not acquainted."[14]

Eventually, Grant moved to more ominous notes. Recalcitrant slaves knew that their punishment could be sale to the Caribbean, where slavery was a different matter. Grant wrote that there were a few instances where slaves, "through levity of mind, or a love of liquor or finery, betrayed their trust, or habitually neglected their duty." While "no severe punishments were inflicted at home," they were sold to Jamaica. In that case, the "culprit" was watched on his way to New York, "lest he should evade the sentence by self-destruction." It was fascinating how Grant skirted around the obvious: that slavery in a place like Jamaica might be so horrific that suicide would be a better choice. To Grant, killing oneself was just a sneaky way to avoid punishment. Even with that threat, most slaves embraced their destiny, Grant explained. Slaves knew "servitude to be their lot for life, and that it could only be sweetened by making themselves particularly useful, and excelling in their department."[15]

I found another book that picked up on those themes. The *Memoirs of Madame de la Tour du Pin* was written by Henriette-Lucy, Marquise de La Tour-du-Pin-Gouvernet, an aristocratic exile from France's Reign of Terror. Madame also lived near Albany, but about thirty years later in the years 1794 to 1796. She managed to twist her talk of slavery into a self-aggrandizing tale. With some hesitation (it "gave me such a strange sensation"), she and her husband purchased an enslaved man and gradually added a few others.[16]

Madame saw herself as the most munificent enslaver, always doing each person she purchased a favor by taking him or her away from a less desirable owner. With one woman she bought, she wrote, "Learning that I had bought her husband and wished to buy her also so that they might be reunited, the poor woman sank fainting on to a chair."[17]

When she and her husband decided it was safe for them to return to Europe and were wrapping up details at the end of their New York sojourn, they announced that they would free their enslaved workers. The slaves burst into tears. She wrote, "Never in my life have I known a happier moment. These people whom I had just freed, surrounded me and wept. They kissed my hands, my feet, my gown; and then, suddenly, their joy vanished and they said: 'We would prefer to remain slaves all our lives and for you to stay here.'"[18]

Hold on—they wanted to remain enslaved? If they did shift from tears of joy to tears of sadness, it might have been because the reality hit them: life as a free Black in the frontier land of New York at the end of the American Revolution was precarious and dangerous. Could they be re-enslaved by a less-beneficent owner? Where would they live? How could they work?

As I read these memoirs, I saw the connection between the rationalizations and the whitewashing. Why make a big deal of northern slavery, after all, if it was "softened into a smile"? These early memoirs made the argument—never challenged—that slavery was akin to going out and hiring a permanent member of the family. Even though these books were not widely known, they had set the tone. If slavery was this intimate, loving, and mutually beneficial, why change it? Or at the very least, why change it so suddenly? Not only that, but why make a big deal out of the darkness of slavery? These early writings filled a vacuum. There was no real counternarrative. Begun by little-known writers and picked up by the giants of American literature, the messages carried through and laid the foundation for the kinder, gentler storyline on New York slavery.

The argument for compromise was the logical next step. Change had to be gradual, not a radical elimination of all slavery. Even the New York Manumission Society, formed in 1785, was populated by enslavers. Many of its members believed that slavery was immoral, but a gradual manumission was better for all. As slavery dwindled in the North and grew in the South, public opinion did not always divide along clear lines. New York City, in fact, wasn't a safe space for abolitionists for much of the nineteenth century. The city was the hub of a clandestine slave trade, where ships were sent off to Africa and the West Indies, money was laundered to hide the illegal process, and slave traders operated with relative impunity. Much of the economic wealth of New York came from cotton trade with the South.

An 1859 editorial in the *New York Times* advocated for the go-slow approach, arguing that southern slavery should be ended "by persuasion rather than by force." The newspaper contended that the fight for full-on abolition slowed down emancipation "and increased the evil it sought to remedy." This rancor was all the fault of the northern abolitionists. "Until the active crusade of Northern and British Abolition was commenced, the public mind in the Southern States was far from having taken on that tone of defiant, resolute hostility to emancipation which it has since assumed."[19]

These extreme abolitionists had forced the South to dig in its heels. "Instead of being left to work out their own social problems for themselves, the Southern States found themselves compelled to assume the attitude of self-defence." And the coup de grace: "The best thing that could possibly be done towards the abolition of Slavery would be *for the North to stop talking about it.*"[20]

There it was: advocating for silence. That idea of letting the South figure out these "social problems" themselves was linked to the reasons why, more than a hundred years later, I had learned nothing in my schooling about the earlier, northern version of slavery. Polite societies change the subject rather than draw attention to that unpleasantness that we are so far beyond now. The way a parent might ignore his toddler's temper tantrum, the newspaper suggested that the best idea was for the South to realize the error of its ways all on its own.

As for the North, there were kernels of truth to the argument that northern slavery was lesser. The North *did* end slavery, and it did so without tearing itself apart with war. New York *was* home to hundreds of stops on the Underground Railroad. Large swaths of the state, especially in the northern and northwestern areas around Albany, Syracuse, and Niagara Falls, were safe homes for abolitionists. The North as protector is also just one of those feel-good stories. Historian Leslie Harris told me that the idea of a free North that ended slavery was "one of the most powerful elements of our culture." The expanded version of that history just "complicates what is otherwise a simple heroic story."[21]

Historians also glossed over the messier stuff because northerners, especially those pious New Englanders, needed to find a way to absolve their ancestors of guilt, historian Marc Ross, author of *Slavery in the North: Forgetting History and Recovering Memory*, told me. Added to that, racist Jim Crow laws and jobs being taken by the new Irish and German immigrants pushed free Blacks out of many areas of the North. Out of sight, they were out of the history books.

But perhaps the biggest reason, Ross said, was that forgetting northern slavery offered an avenue for the North to demonize the southerners during the Civil War. *They* were the ones who were accountable, not us.[22] It all added up to a case of what scholar Joanne Pope Melish called collective amnesia.[23] For the states surrounding New York, many of which abolished slavery earlier and instituted a gradual manumission process sooner than New York did, that narrative became all the easier.

To be certain, the South also created its own form of revisionist history, but that version was formed in the post-Reconstruction era following the Civil War. The belief system known as the Lost Cause argued that the South wasn't fighting to preserve slavery but to retain its rights. Life on southern plantations was idyllic, Confederate soldiers were noble, and slavery in fact protected Blacks and saved them from an uncivilized existence in Africa. That line of thinking has lingered, of course, in the reluctance to remove Confederate statues such as those of Robert E. Lee.

In 2019 the *Washington Post* ran a special supplement about US curriculum, "Teaching America's Truth."[24] Written before the argument over critical race theory became a red herring, the report looked at widely used textbooks from southern states to see how they dealt with slavery. A 1964 history textbook from Virginia, for instance, wrote that slaveholders "knew the best way to control their slaves was to win their confidence and affection." The book went on to add, "A feeling of strong affection existed between masters and slaves in a majority of Virginia homes." In the past I might have read that, shuddered, and then told myself that was what the racist and ignorant South was like—and is still like—in many places. But the more I looked for references to slavery in the North, the more I found evidence proving that this toxic mixture of nostalgia for an imaginary past, false information, and the perpetuation of myths continued in the North also.

One search brought me to an article published in January 1925 in the *New York Genealogical and Biographical Record*. "A Notable Example of Longevity (1737–1852)" described Caesar, an enslaved man owned by the Nicoll family of Bethlehem, New York, just north of my hometown. It repeated, almost word for word, some of the tired old themes that first appeared in Anne Grant's memoirs in 1808. "Slave owners, both Dutch and English, living in the Hudson Valley in the early 18th Century, were extremely kind to their slaves, they were seldom worked in the fields, being kept more as household and personal servants," wrote Dunkin H. Sill, the great-great-great-grandson of Rensselaer Nicoll, a descendant of the Van Rensselaer family and an enslaver. "They were never whipped or severely punished," Sill wrote, "and an adult slave was rarely sold, unless one became incorrigible, in which event the slave was shipped to Jamaica Island, in the West Indies, and there sold."[25]

"As a result of this treatment the slaves were devotedly attached to their masters and their families," he concluded. Here, once again, was the message that slavery just wasn't that bad. Since Sill didn't provide documentation for his proclamations, it's not hard to imagine they were borrowed from the earlier memoirs, or from his inability to think of his family as anything other than benevolent. The language is identical to the tropes used by apologists and diffusers of slavery in the South to this day—"extremely kind," "never whipped," "devotedly attached"—and that's where I thought it remained.

The article was written in 1925, about a hundred years ago. Then I came across an article based on the original one, published on November 12, 1970, in the *Spotlight*, a newspaper in Bethlehem, New York.[26] In it, Allison Bennett, the Bethlehem historian at the time, recycled the 1925 article about Caesar, calling it "Old Caesar—A Slave's Story." She changed a few words here and there but preserved the motif: slave owners "were very kind to their slaves, keeping them as household and personal servants," she paraphrased. "As a result of this treatment, the slaves were devotedly attached to their masters and their families."

I realized that both the 1925 and 1970 articles perpetuated an astonishing error. Caesar, said to have been born in 1737 and to have lived to

Figure 3. An 1851 daguerreotype of Caesar, a New York man enslaved by the Nicoll family of Bethlehem, New York, who may never have been told he was freed by law in 1827. Photo courtesy of the New-York Historical Society.

the extraordinary age of 114, was passed from owner to owner over the course of his life. The 1925 article wrote: "In 1808, under the law, and in keeping with the intent of the United States Constitution, all slaves under sixty-five years of age, in the State of New York, were freed. Those over this age remained slaves, their masters being obliged to provide for them. Caesar being over the age limit in 1808, remained a slave, though his children and grandchildren were freed." This is wrong. The only change in US law in 1808 was the end of the slave trade, with the "Act Prohibiting the Importation of Slaves." In 1817 New York did pass a law that that all remaining slaves in the state would be freed in ten years, by 1827.

The 1970 article, published when I was thirteen, repeated almost every detail of this false story. Both articles explained that Caesar was "passed by will" to his owner's widow in 1844. What neither article mentioned was that every single one of New York's enslaved had been freed seventeen years earlier. In 1851 one of the family members convinced him to have his daguerreotype taken, and that image, of a somber man in a plaid waist-coat, holding a walking stick and staring straight ahead, has appeared in multiple places, an emblem of New York slavery's long reach into the nineteenth century. Caesar passed away the year after the daguerreotype was made. Did anyone ever tell Caesar he was free? Did he die thinking of himself as a slave? In 1925, Sill wrote, "Caesar was without doubt the last person North of the Mason and Dixon line to die a slave." The 1970 article repeated the canard word for word.

The foundation of our lost history, our collective amnesia, was becoming clearer to me. When I published an article about my enslaving ancestors in the *Washington Post Magazine* in 2020,[27] readers reached out immediately, people who had the same reaction: "Why had no one told me about northern slavery?" Dozens of readers wrote to say they were shocked. One wrote that because she had grown up in Connecticut and most of her ancestors were recent immigrants from Europe, she had assumed her family bore little responsibility for slavery. "This discovery changed that assumption!" Another wrote that she "sat at my computer—flabbergasted. I never learned about this at school in New Jersey."

The deliberately shaped narrative that managed to simultaneously ignore and sugarcoat what it couldn't ignore was bolstered by one other fact. There are almost no slave cabins in the North. It's next to impossible to find slave cemeteries. What you can't see is what you can't imagine. The writer Toni Morrison once said, "If you are really alert, then you see the life that exists beyond the life that is on top."[28]

What does exist in my hometown leans toward the fables. I've spent more days than I can count paging through the endless documents at the Greene County Historical Society's home at Vedder Research Library in Coxsackie. On its wall is a banner created in 1956 for nearby Catskill's sesquicentennial. Appliquéd on blue satin is a jaunty Rip Van Winkle, his white beard flowing behind him, straddling a 1950s-era silver rocket ship as it heads up toward the heavens. Underneath this image are the words, "RIP'S AWAKENING." I imagine the organizers of this celebration hoped that when the modern-day Rip awoke 150 years after the incorporation of the village of Catskill, he'd wake to a new world of Cold War space travel.

The banner might be mixing its metaphors a bit, but this was a region that celebrated its heritage—and felt optimistic toward its future. There's irony in the actual moral of the Rip Van Winkle story, as Irving created it. While Rip slept, the world kept changing. Maybe the next banner should be "Rip's Reckoning."

Downriver in Sleepy Hollow, it took more than a few years for the Philipsburg Manor film to be shelved. By the time the film was completed in the 1970s, the civil rights movement had been going on for more than a decade. The effects of social change often took far longer to reach conservative places like upstate New York. Even so, the choice to exclude Black actors from this film is especially galling.

The Mill at Philipsburg Manor was still being shown in the visitor center at Philipsburg Manor through the late 1990s, said Michael Lord, the former education director. At that point, advisors for Historic Hudson Valley, the nonprofit that operates the manor and other sites in the lower Hudson Valley, were beginning to think about ways they could recognize the disenfranchised who were erased from these stories. In the 1980s the manor's annual celebration of Pinkster, the Dutch holiday of Pentecost, moved from a celebration of tulips and wooden clogs and white people to a depiction of the more accurate celebrations that the enslaved embraced in the late eighteenth and early nineteenth centuries.

It was time to shelve the wooden clogs and find the real history.

3

"They Are Calling to Us"

When I first learned about my enslaving ancestors, I imagined that I would write an article concentrating on my Dutch lineage. That felt like enough of a reckoning, my own confrontation with a very personal history and a good way to tell a story of northern slavery. It was also one that not enough people knew. The *Washington Post Magazine*'s editor at the time, Richard Just, had other ideas. He suggested I try to find descendants of the enslaved—those who lived in the area or even those who might have been enslaved by my family.

"Right, sure. Good luck to me," I thought. I figured that the little-known history of northern enslavers in the seventeenth, eighteenth, and early nineteenth centuries was going to be challenge enough. Finding people who could claim a genealogical connection to the enslaved, those who were not registered or recorded in any real way, felt close to impossible. But there was another reason I reacted with ambivalence. I knew that undertaking the search would be uncomfortable. And then: What if I found someone? What would I do next?

At the same time, I remembered the optimistic feel of the Coming to the Table website—multiracial hand-holding! Reconciliation!—and that gave me enough bravery to take a couple of steps. When I first began my research, I hired a genealogist named Sylvia Hasenkopf, who specialized in the families of Greene County. She had compiled a collection of articles she had written for local newspapers into several books titled *Tracing Your Roots in Greene County*,[1] so I suspected she had sources I might not be able to find. And in fact, she did find something intriguing, an affidavit from a woman named Nancy Jackson, who said she had been enslaved by Isaac Collier's son Casper, my four times great-grandfather. Now I had a real hook: a person with a first and last name, and one who very clearly had been enslaved by an ancestor of mine. I asked Hasenkopf to dig further, and she found more details on the Jackson family, including some of her possible children.

With the names of some of Nancy's supposed children and grandchildren—resonant names like Thomas Jefferson Jackson, Richard Henry Jackson, Abraham Jackson, and George Washington Jackson—I had enough detail that I decided to try to see what I could do online. I started building a profile for Nancy Jackson and her family in Ancestry's online genealogy database. I knew that Nancy had been of childbearing age around 1800. I knew Casper Collier had sold her to a man in Albany. I had a few more details about her life, and I wanted to see what else I could find about her descendants.

Hasenkopf told me she estimated that after she was free, Nancy lived out much of her life in the Albany area and in towns just south of the city. She had at least six children and, if the connections were accurate, even sent some of her grandsons off to fight for the Union with the Colored Troops during the Civil War. This amount of information felt like a jackpot.

From those details, I launched off in my own research. I asked myself: how hard could it be? Also, paying for a genealogist when I was a perfectly good detective myself seemed wasteful, especially as I got more confident in knowing where to look, or more intrigued by the hints that showed up in the Ancestry database. As I dove in, I immediately found pages of information, but much of that information was problematic. The biggest issue was that the family name Jackson was a common one taken by recently freed Blacks in the Albany area. Another problem was that Ancestry relies on what I eventually realized was a crowdsourcing method of research. Sometimes the data is backed up by baptismal records, newspaper articles, or census pages. Sometimes it's not. Anyone who is careless in clicking on those hints and adding it to their own databases could compound the errors. I fell into that trap, using the "more is better" approach. I jumped to conclusions because somebody else jumped to conclusions. I kept going nonetheless. Using a series of what I now recognize as rather dubious and presumptive inferences about where Nancy's descendants might have lived and moved from the nineteenth century into the twentieth, combined with an investigation that involved pulling up recent phone records from public databases, I tracked down a Black woman living in the Hudson Valley. According to my rushed approach, she was a descendant of Nancy Jackson. She also had helpfully made her family tree public on the Ancestry site. Not everyone does that.

I called a few numbers, including some that seemed to be her place of work, and left messages. Finally, she called me back. "I heard you were trying to reach me?" she said.[2] I took a deep breath and spilled out my story and my research in one large rush. I told her about Nancy Jackson, about my ancestor Casper Collier, about what I had learned of her life so far, and how I had then traced the Jackson family through the centuries.

"I know it's strange to think that I'm calling you and telling you my ancestors owned your ancestors," I finally blurted out, then stopped. It was quiet for a few seconds on the other end of the line.

She was polite, but cautious. "That's fascinating," she said. She said she especially loved the part about ancestors who fought in the Civil War. It was something she would be able to tell her grandchildren someday. I told her that I had created a Jackson family tree on my Ancestry account and asked her to look at it. Then maybe we could compare notes and talk a little more. She agreed, although she warned me that she had been very busy at work and was about to take her mother on a trip.

Then things got quiet. Weeks would pass. I'd check in from time to time, and she'd eventually get back to me, but she always had reasons why she hadn't dug deeper into her own research or looked at what I had done. Finally, I showed my work to Hasenkopf, the genealogist I had hired. She wrote by email, "Deb, I looked at the family tree you created online, and frankly don't think some of your assumptions are accurate or need more proof to substantiate the claims you've made."[3] For one thing, she explained, with a common name like Jackson, there could be many people with the identical name and similar dates of birth and death. That could cause even an experienced genealogist to lose the trail. I had traced descendants to places like Indiana, which, she said, was an unlikely journey for poor people not long freed from slavery.

In other words, if I was going to do genealogy work, I needed to make sure I knew what I was doing. I was disappointed, and knew I had to admit this setback to the woman I had contacted. When I wrote to her that it looked as though my genealogy work had been rushed and sloppy, she responded with just the word "thanks" and a smiley-face emoji.

When I slowed down and thought about it, I realized that approaching her out of the blue was a questionable tactic, even if my research had been accurate. Likely, she just didn't want to engage with a woman who was twisting an imaginary family tree into knots to create a connection. She hadn't asked for this. What was I trying to prove? My outreach was both clumsy and inappropriate. She was clearly not interested in playing the genealogy parlor game with me.

That encounter led me to start thinking more deeply about my own motivations, beyond what an editor might demand. Was I looking for absolution? Was finding the histories of enslaved people a matter of satisfying my curiosity, or was this step of the investigation part of a more honest and open reckoning? One thing I realized was that finding actual names made the vague concept of slavery more real and more horrifying. But in the larger sense, I didn't have an answer to the internal voice that asked, in the middle of the night, "What are you doing?" Something felt wrong. Slavery was an unspeakable horror—who was I to treat my research like a genealogy reality TV show?

Some white people asked me, "Are you supposed to feel GUILTY?" Those kinds of questions had an underlying assumption: if I did feel guilty, I was also expecting other white people to feel guilty, and they certainly weren't buying into that. My answer was always no, I never felt personally guilty. I never felt as if I had to be individually responsible for something my ancestors did hundreds or even mere dozens of years before me. At the same time, my epiphany about my ancestors had left a residue, a trace. I felt *called*. I'm certainly not the only American who has been horrified to learn of enslavers among her ancestors, but I found myself at the intersection of history, timing, and ability.

Did it mean that Americans whose families are unconnected to slavery are free from obligation? No, I thought, because no one is free of the responsibility to understand the past, especially those who descend from families that benefited from their privilege. The obligation is even greater for those of us from parts of the country not normally associated with slavery. We've felt too removed from the story for too long.

There's a finger-on-the-scale element at play in my mind. Having a genetic link, a familial tie, and a regional link, one that still connects me to my family and my region to this day, underlines the calling. It adds urgency. Many Americans have left their hometowns behind. The search for connections is what puts television shows like PBS's *Finding Your Roots* into its tenth season (as of January 2024). It's why a company like Ancestry is so popular.

My sense of calling also evolved out of some chagrin I felt from my original, romanticized vision of what family means. I went searching for ancient grandmothers in bonnets and doughty grandfathers with axes, expecting coziness and connection. Family stories have always attracted me. When my uncle Bob Van Valkenburg, my mother's brother, was alive, we spent one long afternoon walking through the haphazardly mowed grass of the cemeteries way up in the Catskill Mountains, reading the names on the tombstones and peeking in the window of Lexington-Westkill United Methodist Church. I felt rooted, part of a line that goes back generations. Today I wear the diamond and platinum engagement ring of my Dutch grandmother. She always told me it would go to me at her death. That ring will someday go to my granddaughter. A ring that was purchased in the 1920s will one day go to a girl born one hundred years after that, in 2020. I hope she will be able to give it to her own granddaughter someday. I love the thought that this small ring will span more than a hundred years and multiple generations. Certainly, this thought borders on sentimentality, but it's also concrete. If I can go back hundreds of years in my imagination and then push that imagination forward to the future, nothing is abstract.

Slavery was also not abstract, even though it had felt that way to me in the beginning. I hoped to find others, descendants of the enslaved, who also wanted to push past the abstraction. My first foray into finding that person almost stopped me cold. But social media adds a layer of anonymity and distance that, I realized, could be an entry point. "I've Traced My

Enslaved Ancestors" was that kind of group, people who had already made up their minds that some version of connection was valuable, even if that connection wasn't a direct link. I wasn't sure I'd be able to go deeper and find someone in my family tree who wanted to be found.

That's why the Facebook encounter with Eleanor Mire gave me new resolve. It felt like a chance to try again. After Eleanor and I connected online, I asked if I could call her. She agreed. We both marveled at the serendipity of our finding each other, even if we weren't sure, at first, what that meant exactly. Eleanor told me that she had grown up, and still lived, just north of Boston. Her strong Boston accent reminded me of the years my own family lived in New England. Plus, she was, like me, a Yankees fan—a brave thing to do in Red Sox country. We talked on the phone for a while and continued the conversation that first day with about fifty texts, mixed in with emojis, all-capital letters, and exclamation points, sharing details of the lives she had found in her family, all discovered by that wife of a cousin working with a former librarian in Coxsackie.

Every year, she takes her son on a trip to Washington, DC, where I live, so we arranged to meet on a hot August day in the lobby of the National Museum of the American Indian, a sunken seating area above which the multistory museum soars. I was nervous. But the minute I saw her, I relaxed. She's tall, with high cheekbones, close-cropped hair, and an easy smile. We hugged, still strangers but already wordlessly agreeing that we had started something. We went to the museum's cafeteria, grabbed cups of tea, sent her son Jake and her partner Paul off to explore, and talked.

She lives with her adult son Jake, a young man with high-functioning autism. She is patient with him, indulging his passions: Burger King Whoppers, annual trips, and anything to do with the movie *The War of the Worlds*. She told me she believed autism shouldn't be a source of shame—that hiding it implies that something ought to be hidden.

She also told me more about her family. Her grandmother was a cold and undemonstrative woman, very hard on Eleanor's mother. Eleanor attributed her grandmother's demeanor to the fact that she had lost many of the siblings from her large family very young and, along with that, her own son in a sledding accident when he was little. One great-grandfather, Eleanor said, had been a steam engineer who was probably secretly scalded by Irish coworkers who resented his good job. Someone had left a valve open. She also told me she was related to the Harlem Renaissance photographer James Van Der Zee. The photographer's father had been a servant to former president Ulysses S. Grant in his final years. "I was stopping people on the street and saying, 'Let me tell you about my family,'" she said with a laugh.

We also realized we had another parallel experience. Eleanor grew up knowing about her family roots in the Hudson Valley. But her grandmother insisted that the Vanderzees who had lived in New Baltimore, Kingston, Poughkeepsie, and western Massachusetts had never been enslaved. She took great pride in that, Eleanor said, all part of Vera Washington's image of herself as a "proper New England lady." Her grandmother had almost certainly known her own grandmother, Mary Vanderzee, since Vera was thirteen when Mary Vanderzee died, and Eleanor remembers her grandmother talking about going to visit the family in the Hudson Valley. Mary Vanderzee may not have announced to her granddaughter that she was born of enslaved parents, but she also could have talked about those earliest times.

What I was seeing, then, wasn't just a whitewashing on the part of white people. The erasure happened in other ways, for other reasons, with Black people. Denial of northern slavery had seeped into the collective unconscious of so many. Focusing on slavery meant directing attention on the past, long gone and good riddance.

Another woman had written to me when my *Washington Post* article came out. Cheryl Rollins was another Black Vanderzee descendant. She told me that her mother had warned her about genealogy research when she started asking questions as a teenager. "Be careful what you dig into," her mother said. "You might not want to know the answer."[4]

Eleanor did. So did I, even when I felt as if I might be treading into territory that didn't belong to me. Eleanor told me that she was relieved to meet me. She had encountered others in her research who only seemed to want answers if those answers fit into their worldview. One woman in Connecticut who was tracing her Native American roots connected with Eleanor online, since Eleanor also found Native American ancestors. When she found out Eleanor was Black, she told her it couldn't be the same family. Eleanor said it was, and that was the last she heard from her correspondent. After that, Eleanor stopped revealing her race immediately

Figure 4. Eleanor Mire, the descendant linked to Debra Bruno, stands in the stacks of
Vedder Research Library in Coxsackie, New York. Photo by author.

when she set up a connection, in the hopes of keeping the conversation
going.

We hugged when we met, and we hugged again as we said goodbye
that day. In just a short time, we had found ourselves chatting nonstop
like old friends who were trying to catch up on a few years, or a few hundred years. Untangling a complicated tale was the easy part. There were
still things we didn't address head-on. Almost by unspoken agreement,
it seemed as though Eleanor and I were dancing around the other issue
that came up as we looked. It was very possible that we shared biological
ancestors—me descended from a daughter of Mattias Houghtaling, one of
the first settlers in the area, and Eleanor from the children of her ancestor

Mary Vanderzee, who was most likely raped by a Houghtaling. We had both taken DNA tests, but we never found a direct genetic Houghtaling DNA connection. Early on, we settled instead into roles that were closer to research partners than justice warriors. Hand-wringing and emotional self-indulgence didn't fit our personalities. What did fit was a search for the truth. When I met Eleanor, I felt as if we had both been given a ticket to forge ahead and do the work.

What mattered for both of us, at least at the early stages of our research, was to get at the real story. And the truth was that the history was there in tiny slivers of information, if we kept looking and never stopped. It was almost unspoken that bemoaning the fates of the enslaved was less important than telling their stories, saying their names, giving light to what had been hidden.

My stumbling upon Eleanor Mire and her ancestor Mary Vanderzee—and then writing an article about that—opened a door. In the first few days after the article appeared, many of the comments on the article or the direct emails came from descendants like me: people who hadn't realized their ancestors might have been enslavers, or found out later in life, or who had tried to grapple with the truth. One writer said his ancestors enslaved thousands of people in Alabama and Mississippi, including one trader who was "so hated that his slaves killed him." He had tried to reach the descendants of the enslaved, but none of them wanted to be in touch. He understood: "The last thing they want are condescending white people."

Another writer told me he had reached out to a Black man who shared a family name but never heard back. "Your article inspires me to try again." Another said she had been in touch with descendants of those enslaved by her ancestors. "My life has been so enriched by knowing them. Somehow something good has come from all that horrible-ness."

One wrote: "As an African American, I have ZERO desire to build close relationships with any white descendants of my former enslavers of my ancestors. However, sometimes such people have great records that can help descendants of slaves complete their genealogical trees. Thus, such interactions are ultimately necessary and appreciated."

After a few more days, other messages began to arrive, including other descendants of Mary Vanderzee, such as Cheryl Rollins. The retired college administrator from Upper Marlboro, Maryland, had read the article and realized this was her family. She wrote to me, "My great-grandmother on my mother's side was Melissa Vanderzee Potter." Cheryl's cousin was a woman named Kitt Potter, another descendant of Thomas Vanderzee's daughter Melissa, who married a Potter. Kitt Potter today lives in Kingston, New York, where a branch of the Vanderzee family settled, and is director of the City of Kingston's Department of Arts and Cultural Affairs. Kitt Potter started connecting me to other extended family members.

But it was Eleanor and I who dug most deeply into the research. Our emails were a hodgepodge of random notes, maps of cemeteries, photos of ancestors, clips from newspaper articles, and observations about life in general. We had some basics: a location, some names, some other evidence of lives.

Finding the earliest histories of the enslaved is complicated. If they appear beyond a checkmark in written records, it's often just a reference to a badly spelled first name—"Sawr," "Ceasar," or "Bec"—and almost never a family name. If a full name appears, it's one that a person could have changed once she was freed, making research more complicated and fraught. Rarely did enslaved people merit mention in fusty history books, even if they did fight in the American Revolution or help build an early fort.

It felt close to impossible. How could people with such a truncated and obscured history become real to me? How could I find them? Genealogists talk about the "1870 brick wall" for Black family trees. Before the end of the Civil War, especially in the South, enslaved people were rarely listed on records by more than a first name. As for the Hudson Valley, I knew that I might face similar complications or a lot of confusion over many of the names the enslaved took after emancipation— Dutch names, English names, the family names of their enslavers, and sometimes new names like Freeman. Even more confusing, census takers could be sloppy in their notations, so a family could be marked "B" for Black, or "M" for mulatto, and sometimes with no race noted at all, with the default always being "W" for white. The matter of whether someone was of mixed race could also be based on the census taker's eyeball judgment.

At this point, neither Eleanor nor I had an answer to any of these questions. One day, we were texting back and forth, and I told her that the cover of the *New Yorker* that week was a picture of Sojourner Truth.

"Everything is converging," Eleanor responded. And she attached a photo of the intersection where she had parked to read my text. "Sojourner Truth Court," it said.

"Nice," I wrote. "Where?"

She responded, "I am in Boston, and pulled over to read this. I looked at the name of this very small street. I am freaking right the hell out."

"Holy shit," I wrote. "They are calling to us."

4

"A Vile Slander"

In the waning days of 1725, a baby was born in the village of Loonenburg, the Hudson Valley town named after the Van Loon family.

Isaac Collier was the third child of Jochem Collier and his wife Stynje (or Christina) Vosburgh, both hailing from the families who were early settlers of the region.[1] Here, in the pages of the record book for Zion Lutheran Church, was the earliest mention of that ancestor whose will I first found. His parents were Jochem Kalier (one of the many spellings of the name) and his "wife, a Reformed woman." The baptism of my five times great-grandfather a few weeks later, on Epiphany—January 6, 1726—was recorded by the church's pastor, the Reverend Wilhelm Christoph Berkenmeyer, a German minister who had recently been hired to serve Lutherans and their nascent churches in the Albany area. Berkenmeyer, considered by some to be one of the founders of the Lutheran church in America, added a measure of colonial star power to the tiny village.

What caught my eye, though, were the other entries on the page. On December 5, 1725, Berkenmeyer wrote, "bap at our meeting at Loonenburg, 4 weeks old, Hannes Christian, a child of Pieter Christiansen a bapt negro and wife Elisabeth a German woman."[2] Another interesting item appeared a few lines down: "Dec. 28 bap at Albany at the house of Johan Everts: Jannetje, 3 years old child of an unconverted negro and his wife Betty a baptized negress. Godmother the grandmother Betty also a baptized negress and a widow, servant at Willemtje Braad."[3] Next was "Elisabeth, 4 months old, child of the same parents, servants of Renier Van Euvere whose written consent, signed by his own hand I have received. Witnesses of their promise that they shall faithfully serve their master, and increase . . . in the Christian faith, were Maritje, wife of Johan Everts and many others."[4]

Loonenburg's new pastor was busily welcoming Blacks and interracial couples of the area into the Lutheran church's Christian fold, right alongside their enslavers. But even the hope for eternal salvation had earthly limits. Baptism didn't confer freedom. In some of the cases, the parents needed signed consent from their "master" to join the church. Berkenmeyer described some of them as "servants," but in early eighteenth-century New York, slavery was the rule, not the exception. Before I found these entries, I hadn't realized that marriages of white women and Black men would be common enough to be recorded in eighteenth-century colonial church records without commentary. I also hadn't realized that baptizing a family's enslaved was possible.

Was Zion Lutheran fulfilling its mission as a new Zion, the heavenly city? At first glance, I thought it could be evidence of the early stages of a slowly integrating society, a vision of harmony and stability. I looked more closely at the earliest records of Zion, starting with its first pastor, Justus Falckner. In 1712 he baptized a man named Pieter, who was "about 30 years old" and the slave of Jan Van Loon, the village's founder.[5] This was the Pieter Christiaan I had found earlier. Also baptized in 1712 was a girl named Lea, the child of a slave of Johan Casperson and a woman identified only as Eliesabeth Hoogdeeling. In 1716 Pieter's daughter Anna Catharina was baptized, as well as a "mulatto" child called Jan, whose parents were an unnamed "Indian slave of Jan Caspers" and "Maria," simply described as a negro. From 1712 until the end of the century, Zion baptized 146 slaves, free Blacks, and mixed-race children, along with some teenagers and adults.[6] Here was name after name, some described as "bastard," some as children of an "English father" and an Indian woman, and often christened with enslavers serving as their sponsors.

Was this typical for these prerevolutionary towns in the Hudson Valley? I pictured families of all races sitting together at church, sometimes intermarrying. I continued my research by digging into the 462-page tome *History of Greene County*, written by a group of local historians at the end of the nineteenth century and published by J. B. Beers and Company. The history dove with stultifying detail into the lives of prominent men and the county's roads, mills, churches, and cemeteries. The references to slavery were scattered and rare, the references to mixed-raced marriages nonexistent.

According to the history, very little happened in the world of these Dutch farmers. Life in this region of the mid–Hudson Valley "was not one of excitement and enterprise," wrote William S. Pelletreau, author of the chapter on Athens, as he looked back from his turn-of-the-twentieth-century vantage point. The Hudson Valley was certainly not New England, where community life centered on commerce, conversation, cooperation, and the village green. The Dutch man, Brace explained, "lived alone on his bouwery. His family and his servants composed his social world, except when, on Sundays, he met with the domine of the church, and the few neighbors scattered at wide distances from each other."[7] Life moved slowly, like a calm river.

That's exactly the serenity I found in a painting from that period.

The Van Bergen Overmantel—seven feet long and a little over a foot wide—is an oil-on-cherry depiction of the home and property of Martin Van Bergen.[8] Van Bergen was a prosperous farmer from a well-off family in nearby Leeds, a hamlet tucked between Loonenburg and Gatskill. He commissioned the painting around 1733 to be placed over his fireplace as a vanity piece, much like the professional photographs you might see today of children or dogs in a mega-mansion's great room.

One cool summer morning at the Fenimore Art Museum in Cooperstown, I stood in front of the painting. Here was a farm scene, a primitive work that looked as though it could have been drawn by a child: cows all facing the same direction, human figures looking like miniature colonial paper dolls, a solid mass of thick green trees behind a perfectly rectangular

Figure 5. The Van Bergen Overmantel depicts the eighteenth-century home of Martin Van Bergen and his family. It was one of the first visual images of enslaved people in their daily lives in Leeds, New York, in the foothills of the Catskill Mountains, and possibly the first depiction of slavery in New York State. Photo courtesy Fenimore Art Museum, Cooperstown, New York.

house with a bright-red roof. What a vision of tranquil domestic life in the early eighteenth century. Smoke rises from two chimneys, one on the main house and another on a smaller attached building. A brown-and-white dog looks as though he is chasing something. A man in a dark hat wields a whip to guide two white farm horses pulling a wagon carrying bundles of hay. Children play. And then there are others. White people in brown clothing alongside dark-skinned men and women wearing white muslin. A couple of Native American figures pass through the field in front of the house. The other adults look as though they are all going about their day, preparing to milk the cows, scatter grain to the chickens, and plow the land. A young man has just been thrown from a dark horse. Overlooking the people, animals, and land, as if they are just stepping outside their door, are Martin and Catherine Van Bergen.

The painting would be easy to overlook among the art and furniture in the museum's room devoted to charming early American folk creations. But the Van Bergen Overmantel is significant. The brown-skinned workers in white muslin are not the servants of the Van Bergens. They are their property. The Van Bergen Overmantel is the first visual evidence of slavery on a New York farm.

The Van Bergen family, owners of some of the original patent land purchased by established families from Algonquin tribes and the colonial government, set up farms, cleared fields, grew crops, and married each other. Martin Van Bergen's father was one of the earliest settlers of New Netherland. The Van Bergens prospered in this hamlet snuggled into the foothills of the Catskill Mountains, alongside their neighbors the Van Vechtens, the Van Loons, the Broncks, and occasional English families like the Salisburys. Martin's brother Gerrit built a farm next door to Martin. Some scholars believe that the man approaching the property with two boys on the righthand side of the painting is Gerrit.[9] According to the *History of Greene County*, Gerrit's house was built around the same time, also with a red-tiled roof, and attached to a much-older structure that dated to 1680.[10]

Gerrit Van Bergen used that older attached building as a kitchen and living space for the family's enslaved. At Martin Van Bergen's smaller house, the enslaved spent their days in what had to be a tiny and dank cellar-kitchen beneath the house. Even so, the painting depicted the enslaved looking almost, well, content: well fed, carefully clothed. Maybe they even worshipped alongside the Van Bergens, like the enslaved in nearby Loonenburg's Lutheran church.

Greene County's first historian, Jessie Van Vechten Vedder, for whom the library is named, noted in her book *Historic Catskill* that on cold winter nights "a slave would run the brass warming pan filled with redhot embers between the homespun woolen sheets" in the upstairs room for Gerrit Van Bergen's children.[11] She didn't mention how the enslaved kept warm.

The Van Bergen brothers busied themselves in building a Dutch Reformed church, with the local families contributing land, timber, and labor. To feed the workers as they were building the church, a long table was set up in the hall at Gerrit Van Bergen's house. Vedder described the scene: "huge joints of beef and mutton on pewter platters were brought out with roleitjes [rolls], cider, applesauce and all the good things the Dutch vrouws [women] were capable of making. After dinner came long-stemmed pipes, the little slave boys passing around the hot coals tightly pinched in the pipe-lighters."[12]

The Van Bergen Overmantel wasn't just one of the few early images of slavery in New York. It also signaled the beginning of the growth period for slavery in the area. As the Dutch farmers expanded their property—their mills, their crops, and their products for sale—they also accumulated human property. In the eighteenth century the rural area south of Albany was dotted with farms on both sides of the Hudson, farms with a growing need for labor.

Population tallies are sloppy measures because boundaries kept shifting over the century, but some numbers give us a sense of that expansion.

In 1714 the region of Coxsackie and Livingston Manor, which included the estate of the Livingston family that extended for many miles on the east side of the Hudson across from Coxsackie, counted just 243 people. Out of that number, fifty-three were enslaved, or 21 percent of the total population.[13] By the end of the century, individual towns began to count their numbers, although the tallies from the first federal census in 1790 are almost certainly inaccurate, since a 1911 fire in Albany destroyed the edges of many pages of the census, and it was on those edges that heads of households reported their numbers of enslaved.

But we can get a rough sense. In 1790 Catskill, which at that time included Loonenburg, had a total population of 1,080, including 305 slaves, a full 28 percent of the population.[14] Nearby Coxsackie had 3,406 people, with 303 of them slaves.[15] Even though these numbers seem high, they were dwarfed by farming communities like Brooklyn in New York, where about 30 percent of the households held slaves.[16] Across the state, some seven thousand slaves had been imported into New York over the eighteenth century. By the end of the century, the state had 319,000 slaves, about six percent of its total population. In some areas, like mine, the percentages could be much higher.

At almost the same time that the Van Bergen Overmantel was being painted, another house was being built in nearby Loonenburg, the village that would later be renamed Athens. Albertus Van Loon's home, dating to 1724 and maybe earlier, is one of the oldest eighteenth-century buildings remaining in the area. That building was part of the landscape of my youth, just six houses north of my childhood home. I walked past that low-slung house nearly every day, its walls so close to the sidewalk that my hand could reach out and touch the ivy-covered stones. Albertus Van Loon, the man who built the house, was one of eight children of Jan Van Loon, a blacksmith, and the man for whom the village was named. A portion of his father's house remains in one wall, on the south end of town. Albertus was my seven times great-grandfather, and Jan my eighth.

From the beginning, slavery was part of Loonenburg's story. Justus Falckner, the first Lutheran pastor, started in 1712, just a few years after Zion Lutheran Church was founded in the village. When he baptized Pieter, the slave of my eighth great-grandfather Jan Van Loon, Pieter took the surname Christiaan instead of Van Loon. It's unclear just how Christiaan got to Loonenburg, but records noted he had been born in

Figure 6. The second floor of the home of Albertus Van Loon, the author's seven times great-grandfather, first built around 1724. He was one of seven children of Loonenburg's founder, Jan Van Loon. The village, the author's hometown, is now called Athens. Photo by author.

Madagascar and was about thirty years old. Starting in the 1690s, some of the slaves who arrived in New York had been captured from pirate ships that had kidnapped people from Madagascar. That means that Pieter Christiaan was at most twelve years old when he was taken from his home. What must it have been like for a boy stolen from an island off Africa's southeastern coast to end up in a Hudson Valley village with snow and a frozen river in the winter, among Dutch-speaking farmers who were resolutely Christian?

Falckner noted that Pieter "has promised among other things that he will hereafter, as well as he has done before, faithfully serve his master and mistress as servant." Falckner added this prayer: "Grant, O God, that this black and hard Negro-heart be and remain a Christian heart."[17] Was this terminology—a "black and hard" heart—a sign that Pieter might have already made a name for himself around the village, creating some unease in the pastor's mind? Or was it simple racism? Maybe his words meant: I'll baptize the guy, but I'll need God's help in keeping this Black man a Christian.

Two years after his baptism, Pieter married a German widow named Anna Barbara Asmer. It's unclear whether an enslaved man would have been free to marry a white woman, or whether he was freed as early as 1714. She died not long after, and Pieter married another German woman named Elizabeth Brandemoes. Pieter Christiaan was described in later records as a free Black. In 1720 Jan Van Loon gave all his land to his sons, and it's possible he freed Pieter at the same time.

Slavery—at least in terms of a young man who found himself far away from his African island home—seemed to be a fluid state, something that Pieter Christiaan proved adept at casting off. I don't know if this avenue to freedom was available to the other enslaved people of Loonenburg. I could find Pieter Christiaan in the records because he had a family name. His name even shows up in the list of those who served at meetings of the Zion Lutheran Church council in 1732 and 1734.[18] Other enslaved people remained in the shadows—at least when I first looked.

Meanwhile, the Van Loon family was busy establishing the Lutheran church, which had been holding services inside homes. They donated land to build a church and hire a new pastor after Falckner died young. Berkenmeyer, the star pastor from Germany, filled the opening. It's not clear why Berkenmeyer chose little Loonenburg—maybe because it was halfway between Albany and New York City. Or maybe because he liked the opportunity to be a big fish in a very small pond.

From the start, life didn't go as planned. John P. Dern, who in 1971 wrote the introduction to the *Albany Protocol*, Berkenmeyer's journal from his years in Loonenburg, noted that the twenty years of Berkenmeyer's pastorship were "marred by the conflict between a frontier environment and his background of religious training."[19] That's one way to put it. The free-spirited mentality of people living in a barely settled village where the rules were shifting and daily life was a struggle met up with a pastor who was said to be autocratic, staunchly traditional, and anything but a bon vivant. Berkenmeyer was especially zealous about his religious beliefs, in contrast to a wave of new Lutheranism that was beginning to move through the land, a movement called Pietism that emphasized individual faith over church-sanctioned belief.

He found himself dealing with a congregation in which illegitimate babies, battles over property, and hunger were constant headaches. Not to mention the perpetual gossip that runs through any small town. The schoolmaster the Van Loon family had hired for Loonenburg, Sam Bekman, ran off after he got Jan Van Loon's daughter pregnant. Berkenmeyer himself struggled with poverty: it looks as though parishioners barely provided him with resources to live, even though the small congregation had promised him both food and property. One entry from the *Albany Protocol* from 1732 noted: "Concerning the hauling and splitting of wood, the brethren promised to do better in the coming year."[20]

Loonenburg was populated by uneducated farmers who spoke more Dutch than English, many of them unable to read or write in either language. This German intellectual, in contrast, brought with him a library of about three hundred books in Latin, Greek, Hebrew, and German, an impressive number for any village in the early 1700s. Rather than being a big fish in a small pond, Berkenmeyer was more like a fish out of water.

His uncompromising religious convictions also caused problems. Here was a man who could simultaneously own humans and baptize them— and those incongruities caused a fair amount of grumbling in Loonenburg. Berkenmeyer baptized freed and enslaved Blacks as well as illegitimate children, and even the unbaptized were allowed to occupy a bench at church. He addressed the issue in his journal: "And is it evil-mindedness or just ignorance when they say, for example, that the Negroes are received and accepted into our congregation and that we take so much trouble over them?"[21] The defensive tone shows Berkenmeyer was getting some pushback for welcoming Blacks into the church. On April 19, 1742, eight slaves were baptized in the church, each of them changing their first names to biblical ones: "Pieter, formerly Jak," was Albertus Van Loon's slave; Abraham, formerly Jak, Matthys Van Loon's slave.[22]

One section of minutes from a church meeting noted: "The Pastor asked whether the Church Council would express its feeling about the allotment of a bench in the church to the Negro [slaves], baptized or unbaptized. It was decided that no definite place would be designated for the colored people since only a few [white] members have their own seats. So those masters who send their Negroes to church will advise them not to stay in the rear but to occupy the first bench and the stairs. Their masters will tell them also that they must clear the front bench if other Christians come looking for a seat."[23] Maybe the pastor felt the enslaved needed to hear his religious teachings; maybe he felt it was the best way to keep an eye on people who might be testing the boundaries of slavery.

At the same time Berkenmeyer was pushing for one level of racial inclusion, he also owned at least three enslaved men and women. That also brought grumbling. One note from a church council meeting in 1743 gave a hint of that. A woman named Jannetje Van Hoesen mentioned that Berkenmeyer had received a slave in payment for some church ground he had earlier sold in Albany. Loonenburg's first "sainted" pastor Justus Falkner, she complained, "never would have done such." In another tiff with members of his congregation, Berkenmeyer complained that he was forced to live in "destitution" and wasn't given enough wages to keep himself in candles and firewood. He wrote in his journal, "People say: The Pastor has a Negro; let him split the wood." Berkenmeyer answered that charge by writing, "I thank God for him," and then added that his purchase of a slave was no thanks to his parishioners, who wouldn't even donate a penny to help him buy the man.[24]

Meanwhile, Berkenmeyer also clashed with the same Black parishioners he was trying to include in the church—especially the family of Pieter Christiaan. Berkenmeyer had hired two of Christiaan's daughters, Catharina and Margarita, as servants. Catharina used her vantage point from inside the pastor's house to spread gossip about her boss's sexual behavior, gossip that the pastor meticulously noted, writing, "Pieter's Catharina was supposed to have said . . . that if people knew what was going on in the parsonage between my wife and myself, then my wife would deserve to be flogged and I would deserve to be hanged." He went on, "Such 'beautiful news' was kept quiet for more than two years by people who wanted to be the Pastor's bosom friends."[25]

Catharina kept getting pregnant, and no one in Loonenburg seemed to know who had fathered the babies. The second time she got pregnant, she reportedly told others that "she would kill herself or go away because she could not free herself from people who tried to stain her innocence." Catharina may have been a free biracial woman, but she clearly was being raped if she threatened to kill herself to escape the abuse. In February 1744 she gave birth to a baby described as white.[26] Maybe this was why she spread gossip about the pastor's sexual habits: maybe he was the father. Catharina, of course, was the one who faced the blame for her pregnancy and birth.

But before the child could be baptized, it died. Catharina's father Pieter told the pastor that the child had been healthy when he left home on a Sunday. When he returned on Monday, "he found his family busy with the burial." Others reported seeing Catharina "go down the River on the ice to Catskill without visiting anyone's home along the shore."[27]

Did Catharina kill her baby? It may have been the only way for an unmarried woman to deal with an unwanted pregnancy. The reaction to this shocking news from Zion's congregation was oddly muted. They told Catharina to "improve" and "not to provoke God's anger further by more sin." Berkenmeyer defended her, arguing that it was "not fitting" for the church council to call her a prostitute or accuse her of murder. In fact, he argued that Catharina should be allowed to receive communion, even though she had slandered him in the past. He didn't want to be seen as acting out of "vengeance, meanness, and worldly zeal," instead of "zeal for the Lord." Maybe the pastor was taking the Christian high road, or maybe the entire community was relieved that this problem had gone away.

All that lukewarm support for Catharina came to a breaking point in the winter of 1745. Catharina's younger sister Margarita, called Grit, admitted she too was pregnant. Grit then dropped a bigger bombshell: she accused the fifty-eight-year-old pastor of being the father of her child. Grit, twenty-one, had been working for the Berkenmeyers since she was seven years old. Berkenmeyer denied it and called Grit a "prostitute." Berkenmeyer said Grit was urged "to revenge her Negro race by a vile slander on our whole congregation."[28]

Finally, on a Sunday in June 1745, Mother Betty Van Loon, Loonenburg's white midwife and widow of Jan Van Loon, the son of the village's father, was called from church to help deliver Grit's baby. As Grit was in labor, Mother Betty demanded that Grit name the baby's father, even though she had already named Berkenmeyer. This time, Grit refused. She said she must have gotten pregnant while she was asleep. As she was in labor, Grit's father Pieter sat outside his house, calling to parishioners on their way to church to "rejoice with him." Pieter may have thought the arrival of this infant would be enough to shame Berkenmeyer and give his own family some kind of vengeance.

When the baby boy was born, Mother Betty announced that "she had never seen a blacker baby even among the blackest of Negroes." This was absolute proof, at least to the denizens of Loonenburg, that the pastor could not have been the father. Like a moment in a reality TV show, Pieter, thwarted in his chance to shame the pastor, turned on Grit instead, saying, "The prostitute should be whipped or hanged or burned!" After church services were over, the townspeople "climbed over the fence" to avoid passing Pieter's house, Berkenmeyer reported. Suddenly, I could picture townspeople falling all over themselves to stay out of this battle. There was no comfortable way for them to take sides.[29]

Berkenmeyer felt he had won. He piled on to the condemnation of Grit, writing, "Does not the black skin and the Negro head of her illegitimate child betray the father, even though the prostitute did not want to name him? This has silenced the prostitute and consequently everyone else. And toward the Pastor, toward his home, and toward our congregation and faith does this not reveal her lying and vile heart?"[30]

Berkenmeyer stewed in his journal for quite some time about the accusations. He compared his sufferings to those of Christ. He tallied a long list of people that he said he would forgive, but he sounded more like he was settling scores than offering forgiveness. For instance, he forgave "those who, in taprooms, in houses of prostitution, and elsewhere, made merry over this news about the Pastor and said, for example, that I had well deserved this punishment because I took too great pains in behalf of the blacks." He asked the church council to refuse to allow the Christiaan family to come to worship because "much evil is rooted in this race of Piet's and also that no good can come from, or make a lasting impression on them, especially since they misuse their coming to church as a cover for their evil."[31]

A month later, Mother Betty came to the pastor and asked if he would baptize the baby. She also asked him what they should name him. Berkenmeyer said, "What do I have to do with the name-giving?" Maybe he thought Mother Betty was implying he was the father. She suggested naming the child after Andries, a local enslaved man. The pastor replied, "It is all the same to me." But then he listed his rules: the baptism would have to be performed without witnesses present, outside the walls of the church, and Grit would need to repent and to stay away from him and the church. Finally, her family would be banished from the church for a year and three months.[32]

The baptism, unsurprisingly, never happened. One year later, members of the church council told Berkenmeyer that the child was ill and needed to be baptized so he could die a Christian. The pastor hedged again. The baptism "should not be made too easy," he said, and suggested Grit take the child elsewhere, such as to the town of Schoharie, nearly fifty miles north of Loonenburg.[33]

There was no more sign of this baby. Three years later, the Christiaan family asked the church if they could come back to services and be reconciled. At that point, Berkenmeyer seemed inclined to say no, especially since "the prostitute" let her child die without being baptized, a classic case of victim blaming.[34] After the incident with Grit, nothing was the same between the pastor and his congregation. Membership in the congregation dropped off, and little Loonenburg struggled to find another resident pastor after Berkenmeyer died in 1751, at the age of sixty-four. In the battle between Wilhelm Berkenmeyer and Pieter Christiaan, the former slave won, even if it was a pyrrhic victory.

Gethen Proper, an Athens woman who serves on the board of Zion, suggested I look at the church's baptismal records to see if there was anything else I had missed.[35] I made an appointment with the church secretary and spent a morning copying church records. I hadn't realized how much I had missed in my online searches. The pages were filled with baptism after baptism of Blacks—free, enslaved, and "mulatto," along with those whose identity was not fully explained, other than the absence of a family name.

What I found was far different from what I had read when I first learned of the Pieter Christiaan story. An article called "The Pastor and the Prostitute," written in 1999 by historian Graham Russell Hodges for a book called *Sex, Love, Race: Crossing Boundaries in North American History* noted that after the incident with Grit, no other Black babies were baptized at Zion.[36] Hodges was wrong, though. The record of their baptisms was whitewashed from the records of the New York Genealogical and Biographical Society. When I notified Hodges of this discovery, he was generous in his response. "Good for you. These are interesting and valuable discoveries," he wrote. In its 1951 listing of the baptismal records of Zion, the editors of NYG&B wrote: "Slave baptisms have been omitted except where it is apparent that the slave acquired a surname and founded a recognized family."[37] Perhaps the society assumed it would be too complex or confusing to enter first names into any kind of record. Without a family name, they are lost. They don't exist.

Here was another erasure. Since the enslaved lacked family names, they were deliberately left off the record. Not only is that inexcusable, but it also led to at least one scholar making false assessments about Loonenburg. Without the original church records, no one would have known that more than one hundred enslaved babies were baptized in Loonenburg and nearby areas over the course of the eighteenth century, babies who were simply recorded as infants born of enslaved mothers with a first name. I contacted NYG&B to see if I could understand why that had happened. The society's president, Josh Taylor, told me this wasn't the only time slave names had been left out. "I have scoured our history," he said. "I was mortified to learn of this, and I haven't been able to find any official discussion of it in our materials." Could it have been because the enslaved had no family names? No, he said. "We indexed females with no maiden name all the time. I don't really buy the excuse that just because they didn't have a family name, they shouldn't be included," he said. The society is working to update and correct that record, he added.[38]

Having two names—given and family—certainly helped put a stamp on a someone's personhood. Maybe this is the reason why Pieter, the former slave, was careful to take a family name—Christiaan—and to show up at church council meetings. He openly challenged the authority of the most powerful man in town. All of Pieter Christiaan's actions—becoming free, converting to Christianity, marrying two German women, inserting himself into his daughters' lives—were those of a man who was resilient, resourceful, self-confident, and proud. In this tiny town, slavery and racial relations were intimate, complex, and evolving moment by moment. What I didn't know was whether that meant slavery was less entrenched than I thought.

While Zion Lutheran Church continued to baptize free Blacks and enslaved people throughout the eighteenth century, the Dutch Reformed Church, which in its earliest records had a scattering of baptisms of enslaved babies, had almost no baptism of Blacks in the eighteenth century. One reason may have been that some enslaved people saw baptism as an avenue to freedom. Even so, whatever hint of an opening I saw there, I realized that the pendulum was swinging back in the other direction. What I found inside the pages of the baptismal records of one old church was apparently representative of that one time and place, and little else.

Pieter Christiaan and his family were an aberration in the march toward a more formalized slavery. Even the free Black men, women, and children baptized at Zion were rarely listed with a family name. To add to the complexity, the Zion records show that enslaved couples were rarely owned by the same person, so an intact family life was practically impossible. Beyond these baptisms, few people show up.

Mother Betty—the midwife who saw villagers at their most vulnerable and most honest—was one of the few in Loonenburg who seemed to successfully navigate the intimate and complex relations between races. Born Rebecca Hallenbeck, she married Jan Van Loon and thus into Loonenburg's first family. Rebecca Hallenbeck was a member of an enslaving family and had married into another enslaving family. I wondered if she had heard of the Hallenbeck family story from sixty-three years earlier, the one in which two Hallenbeck children were murdered by the family's slave. Mother Betty's cousin Maria Hallenbeck, married to Albert Van Loon, was the daughter of Jacob Casperse Hallenbeck, the man whose children were murdered. Maria Hallenbeck was my seventh great-grandmother. Had the horrific story been passed down in family lore, or was that too whitewashed away? Sitting on the church council that brought Berkenmeyer to town was Jan Casperse Hallenbeck, brother of the man whose babies had been murdered by an enslaved man. The Hallenbeck family continued to enslave humans, right up until New York's full emancipation.

The Van Loon family also had a link to another name that caught my eye. In the Van Loon family, a young woman named Elsie, daughter of the village's founder, married a man named Barend Egbertson in June 1727.[39] Maybe this could lead me to the origins of Mary Vanderzee's father, Cesar Egberts, I thought. When she died in 1739, Elsie Van Loon left her bedding and other household goods to her "negro man" Tobias Norman, who had married her enslaved woman, Maria.[40] Life in the early colony was not what I expected. Murders, baptisms, generous gifts: I struggled to make it all add up to something cohesive.

Of course, most of the enslaved were not collecting gifts, achieving freedom, or baptizing their babies in the local churches. Most of them, in fact, were enslaved forever. For white families, owning humans as property was one of the surest ways for them to pass down their wealth. As historian David N. Gellman said, slavery provided New Yorkers, both "quasi-feudal lords and ordinary farmers, with a means to generate wealth and to spend it."[41] In Catskill, Samuel Van Vechten, my seven-times great-granduncle, died a rich bachelor in 1741. He left most of his estate to his nephew Teunis, and it was substantial: "lands at Katskill with all the houses, out house, grist mill, barns, barracks, orchard, garden and so forth" plus "household goods, furniture, utensils and implements, namely: beds, bedding, linen, wollen, iron, brass, puter [pewter], wooden ware, wagons, slays, plows, harrows, with all my personal chattel as negro slaves, male and female, horses, cows, sheep, swine, poultry" and "every other part of my moveable and personal estate."[42] He was not the only one to categorize his enslaved "personal chattel" alongside the horses and swine.

The Van Bergen brothers of the pastoral scene were also careful to ensure that their enslaved remained valuable assets for the family, a symbol of wealth and a living, breathing way to pass that wealth on to their descendants. Gerrit Van Bergen died in 1758 at the age of seventy-one. His will named ten enslaved people, most likely members of one large family that was split up: one here, two there, and sometimes three or four together but never more.[43] The enslaved went to his five children and one granddaughter. Gerrit's son Martin got people named Anthony, John Tap, Gin, and a boy also named John Tap. His son William got Peter and Joseph. His daughter Debora got Will. His daughter Ann got Sarah. His granddaughter Annake Bronk got a girl named Amgall. And his daughter

Neeltje, who had married a man named David Abeel, got a girl named Sarah. Gerrit also made sure to leave any leftover funds to the Dutch Reformed Church at Catskill.

Martin Van Bergen died twelve years later in 1770, at the age of seventy-eight. Like the wills of many of the early Dutch settlers in the area, Martin's will carried on for ten pages. Martin listed the names of his enslaved as he divided them: Jap, Harry, Frans, Tom, Dido, GrisBeth, and John to his son and daughters and widowed daughter-in-law. If his widow Catherine remarried—meaning her property now belonged to her husband—her slaves would instead go to her children. However, not one of their names is mentioned in New York's abstract of wills. The database, a summary of wills, turned out to be another form of erasure, I learned.[44] I found the complete version of the will, written in the graceful swoops and slopes of eighteenth-century handwriting, online on Ancestry and digitized from the New York Surrogate's Book of Wills.[45] I was getting to the point where I expected the details of slavery to be hidden or diminished with a shrug. Someone made the decision in compiling the abstract to include the land, the mill, the waterfalls, the farm, the streams, and the house—but leave out the seven human beings. This was deliberate. It was a general disregard of the value of human life owned by another. And maybe, just maybe, they were ashamed of this strange custom of passing humans down to descendants.

I was getting better at seeing what was beneath the easily visible. I thought back to my first look at the Van Bergen Overmantel. When I first learned about the painting, I thought it was an interesting image, nothing more than a colorful portrait of that world. If the gift shop at the Fenimore museum had sold framed prints of the overmantel, I would have whipped out my credit card. Granted, the painting was even more compelling because it showed a place just a few miles from my hometown. I wanted that landscape on the walls of my study as I wrote about slavery in New York. In the early stages of my research, I hadn't put together the fact that the Van Bergen family also populates my family tree. But I figured that those tiny figures of the enslaved in white muslin didn't have names. I assumed I had no way to find out how they lived and died.

Then I stopped cold. How had I not remembered this? I thought back to a conversation I had with Eleanor when we first connected.

Van Bergen. I realized why this name sounded so familiar. Van Bergen was the name of Mary Vanderzee's first husband. Mary Vanderzee was Eleanor Mire's three-times great-grandmother. John Van Bergen's children married Vanderzee children. He was Eleanor's step-great-great-great-grandfather. John Van Bergen, born enslaved, was almost certainly descended from one of the enslaved people owned by Martin, Gerrit, or their third brother, Peter Van Bergen. My family members populated the Van Bergen Overmantel. But so too did Eleanor's family.

"We May Be Van Bergens after All"

The wedding of February 1786 was the social event of the season. For three days, "the wine & Other Liquers was near as planty as water," one guest wrote to a friend. The party started on a Monday and "continued with force till Wednesday morning," with fiddlers playing music for the young people in one room and the "Old Folks" in another.[1]

The Coxsackie marriage of Peter Anthony Van Bergen and Hester Houghtaling also signaled the union of two powerful families. Peter was the only son of Anthony Van Bergen, a Revolutionary War hero, and his wife Maria Salisbury.[2] He was named for his grandfather Peter, younger brother to Martin and Gerrit Van Bergen in the Overmantel painting. Hester Houghtaling was one of two daughters of Thomas Houghtaling, the descendant of that first young orphan who came to New Netherland in 1655. Nine years earlier, Thomas Houghtaling had fought in the Revolutionary War under Col. Anthony Van Bergen, Peter's father, in the second battle of Saratoga.[3] Did the men, as they marched through the fields, work out a plan for the union of their children? It's possible, because

Colonel Van Bergen's daughter Catherine also married into the Houghtaling family, to Thomas's third son, Conraedt.[4] These sorts of marriage contracts were also the way things were done—powerful families matched up their sons and daughters, building wealth and creating an enormous and confounding cobweb of names and surnames.

These ancestors of mine also retained their essential Dutchness: William S. Pelletreau, the author of the chapter on Coxsackie in the *History of Greene County*, wrote that "the population was composed of the few families that descended from the Dutch settlers, who retained their ancient customs, spoke the Dutch language of their forefathers, and read with pious care, and treasured with zealous pride, the old, ponderous, brazen-clasped Bibles brought from the Fatherland." Others might ridicule the Dutch for their "peculiarities," he said. That simply meant they didn't appreciate "the force of character and determined will of the race that contended so valiantly for freedom."[5]

That was freedom for themselves, of course. As the families built their wealth, they added to their population of enslaved workers, a move that demonstrated their power and stature in the community as they continued to expand their prosperity. In 1786 Coxsackie had 2,893 white people and 395 enslaved people. Slaves were 12 percent of the population.[6]

In New York State overall, the 1790 census counted 21,324 enslaved.[7] The 1790 census for Coxsackie managed to tabulate just 189 enslaved,[8] although that number is almost undoubtedly inaccurate, thanks to the forever-deleted edges from that 1911 fire. The 1800 census counted 549 enslaved people in Coxsackie.[9]

For these wealthy families with the largest numbers of enslaved, the increase in human property also translated into an increase in their leisure time. They became the landed gentry of the colonial world. While they may have worked alongside their enslaved in the earliest days of the colonies, many farmers now were able to leave the heavy lifting to their enslaved men and become overseers of their properties with ample time on their hands. Even with extra time, these Dutch farmers rarely wrote things down. As Shane White, author of *Somewhat More Independent*, wrote, "The small farmers of New York's hinterland were not prone to self-reflection and generally had neither the time nor the inclination to keep detailed records."[10]

Fortunately, one man's diary painted a vivid portrait of the slaveholders' transition from labor to leisure. From 1785 to 1831, a Scottish-born
man named Alexander Coventry served as a doctor in that stretch of the
Hudson Valley and kept a detailed account of the area's day-to-day life
and his own pursuits. He recorded the days he spent reading the *Specta-
tor*, a British periodical, or a new book in French while Cuff, his enslaved
man, toiled on his farm. Coventry also seemed to relish the chance to mix
business with pleasure, attending to sick patients, bleeding them or applying a poultice, while simultaneously being hosted by the wealthy families
on both sides of the river. He had a front-row seat to the life of these
Dutch farmers. He recounted a visit to Thomas Houghtaling in 1787, the
year after he married off his daughter Hester in that three-day celebration.
Houghtaling—a member of one of the "respectable Dutch families" that
Coventry described in Coxsackie—was "very rich; owns a large tract of
land, has a large substantial stone house, richly furnished," he said.[11]

Coventry noted that it was not "burdensome for them to entertain."
He explained: "Each individual family had more or less black slaves who
did all the work on the farm, and in the house." Owning the labor for
their large farms in the fertile Hudson Valley "saved the masters and mistresses from the insolences of what is called hired help." Servants—in
other words, those who are not the property of their employers—"must be
humored like spoiled children, or they will leave you at their own will."[12]

How much easier it was to have servants who couldn't leave. In the
1790 census, Thomas Houghtaling, my cousin seven times removed, listed
seven slaves, more than almost all of his neighbors in Coxsackie.[13]

The diarist Anne Grant, who had portrayed slavery as an affectionate
bond between a slave and his owner, also waxed eloquent on this American way of life, writing, "An American loves his country, or prefers it
rather, because its rivers are wide and deep, and abound in fish; because
he has the forests to retire to, if the god of gainful commerce should prove
unpropitious on the shore. He loves it because if his negro is disrespectful
or disobedient, he can sell him and buy another."[14]

William Strickland, a British farmer who kept a journal of his travels
through America from 1794 to 1795, was far more offended by this way
of life, but not because of slavery's immorality. When he first encountered
Dutch farmers in New Jersey, he described them this way: "No man is to
be seen here on horseback, all people travelling in waggons [*sic*] drawn by

two horses abreast," with a bench across the wagon for a seat, he wrote. "A fat Dutchman and his fat wife, and two or three clumsy sons and daughters may frequently be seen thus driven and jolted by a not less fat negroe Slave."[15]

To Strickland, the Dutch had been corrupted by slavery because it allowed them to become lazy and ignorant of their surroundings. "Many of the old Dutch farmers in this country, have 20 or 30 Slaves about their house. To their care and management every thing is left; the oldest farmer manages the lands, directs the cultivation of it and without consulting him the master can do nothing; he is in fact in general the more intelligent of the two; and so as the master can but exist in the enjoyment of content-ment and ease, he is content to become the Slave of this Slave; nothing can exceed the state of indolence and ignorance in which these Dutchmen are described to live." Strickland added: "Many of them are supposed to live and die without having been five miles from their own houses, unless compelled at any time to go to Albany or to their county town upon pub-lic business. I have several times called at Dutch houses to make enquiries, when the owner, unable, though otherwise willing, to give the information wanted, has called for Con, or Funk his oldest Slave, to answer my ques-tions, or point out the road to the place I was going not perhaps distant more than a very few miles."[16]

Both Coventry and Strickland took pains to point out that everyone was content in this arrangement. Coventry wrote, "Although the blacks were slaves, yet I feel warranted in asserting that the laboring class in no country lived more easy, were better clothed and fed, or had more of life, than these slaves."[17]

When I found a mention of enslaved people in works from the eigh-teenth and nineteenth centuries, it was often for the purpose of making them the butt of jokes or a reason for a laugh. A story from a genealogy book published in 1911 about some of the old Albany families talked about an enslaved man owned by Arent Schuyler, who had moved to New Jersey. The man found a copper deposit while he was plowing a field, and that resource made Schuyler rich. "Desiring to reward the slave," Schuyler said he could have three wishes. The man, who is never named, reportedly said: "First, that he might remain with his master so long as he lived; second, that he might have all the tobacco he could smoke; third, that he might be given a dressing-gown, with big, brass buttons, like his master's." Schuyler told the man he could ask for more than that, so the man asked for "a little more tobacco."[18]

Give me a break. He didn't ask for freedom? It's possible any idea of freedom was beyond imagining. It's possible he felt safer in the household of a rich man than trying to strike out on his own. But it's also possible that this story is entirely fabricated. Those sorts of fanciful stories kept popping up, again and again. I wondered what was below the surface. I needed the stories of those who didn't see their enslavement as a kind of lifelong guarantee of job security that was "softened into a smile," as Grant had written.

Cadwallader Colden gave a better picture of what was really happening. Colden, who later would become governor of the Province of New York, was one of the most respected men in the colonial world. Considered a true son of Enlightenment thinking, a revered botanist, physician, and political leader, he moved fluidly between the urbane worlds of New York and Philadelphia.

In 1717 he needed to sell off one of his female slaves, along with her infant. He wished he had been able to beat her into submission. "Were it not for her Alusive Tongue her sullenness & the Custome of the Country that will not allow us to use our Negroes as you doe in Barbados . . . I would not have parted with her," he wrote to the man who was willing to bring her and the baby to the Caribbean.[19] In the Caribbean, enslaved people could be "hardened" by whippings and deprivation. Many enslaved people didn't survive long. French Caribbean enslavers in 1789, for instance, objected to a law that limited punishment to fifty lashes.[20] Colden assured the new purchaser that this woman had potential. "I doubt not she'l make as good a slave as any in the Island after a little of your Discipline or without it when she sees she cannot avoid," he wrote. Then came the cruelest line, as well as a likely explanation for why she might have seemed "sullen" to Colden: "I have several other of her Children . . . & I know if she should stay in this country she would spoil them," he wrote. The callousness of that line stopped me cold.

Colden illustrated a common mindset of this world: eighteenth-century New Yorkers' double standard when it came to enlightenment. Colden's understanding of reason and human happiness, Enlightenment ideals, remained entrenched in botany and good governance. Those views did not extend to the concept that slavery and its horrors might be anything other than the true order of the world. Property was property. Born in Scotland and the son of a cleric, Colden was comfortable corresponding with Benjamin Franklin and English botanists. Because of that, we have a record of his dealings with recalcitrant slaves. I wonder how many others, possibly illiterate enslavers, engaged in these instances of casual cruelty without the devastating evidence on paper.

The diarist Anne Grant described the "unspeakable horror" of the enslaved when colonists were preparing a ship with lumber, flour, and other provisions for the West India market. With the ship went "all the stubborn or otherwise unmanageable slaves, to be sold by way of punishment. This produced such salutary terror, that preparing the lading of this fatal vessel generally operated a temporary reform at least."[21]

Fifty years after Colden sent his enslaved woman off, George Washington did the same thing. In 1766 Washington sold a young man named Tom to the West Indies as a punishment for having run away. Washington wrote, "That this Fellow is both a Rogue & Runaway . . . I shall not pretend to deny—But that he is exceeding healthy, strong, and good at the Hoe, the whole neighbourhood can testifie . . . which gives me reason to hope he may, with your good management, sell well, if kept clean & trim'd up a little when offerd to Sale." Washington added that Tom should be kept in cuffs until the ship got to sea.[22] Washington knew Tom would try to escape this fate.

There were other forms of cruelty too. Closer to my home, Leonard Van Buren wrote a letter in 1787 to his cousin Leonard Bronk, the scion of the large and growing Bronk family in Coxsackie. "Our Negro Ben, is in such a bad state of health, that its thought he will not survive many days." Dick, another of Van Buren's enslaved men, "is very anctious that I should write to you, that you'll please to inform his Parents and Brother of his illness." Van Buren went on to explain that a "Wench in the Neighborhood" had "unfortunately kick'd him against his private parts, out of which his illness stands forth."[23]

Van Buren ended his letter in a cheerful pivot: "The rest of our family are all well my kind Complements to your father, Mother & your Wife and to all enquiring friends." An illness, an infected wound that had taken a turn for the worse—none of that would be unusual in eighteenth-century farming communities. What struck me, though, was the order of facts in Van Buren's letter: an enslaved man was dying, someone should let his parents know, but everybody else (read: the white people) is fine. No need to have the family come and say goodbye, no call for a doctor, just an unfortunate situation.

Alexander Coventry offered another story from 1787, when he visited a home near Schenectady. The owner "ordered his negro boy to put my mare into the stable," Coventry said. But instead, "the little scoundrel" led the horse into the barnyard and didn't feed her, "which vexed me exceedingly."[24] The boy was whipped for his transgression. This kind of casual heartlessness was described in offhand ways and jotted down in everyday letters as an afterthought. It rarely made its way into the history books. One reason the Dutch enslavers were able to build their wealth and acquire human chattel was because that part of the past was tucked away. Instead, the Dutch vaunted their patriotism, taking care to note their service in the Revolutionary War, and then the War of 1812, and the Civil War. There was no need to acknowledge the human beings upon whose backs that wealth and success was built. I suspect that if they thought about it at all, the Dutch farmers would have to see how that suffering undermined their own accomplishments.

The best way to begin to repair this imbalance, then, is to say their names and tell the stories of those who were missing. John Van Bergen. Cesar Egberts. Pieter Christiaan. Nancy Jackson. Mary Vanderzee. They are the reason Eleanor and I were chasing after every detail we could dig up. It wasn't easy.

We were assembling a puzzle with thousands of pieces, many of them missing. We could find offhand references to sales and death, but we were stymied in building a fuller picture. Census records offered tantalizing lists of vague bits of information. The federal records, for instance, listed only "heads of family" in 1790, 1800, 1810, and 1820. If we wanted to find slaves in these Dutch families, we were going to have to be forensic scientists, historians, genealogists, and mediums at the same time.

Four years after he married, Peter Van Bergen listed four slaves in the 1790 census.[25] By that time, Peter and Hester also had a three-year-old called Anthony, named after Peter's grandfather, the Revolutionary War hero. Anthony would be the couple's only child.

The burned edges of the 1790 census for Coxsackie obscured the slave column for two Van Bergen men, but two others, Peter Anthony Van

Bergen and Peter H. Van Bergen, listed four and two, respectively. It was a start: six possible enslaved people in 1790 Coxsackie who might have taken the last name of Van Bergen. Those Van Bergen records gave me a start in trying to seek the Black Van Bergen family.

In the 1800 census ten years later, Matthew Van Bergen listed four enslaved, Peter Van Bergen had six slaves, and Peter H. Van Bergen had another two. This meant I had as many as twelve possible Black people who might take the Van Bergen name. Coxsackie also enumerated eighteen free Black people, all but one living with a white family, alongside its 301 enslaved in 1800. I was building a skeletal tree out of these mysterious checkmarks.

Inside Vedder Library, I found more intriguing hints of Coxsackie's Black community. I hunted for the names from Eleanor's tree: Van Bergen, Vanderzee, Egberts, Dunham. Some people, even the enslaved, became members of Coxsackie's Dutch Reformed Church. For instance, I found a short entry from 1784 for the baptism of Maria, daughter of Susanna, and Susanna, daughter of Diaen.[26] The record didn't list their family names or fathers, but the transcriber wrote, "may be baptisms of slave's children."

After 1784 the baptisms of Coxsackie slaves halted for more than thirty years, until 1818, when a notation appears for Samuel and Caty, born in 1806. The parents, listed as Dick and Maria, are "slaves of Ab'm Hallenbeck," the book noted. Abraham Hallenbeck, my first cousin six times removed, was a wealthy slaveholder in the town who had inherited a "negro boy Jack," a "negro man Boats[,] and a negro woman Diana" in his father Martin's 1785 will.[27] Did they take the last name Hallenbeck too?

First names were also troublesome. So many enslaved women were named Bet (possibly Elizabeth) and Gin (possibly Virginia), while many enslaved men were named Caesar and Cato. As for last names, I had more problems: I couldn't assume the enslaved would take the last names of their enslavers' families after their emancipation. Often they did, but others took on wholly new names, chose a family name from other white families in the community, or took one from their professions: cook, baker, potter, smith. There were no rules and no consistency. As Malcolm X said more than a hundred years later, "The real names of our people were destroyed."[28] I thought back to those Van Bergen brothers who lived in Leeds, a few miles south. In their wills they listed first names.

Gerrit named Anthony, John Tap, Gin, John Tap Jr., Peter, Joseph, Will, Sarah, Angall, and another Sarah. Martin named Jap, Harry, Frans, Tom, Dido, GrisBeth, and John. How many of them survived long enough to become free and whether they chose the name Van Bergen was almost unknowable.

Some of them did. And one of them could have been a clue to Eleanor's family tree. We knew so little about Mary's first husband, John Van Bergen. Eleanor thought that he may have died young. He had been born into slavery around 1793, that was certain. He could have been enslaved by a Van Bergen—but which one? He could have been born into the household of any of the Van Bergens in Coxsackie or nearby Leeds. His parents could have been born in Leeds and then passed on to descendants who moved a few miles north to Coxsackie.

But what else could we find of him? How long did he remain enslaved? Since this John Van Bergen almost certainly was born before New York began its gradual emancipation of the enslaved, there was no requirement that his name be recorded or noted anywhere. All we had was a possible checkmark in census records.

In 1799 New York began its gradual manumission of infants born to enslaved women. Because these babies were born in a kind of twilight period of slavery, I had records, a new way to glean some information about the enslaved in the area. A remarkable document called the Coxsackie Record of Free Born Slaves, created to keep track of those infants born after 1799, gave me more information.[29] With that document, I had a list of slaveholders, the first names of their enslaved women, and the gender and first names of the babies born to them. It wouldn't give us information on John, but it could give us details on Mary, who had been born in that hazy period. At first Eleanor and I thought the list might give us a toehold in our research. Instead, things got even murkier.

Mary Vanderzee had claimed her parents as Cesar Egberts and Rebecca Dunbar. That was a start. The record has several infants born to an enslaved woman listed as "Beck," who might have been her mother Rebecca. The mother's enslaver was Conraedt Houghtaling, Thomas's son who had married Catherine Van Bergen. Beck's babies were born in 1800 and 1802, but only the baby born in 1800, named Bet, was female. Wrong name. We looked for other babies on the list named Mary and found only

Figure 7. The Coxsackie Record of Free Born Slaves was created to register the births of children born to enslaved women in the twilight period of slavery. It lists babies born from 1799 to 1827, including a number of my ancestors: Van Bergen, Colyer, Houghtaling. Photograph courtesy of Franklin D. Roosevelt Presidential Library and Museum.

one infant, a girl born in 1802 to an enslaved woman named Gin owned by Robert Vandenberg. Nothing added up.

One other piece of information intrigued us. We know that after she was born, Mary lived with the family of Conraedt Houghtaling, the same man who enslaved Beck. If Mary Vanderzee had been born to Rebecca and raised in the family of Conraedt Houghtaling, was she actually the baby named Bet, born in 1800? The problem was that Mary Vanderzee had claimed her birthdate as May 25, 1802. Neither the name nor the date linked up. Also, Beck had given birth to a boy named Seasor (likely Cesar, named after his father) in January 1802. She could not have then had another baby a few months later.

Then Eleanor had an epiphany. As we worked our way through the names on the record, one date jumped out to her. She wrote to me: "I FOUND AN OVERLOOKED PROBLEM! CAN OF WORMS! I assumed, but there was something right in my face." Mary Vanderzee's death certificate recorded that she died on November 14, 1907, at the age of 105 years, five months, and eighteen days. "That is very specific," Eleanor said. "That would make her birthday May 25, 1802."[30]

There is no Mary born to an enslaved woman named Rebecca on that date in the Coxsackie Record, but there is one baby with a very close birth date. Gin, owned by Peter W. Van Bergen, gave birth to an infant she named Nan on May 26, 1802. "That would be 105 years, 5 months, and 19 days to the day of Mary Vanderzee's death," Eleanor wrote. "Cannot be a coincidence that they were so specific with the dates." It was only one day off from the registry. There are no other female babies born anywhere near that time. Now we had a new theory. Mary was "Nan," and her birth mother was Gin, enslaved by Peter W. Van Bergen. The mysterious Gin did not have another recorded baby in the record, so she may have died. "This is one big mishegas!" Eleanor wrote.

Who was Gin? Did she die after she gave birth? Gin was also a common name. But why did Mary claim Cesar and Rebecca Egberts as her parents? And what was the relationship between the man who was her first husband, John Van Bergen, and the Peter Van Bergen who listed a baby born to a woman he owned? Why is her name Mary?

This was definitely a can of worms. Eleanor wrote, "It looks like we may be Van Bergens, not Houghtalings after all!"

If Mary was born into a Van Bergen household, all our other calculations might have to change. We may never know Mary's origin. She may have been adopted and given a new name by Cesar Egberts and Rebecca Dunbar. Even the couple she called her parents were a mystery. I found the white Egberts and Egbertson family—often the names were interchangeable—scattered through Athens, Coxsackie, and towns north. I knew that any of them could have been Cesar's enslavers.

As far as the name Dunbar, Rebecca's family name, Eleanor told me that she had come from an area called "Flatbush." We didn't know whether that was the neighborhood in Brooklyn, which was full of Dutch farmers and their enslaved people, or possibly Flatbush Road, which today runs for a short distance just north of Coxsackie, very close to the road leading to the Van Bergen house. The name Dunbar also jumped out at me for another reason. The Van Valkenburg family high in the Catskills, where my ancestors lived, had two men named James Dunbar Van Valkenburg, father and son. Could Rebecca have been enslaved by them?

We kept hitting roadblocks. The facts and partial evidence we found offered just enough information for us to believe some people were linked, but not enough to truly connect the dots. We really could have used a medium to commune with the dead.

One year after I stood in front of the Van Bergen Overmantel, I was there again. This time, I stood there with Eleanor, her son Jake, and her sister Beverly. Beverly Mire is shorter and slighter than her younger sister, with pretty, hazel eyes and an expansive curiosity. Eleanor had wanted her sister to come from her home in Cambridge, Massachusetts, to meet me and to get a sense of the family histories that Eleanor and I had been chasing for years. Mixing in a visit to the Baseball Hall of Fame was added incentive to Bev, a big baseball fan.

The Fenimore Art Museum staff welcomed us like celebrities. They had taken the painting out of its archives, where it had been put away after having been on display. We were being treated to a special showing. With us was Paul D'Ambrosio, president of the museum and a scholar of early American folk art. "This is one of the great early American scenes of everyday life," he said. "It's also one of the earliest scenes of the Catskill Mountains."

In the year between my visits to the painting, I had gathered more information on what we were seeing. Adam Grimes, a graduate student at the University of Delaware, wrote about the overmantel in an unpublished master's thesis.[31] His dive into Van Bergen family daybook accounts in the New York State Library showed that the family was deeply involved in all sorts of trade, thanks to the farm's proximity to the Hudson River and sloops that ran goods to New York City and beyond. Tea, rum, sugar, snuff, tobacco, wheat, furs, and lumber all meant that, Grimes wrote, "the Van Bergens were implicated in a vast web of commodity exchange, and in the process, the perpetuation of enslaved labor on large-scale plantations in the Caribbean."

Even more powerfully, I found a receipt in the New York State Library for a sale in 1762: "Received Albany 20 June 1762 from Capt. Garrison V. Bergen [Martin Gerritson Van Bergen] two Negro Lads Ship'd on board his Sloop by John Henidy at New York." The other commodities that the

Van Bergen family shipped down the river to New York were enslaved human beings.[32] The Van Bergens had both direct and indirect roles in the slave trade.

I also learned more about how the overmantel had been discovered, and how it had nearly been lost to history. Ann Cannon, assistant curator of American art at Fenimore, sent me a master's thesis paper written by Kristin Lunde Gibbons in 1966, along with a related report, both of which added more detail about how the painting came to Cooperstown.[33]

Mabel Parker Smith, an early Greene County historian, attended a seminar in 1954 in which a folk art scholar named Nina Fletcher Little wondered why New York State had no folk art overmantels like the ones found all over New England. Smith recalled visiting elderly brothers in Greene County who showed her a painting that had been in the family since the eighteenth century. The painting had been so darkened by smoke, household grease, and varnish that it was almost impossible to discern any shapes. The brothers eventually decided to sell it, so the New York State Historical Association paid $100 for it and sent it to specialists for conservation.

Once it was cleaned, the images appeared like apparitions. Scholars realized what they had on their hands. "So far as we now can ascertain it is the earliest known painting of the Catskills which were to play so important a role in American painting in the next century, it is the earliest known American conversation piece, the only known contemporary view of rural life among the 18th century Dutch in the Hudson Valley, one of only three or four known paintings by one of the Patroon painters which is other than a portrait or a religious scene," the scholars wrote. "It is the only record we have to date of slaves, indentured servants and Catskill Indians in their everyday garbs." It could have been lost forever.

The discovery of the painting was Greene County historian Mabel Parker Smith's finest moment, Paul D'Ambrosio told us. When she died, she had a reproduction of the painting on display at her wake and funeral.

But Smith was also an apologist for slavery. In her story of the overmantel, she wrote, "In Coxsackie every big family had slaves and they were seldom ill treated. The duties of slaves were cooking, washing, cutting wood, and care of the horses and cows." After manumission, she wrote, "they remained in the family with no perceptible change in their lives except that they received wages and took their former owner's surname."[34]

Smith added a story she had heard about one of the Van Bergens' enslaved men. This elderly man, never named, had been given an elm tree on the Van Bergen property. Its trunk was 13 feet wide with branches spreading more than 74 feet. Someone had been sent to cut down the tree, but the man stopped him. It belonged to him. "In his old age the slave, who could then walk only with the aid of two staves, spent most of his time sitting under the elm in a hickory arm-chair." He spent his days carving ladles and bowls "out of wood brought by fellow slaves from the forest," which he sold "for enough money to keep him in tobacco and rum."

In Cooperstown that day, we were quiet for a few minutes, examining the details of the painting. In the bright light of the museum's storage vault, the images were vivid. We peered at the front stoop, the farm wagon, the horses, the dogs, the pails carried by the enslaved women, the strong arms of the Black man who was likely the smithy, D'Ambrosio told us.

When I looked at the painting this time, I saw there was much more going on than I had realized. The young man being thrown from a horse is probably Martin Van Bergen's youngest son. Gerrit Van Bergen and two of his sons are approaching from a path in the bottom right corner. Two other horses are fighting, their hooves in the air. The enslaved and indentured servants all appear to be mid-task. Why were there so many active moments? we asked D'Ambrosio. And why were the servants and slaves included in the painting? "Maybe the members of the Van Bergen family were standing over the painter's shoulder as he painted," he said. "The fact that they wanted to show everyone was remarkable."

We stared at the windows that revealed a deep cellar, where the enslaved might have lived. There were twenty people scattered around: Van Bergen and his wife and their seven children (four girls and three boys), Gerrit Van Bergen and his two sons, two Native Americans, two indentured servants, and four enslaved people. Of the four slaves, all wearing white muslin, there were two women with pails that could have been for milking cows or gathering eggs, one man, and, at the very bottom of the painting, a dark woman sitting on the ground, holding a glass bottle. She was so tiny.

"We know her name," D'Ambrosio said. "It was Angallo." Ann Cannon, assistant curator of American art at the museum, said that Angallo had been a gift from Catherine's father, Wilhelmus De Meyer, a wealthy Kingston man, when she married Martin Van Bergen.

Later, I found De Meyer's will. "And when my daughter Catrine happens to marry, she shall take with her her negress by the name Angallo," said the will, dated January 10, 1705, thirty years before the painting. Angallo. Was that the same name as the girl Amgall that Gerrit Van Bergen bequeathed in 1758 to his granddaughter Annake Bronk? In the painting, Angallo was clearly an older woman. Was the "girl" from the will her daughter or granddaughter? What kind of name was it? African? There is no Angallo named in Martin Van Bergen's 1770 will, so she was probably gone by then. She was a small thread in this worn and intricate tapestry.

We stood as close as we could to the painting, squinting at the details. I told the group that another author had not wanted the painting used as an illustration in her book because it showed too rosy a portrait of slavery in precolonial times.

"It *is* too positive a picture of slavery," Bev agreed.

Later, I found more detail about the land itself. In 1678 Martin Gerritson Van Bergen, father of the Van Bergen brothers, and a neighbor bought the land from the Lenni Lenape leader named Maetsapeek for 300 guilders in wampum, some woolen cloth, ten blankets, and other items, according to the *History of Greene County*. The author added: "These shiftless and drunken Indians no longer had a dwelling place. Whither they went or what was their fate, is no longer known." The writer did add that there was an "indistinct tradition" that years ago some of them came back every summer from their home "beyond the Mohawk" and camped on nearby land for a few weeks, telling people their forefathers had once owned that land.[35]

The descendants of the Lenape who had lived on the land could have been the figures passing through the frame. My understanding was growing.

As for the painting itself, it was a work done by a white man for a white family. It was almost unthinkable that anyone in the early eighteenth century of that status would want a portrayal of the enslaved in any way that might reflect badly on them. Nor would they have thought of themselves as usurpers of land that had once held a village. What is remarkable is that they thought to include everyone, even in a sanitized picture of farm life in the early eighteenth century. We also knew on that summer day, though, that we were looking at something else. We were looking at Van Bergens, Black and white.

The tiny dark woman in the white dress tossing grain to the chickens could have been the ancestor of Eleanor, Bev, and Jake. The white man and woman standing in front of the house were certainly mine.

The Van Bergen house that Hester's father Thomas gave the newlyweds as a wedding gift stands today, perched on a high hill overlooking the entrance to the New York State Thruway in Coxsackie. The hum of traffic on the Thruway and on nearby Route 9W is constant. The house, which had long been neglected and deserted, is one of the few remaining signs of the prosperity of the Van Bergen and Houghtaling families. It has been renovated in recent years, and it looks as though a skylit third floor has been tucked under the eaves, maybe even the very spot where the slaves had rested. When I tried to go knock on the door, a fence blocked off the long driveway.

I thought back to Mabel Smith's romantic account of the elderly enslaved man. This hill, which today looks out over an antique center, an RV sales park, and a gas station, might have been just the place where the old man spent his last days. Each time I drive past there now, I think of him sitting under the tree more often than I think of Peter and Hester Van Bergen and their grand home.

6

Resistance and Running

The Van Bergen Overmantel was the picture the white enslavers wanted to show to the world. But in truth, an insidious cold war developed between the enslavers and the enslaved.[1] Occasionally, the resistance would bubble over into active war, such as the slave uprisings in New York City in 1714 and 1741, and the revolt in Saint-Domingue, now Haiti, in 1791.

Closer to the Hudson Valley, enslavers faced occasional cases of arson, stabbings, and murder, but they were rare. More common were subtle forms of resistance. These actions were sometimes almost undetectable, like sabotage of farming equipment or an imperceptible slowing down over the course of a workday. Sometimes an enslaved man might take an extra day or two to visit family around Christmas or Pinkster, the springtime festival that comes at Pentecost, fifty days after Easter.

Most of the time, however, escape was the first and last act in the undeclared war. It didn't matter that a man's or woman's life was tolerable on the surface. Enslaved people showed, by running, that they were not resigned to their life. Slavery, however easy in the eyes of white enslavers, was still enslavement.

Those who ran often did so even when the odds were stacked high against them. In 1761 a man named Anthony ran away from Coxsackie's Hendrick Houghtaling. Hendrick was a grandson of the original Cox-sackie Houghtaling and the father of Thomas, the man who liked to wine and dine visitors. Houghtaling took out an advertisement in the *New York Mercury*, describing Anthony as a "mulatto" man who spoke good Spanish but very bad Dutch and English.[2] Anthony seemed to have had a hard life in his twenty-eight years: he was missing an eye and was "very much Marked in the Face with the Small-pox." The reward for capturing Anthony was three pounds. I don't know whether this one-eyed, pock-marked, mixed-race man who spoke Spanish was able to get far enough away that he could escape detection. Maybe he did. I didn't find a reference to Anthony again.

The onset of the Revolutionary War also set up a clear paradox: cries calling for freedom from colonists who didn't believe in freedom for their enslaved men and women. While colonists, first in New England and then in New York, started to chafe against the taxes, laws, and control coming from England, the mood in the Hudson Valley was divided between Loyalists and Patriots.

My family tree had as many Loyalists as Patriots. Entire branches of the Hallenbecks and Van Valkenburgs hoped to remain under England's watch, or at least be left alone to live their lives. A large segment of the Van Valkenburg family headed to Canada and eventually changed their names to more English-sounding ones like Falkenbury, Vollick, and Fortenberry.[3] Even for the Patriots, there was plenty of grumbling about the costs of the war. I suspect that they knew these enormous changes would bring about equally disruptive shifts in the North's attitudes toward slavery.

"During the war both sides had sympathizers," wrote William S. Pelletreau. In the Hallenbeck family, for instance, the ones who lived in Loonenburg were "noted patriots," Pelletreau wrote, while some of the Hallenbecks who lived in Klinkenberg, just a few miles north of Loonenburg, "were equally noted tories." An old stone house owned by Jacob Hallenbeck on the Hudson welcomed "the friends of the royal government."[4] After the war, the Loyalist members of the Hallenbeck family ended up losing their homes and lands, confiscated by Patriots who might also have been their first cousins.

It's possible that their ambivalence about revolution was tempered with a realization that their enslaved also heard the words of independence. The British played into this split, realizing they had a way to weaken the rebellious colonists by undermining the institution of slavery. In 1775 Lord Dunmore, Virginia's British royal governor, was first to carry out this psychological coup by offering freedom for Blacks who fought on the Loyalist side. Initially, Dunmore's offer had limited success because it was limited to fighting men only. Those men would be forced to leave their wives and children. Four years later, British general Sir Henry Clinton expanded on Dunmore's ploy, offering freedom to all those enslaved by Patriots who would run away and serve the British in "any occupation which he shall think proper," including entire families. Clinton made this declaration, called the Philipsburg Proclamation, from his headquarters at Philipsburg Manor. The Philipse family supported the Crown. I wonder what the owners of the largest slave plantation in New York thought about Clinton's move.[5] Some reports noted that twenty thousand escaped slaves did end up fighting with the Loyalists.[6]

However brilliant a move by the British, not everyone was on board. Not all Loyalists were quick to volunteer their slaves. Some Loyalists promised freedom for their slaves and reneged later. Most were anything but abolitionists. Other Loyalists saw they were about to lose and fled the nascent country—but not before selling off their slaves.

Even so, enslaved people owned by Thomas Jefferson, Patrick Henry, and even General George Washington (at least seventeen people from his estate) took up the offer to cast their lot with the British. Washington's enslaved man named Henry Washington became a corporal in the Loyalists' unit called the Black Pioneers.[7] After the war, Henry Washington moved first to Nova Scotia and then eventually to Sierra Leone, where he fought against British colonization. Many of the slaves who fought for the British resettled in Nova Scotia, London, and Africa.

The Patriots eventually realized that they needed to match the offer: enlist enslaved people in exchange for freedom. They risked losing even more people to the Loyalists if they didn't. In 1781 they offered to pay slaveholders in money or land to allow their enslaved to fight in the Continental army and earn their freedom. For the enslaved, choosing any side was still a gamble. Even as they were fighting for the Patriots, they may have asked themselves why they should risk their lives for a country that had enslaved them. Nevertheless, New York's branch of the Continental army organized two regiments of Black soldiers. In return, those slaves would be manumitted after the war. This late move turned out to be less of a triumph for the Patriots: only about five thousand slaves ended up fighting for the Continental army.[8] Interestingly, both the National Museum of African American History and Culture in Washington and the Museum of the American Revolution in Philadelphia give nearly equal emphasis to the histories of the Black Loyalists as to the Black Patriots, with slightly greater attention on the Patriots, even though their numbers were far fewer.

I haven't found any records that my ancestors took up the offer to send their enslaved men to fight for either side. I also didn't find any records of Black revolutionary soldiers from my towns applying for pensions.

I suspect it was one man more than any other who dragged the colonists of the area into the fight for independence. Dominie (Reverend) Johannes Schuneman, known as the "Dutch Dominie of the Catskills,"[9] had answered a call of the Catskill Dutch Reformed Church for a pastor. He ended up marrying Anna Maria Van Bergen, one of the little girls traipsing next to her father Martin Van Bergen in the overmantel painting. Schuneman served both Catskill's and Coxsackie's Dutch Reformed churches. When Martin Van Bergen died, says the *History of Greene County*, this daughter inherited a good portion of his land as well as "the boy called Tom." The wealth added up. "Dominie Schuneman thus became, as the times went, a rich man."[10]

He was also a fervent Patriot. "All his zeal and superabounding energy flamed out in behalf of his country," wrote Henry Brace, the Catskill historian. "He preached constantly the high duty of strenuous defense, exhorted his neighbors and parishioners in behalf of a good cause, became a member of the local Committee of Safety, made his house a shelter for the few soldiers who passed by on their way northward to . . . Saratoga, and a hospital when they came back sick with fever." His enthusiasm drew anger against him from the Loyalists of the area, so he carried his guns with him even as he rode to preach the Gospel.[11]

Besides the Bible, he carried another document to his churches in Catskill and Coxsackie. In the year before the Declaration of Independence was signed, a special document circulated through Coxsackie. Called the Coxsackie Declaration, it was signed by 225 yeomen of Coxsackie in 1775.[12] Much like the national one a year later, the signers vowed to, "in the most solemn manner, resolve never to become Slaves." Of the 211 legible names listed there—some of them with an X, proof of their illiteracy—dozens of them were enslavers. And just as many of them were my kin. I found my five times great-grandfather Isaac Collier, plus a long roster of other family names: Van Loon, Hallenbeck, Spoor, Salisbury, Vosburgh, Dubois, Van Vechten, Conine, Vandenberg, Bronck, and Van Valkenburg.

Did these enslavers—especially Dominie Schuneman—see the hypocrisy in resolving never to become slaves? Did the enslaved of Coxsackie know about the Coxsackie Declaration, or about the offer from both sides of the fight that gave them a path to freedom? If they didn't know just how the war would play out, they must have sensed the rumblings. Fighting between the Loyalists and the Patriots could upend allegiances and tip the balance. Chaos can be useful when you're on the bottom of the heap.

One fascinating story from Leeds showed me as much about how slaves felt about their lives as it did about the chaotic energy of revolutionary times. On a Sunday evening in the winter of 1780, when the British had been making raids south from Canada all through upstate New York, a group of Native Americans and local Loyalists disguised as Natives moved through Leeds, near the farms of the Van Bergens. They wanted to ransack the houses and take prisoners.[13]

They finally got to the home of David Abeel, a Van Bergen neighbor who had married Gerret Van Bergen's daughter Neeltje. The family was having supper after the usual Sunday prayer services. The men, according to Henry Brace, were so surprised by the Native Americans and Loyalists disguised as Natives bursting through their door that they had no time to take down their guns. It wouldn't have mattered. The Abeel slaves had known about the plan to attack and decided to stuff the barrels of the guns with ash while the family was at church.

It was the perfect act of sabotage, and maybe a reason why Pastor Berkenmeyer in Loonenburg decided he wanted the village's enslaved people sitting on the front bench of Zion Lutheran. For the Abeels, leaving their enslaved unsupervised back at the house while they sat in church turned out to be a dangerous mistake. The sabotage left them with no usable guns.

One "large and powerful" enslaved man named Lon helped tie up David Abeel and his son Anthony. Then the truth emerged: Lon told his enslaver just what he thought of him. "The negro heaped upon his master all manner of abuse, complaining chiefly that he had not been allowed enough to eat," Brace wrote. Lon finally "snatched his master's hat from his head, giving him his own in exchange, and saying in Dutch, 'I am master now, wear that.' "[14]

The attackers took the two Abeel men as prisoners, along with Lon and an enslaved girl named Jannetje, and marched them 250 miles north to Montreal. Lon may have willingly left with the group. The small group struggled with wintery cold and hunger on their way to Canada, killing and eating their companion dogs one by one. The son, Anthony, eventually escaped. David Abeel, the father, was released because of his advanced age of fifty-three. Nothing further was ever heard of Lon. It's possible that the man, being both large and enslaved, was last to be fed. He may have starved to death. It's also possible that Lon decided his chances were better as a free man in Canada.

Jannetje eventually escaped from Canada and made her way back to the area. According to one account, Jannetje reached a settler's cabin along Lake Champlain. When she got back to Catskill, she worked for the Van Vechten family in Catskill, where, according to *Historic Catskill*, she "was taken in and kept for many years, for she could not trace her relatives."[15] Jannetje may have returned to Catskill because she figured she had no other options. Brace reported that in her later years would use the stories of her capture in the frigid winter to chasten and frighten the family's children.[16]

The story jumped out at me for more than one reason. First, it was an example of resistance—hidden at first and revealing itself in a dramatic moment. This enslaved man, feeling that he had the upper hand, used that chance to show his true feelings for his enslaver. Like the tale of the enslaved man who slit the throats of the Hallenbeck children, this story was another example of a calm surface hiding a deeper hatred, waters that seem placid at first glance but are roiling beneath. As James Fenimore Cooper had written, "The treatment of the negro is of the kindest character." Maybe not. The disruptions of the revolution looked like a harbinger of disruptions for the enslaved as well.

There was a second reason the story grabbed my attention: Jannetje's full name, according to Henry Brace, was Jannetje Van Valkenburg. This enslaved woman shared my family name. Chances are that at one point, Jannetje had been owned by a person in the Van Valkenburg family. The discovery marked the end of my theory that the Van Valkenburg family had managed to escape the taint of slavery.

Before I came upon the story of Lon and Jannetje, I knew this truth on some level. But each story I found forced me to continue to recalibrate my thinking. In my hometown, with my web of family ties and intermarriages and centuries-long connections, I would not find a single family that didn't have some link to enslavement. And each time I found a new tie between my family and slavery, I also knew that there would be more, tucked away as if behind a hidden door or just below the waves, like the treacherous currents of the Hudson. There was the placid surface and an altogether different situation underneath. I just needed to keep looking.

Meanwhile, David Abeel returned home from his ordeal and prospered. Lon's insult may have severed any imagined ties of affection between him and any people he enslaved, but it didn't dissuade David Abeel from owning human beings. Ten years after the incident, in the 1790 federal census, he listed thirteen slaves; in 1800 he had ten; and in 1810 he counted eight slaves.[17] When he died in 1813, he bequeathed his slaves to his children, even as New York slavery was in its final years.[18]

Yet the world was changing. Outside of New York, the surrounding states were starting to abolish slavery. Vermont was first, prohibiting slavery in its 1777 constitution. In 1780 Pennsylvania began a system of gradual manumission. Massachusetts (1783), Connecticut (1784), and Rhode Island (1784) also ended slavery through gradual manumission systems. New Hampshire seems to have ended it by attrition, as the number of slaves dwindled to almost none at the end of the eighteenth century. Only New Jersey clung to its slavery laws for longer than New York.

As the Revolutionary War reached its peak, so too did the number of escapes—and attempted escapes—from slavery. In 1780 a six-foot-tall, "spare and ragged" twenty-six-year-old man named Peter was "taken up in the woods near Catskill" by a man named John Baptiste Dumond. I found Dumond's handwritten report on a paper in the records of Greene County's historical documents at Vedder Library in Coxsackie. Peter didn't belong to Dumond, but it's clear that the Catskill man hoped that by grabbing Peter and holding him at his Catskill home, he would be rewarded. According to Dumond, Peter "speaks nothing but English and his Mother Tongue." As for his English, "he speaks so improper that he cannot be understood only here and there a word and the latter is such a tongue that our Negroes here cannot understand."[19]

To Greene County's historian Jonathan Palmer, the man's garbled language could have been a clue that Peter spoke an African language, Spanish, or Portuguese. Peter's limited language skills also meant he was easier to catch. Spare and ragged, he lost his chance at a new life. Even if his enslaver never saw the newspaper advertisement and didn't retrieve him, it's unlikely that Dumond would simply let him go free.

Elizabeth Freeman found a different form of resistance, one that ended in a happier way. Her gravesite is nestled inside a quiet grove in Stockbridge Cemetery, in western Massachusetts, not far from the Red Lion Inn (established in 1773) and the Norman Rockwell Museum. According to some stories, Freeman, originally called Mumbet, was born around 1744, just across the river from my hometown, in the village of Claverack.

The stone is rectangular and spare, its top ridge covered with pebbles (including a bright purple one), larger stones, and pinecones. Dried flowers rest at its base. The spot, inside what's known as the Sedgwick Circle, has become a kind of pilgrimage place, probably the only place in the state where people can pay their respects to a woman who sued her way to freedom. Her 1781 lawsuit, championed by Theodore Sedgwick, who is buried just in front of her in the center of the Sedgwick Circle, was part of the push that led to the end of slavery in Massachusetts.

I had never heard of this woman until Eleanor mentioned her. For her sixtieth birthday, she told me, she treated herself to a visit to Stockbridge so she could pay her respects to this emblem of resistance and perseverance. "She is a personal hero," she said. When Eleanor first mentioned her, I thought the story was an interesting anecdote, but since it was set in Massachusetts, I figured it had nothing to do with my history, or our shared history. I was wrong.

Her story was told by Catherine Sedgwick, one of America's earliest novelists. Elizabeth Freeman never learned to read or write. Sedgwick's saccharine story of Mumbet, sometimes shortened to Bett, reminded me of the melodrama of *Uncle Tom's Cabin*.[20]

We have a few facts. Annatie Hoogeboom was the daughter of a Claverack man named Pieter Hoogeboom. In his 1746 will Hoogeboom

Figure 8. The Stockbridge, Massachusetts, grave site of Elizabeth Freeman, also known as Mumbet, who was one of the first enslaved women in Massachusetts to sue for her freedom and win. The stone is part of the Sedgwick family plot. Photo by author.

(later spelled Hogeboom) bequeathed his slaves to his twelve children, five sons and seven daughters: "all my negroes and negresses, big and little, young and old," he wrote.[21] Annatie (also called Hannah) married John Ashley, a Massachusetts man who also owned slaves. The Ashleys enslaved Elizabeth and a younger girl named Lizzie, who may have been part of Hannah's inheritance from the Claverack estate.

According to Catherine Sedgwick's account, Bett resisted her enslavers from the start. One story mentioned she had raised her arm to prevent Hannah Ashley from striking Lizzie with a hot pan, and the pan hit her instead, burning her arm and creating a large wound. Bett refused to cover up the wound so that visitors to the house would ask about what had happened, thus embarrassing the Ashleys.

Eventually, Bett, with the help of Catherine Sedgwick's father Theodore, sued for her freedom. The state constitution, noting that "all men are born free and equal," had been written the year before. According to Catherine Sedgwick, Bett said, "I heard that paper read yesterday that all men are born equal and that every man has a right to freedom. I am not a dumb critter. Won't the law give me my freedom?"

The case was tried at the County Court of Common Pleas in Great Barrington; Theodore Sedgwick argued that the new state constitution outlawed slavery. The jury decided that Bett and another enslaved man named Brom were not property, and they were released. After a third related case went to the state Supreme Court, slavery was effectively abolished in Massachusetts. Bett changed her name to Elizabeth Freeman and went to work for the Sedgwick family. Would she have succeeded without the Sedgwicks? Unlike Sojourner Truth, she spent the rest of her days quietly serving the Sedgwick family.

Even if Freeman's story was shaped and sentimentalized by the Sedgwick family, I found the story of Elizabeth Freeman fascinating. Her journey took her from a Dutch household in the middle of a very quiet stretch of the Hudson Valley—quiet in the eighteenth century and nearly as quiet today—to a place of freedom. She became an icon. I wondered if I could find a story like that in New York. Did the enslaved in the Hudson Valley find a way to make themselves heard? I wondered what might have happened to the other people enslaved by the Hogeboom family, one of the oldest and wealthiest families on the eastern shore of the Hudson.

It didn't take me too long to trace the Hogebooms to my side of the river. Another of Pieter Hoogeboom's daughters, Hannah Ashley's sister Catherina, also called Catryntie, married Philip Conine of Coxsackie in 1720.[22] Not only did I find the family link, but I also found further proof that Elizabeth Freeman's life would have had a different outcome in my hometowns. Philip Conine and Catherina Hogeboom were my six times great-grandparents. Pieter Hogeboom was my seven times great-grandfather. The Conine family in Coxsackie, like so many of the area, had a generations-long history as enslavers. I found five generations of Conines, all with children named Philip, and every one of those generations, from the early eighteenth century well into the nineteenth, enslaved human beings. It's also very likely that Catherina, like her sister, brought her own enslaved people with her to Coxsackie upon her marriage to Philip Conine. The enslaved that Catherina undoubtedly inherited remained in New York. No one took up their case, and none of the Conine family slaves became icons like Elizabeth Freeman.

I sent Eleanor a text: I had found a Coxsackie connection to Mumbet and the Massachusetts story. The difference, of course, was that no one in Coxsackie was thinking about lawsuits that could free slaves. Eleanor wrote back: "I remember my grandmother talking about an Aunt Nancy Conine in Coxsackie." We had seen her gravesite in the section of Riverside Cemetery where we had found other Black families. Nancy Conine (1828–1911) is listed separately on a gravestone with William Egberts (1852–1934). Eleanor told me that Nancy had been married to a man named Joseph Conine.

I looked at the Coxsackie Record. Philip Conine, the son of the Philip Conine who married Catherina Hogeboom, along with his son, also named Philip (lord, help me), listed seven babies born to their enslaved women. One of these babies was a boy Joseph, born to a woman named Bett, on March 13, 1802. It could have been Joseph Conine, married to Aunt Nancy.

It had happened again. A name would come up in my research, and I would track down an ancestor. Then Eleanor would mention she also found a person with that last name in her family tree. We were linked again. It became a bit of a game: Find the connection between enslaver and enslaved. Find the larger link to history. We became almost giddy with the thought of the stickiness of this cobweb. Although we were researching one of the darkest, most shameful periods of American history, we were undertaking it with something close to a sense of triumph, as if it were almost funny. Or maybe it was more like a form of gallows humor, the idea that we might get excited when we found another example of a slave, a sale, a human being bequeathed in a will. In that way we were in perfect sync, more than kindred spirits. We were doing something necessary. We were tracing the tiniest footprints of evidence, but we were also giving names to the unnamed. Toni Morrison's line about looking for what existed below the surface was, as so many things with Morrison, exactly right.

At one point in the evening, Eleanor wrote, "There is a white Joseph Conine in Athens. Have to be careful not to mix them up." I responded, "Oh dear god help us." She answered, "He hates us. He really does." Maybe, I thought. But at least we had Toni Morrison on our side.

Philip and Catherina Conine's daughter, also named Catherina, married Philip Bronk. One of their children was my four times great-grandmother, Anna Bronk, married to Casper Collier. Casper was the son of Isaac, the first slaveholder ancestor I had found. They were all connected and all conspiring from the grave to keep us from learning the truth.

That night I dreamed I was peeling up a long sidewalk and staring at the dirt beneath it. In the dream, all I saw was dirt.

There may have been no other Mumbets, but change was in the air during the Revolution, coupled with more insistent debates in the New York legislature about gradual manumission. Finally, there were some results on the ground. A law passed in 1785 allowed manumission of slaves without penalty. Before then, slaveholders had a pay a bond and faced financial loss if they chose to manumit their enslaved. It was a way to ensure that workers past their prime wouldn't become a public burden. If they could assure that their enslaved would be able to support themselves, they could release them.

For many who fled, these gradual changes were not enough to convince them to wait it out. While there might have been an increase in manumissions, there was also a surge in runaways.

The doctor Alexander Coventry wrote in his diary that he had treated a farmer on the other side of the Hudson, a man named John Van Valkenburgh, who had a festering wound after being stabbed in the thigh by his enslaved man.[23] In 1787, according to Coventry, "The negro and his wench had run away, and escaped into Boston state [Massachusetts] where negroes are free." Thanks in part to Mumbet, Massachusetts had abolished slavery just three years earlier. Maybe this couple had even heard about Elizabeth Freeman's legal victory. In this case, though, their freedom was temporary. John Van Valkenburgh and his brother William went in pursuit. They caught up with them but the enslaved man "drew out a large knife and made two or three stabs at him." One stab landed in John Van Valkenburgh's thigh. Despite the attack, the brothers captured them.

Six weeks after the incident, John Van Valkenburgh's wound continued to fester. "He has had several surgeons," Coventry reported, "but the wound is worse than at the beginning; the orifice is almost closed, though the internal wound is as large as ever." We don't know what happened to John Van Valkenburgh, undoubtedly a member of my extended family, or the recaptured slaves, but neither seemed good. Stabbing his enslaver in the thigh made it evident that this man was going to do what he could to avoid recapture.

Others who ran probably succeeded. Also in 1787, Harry, a man enslaved by Dirck Spoor of Coxsackie, ran away. Spoor advertised for the return of Harry, who "speaks good English, High and Low Dutch," meaning both German and Dutch. Harry had a large scar on one on his feet and took a fiddle with him. He advertised for Harry again in 1790, describing different clothing the man was wearing, which seemed to prove Harry had been recaptured and had run a second time.[24] I'd like to think that after multiple tries, Harry got free. Maybe he could support himself with his fiddle. Oddly, Spoor listed no enslaved on the 1790 census— which might mean Harry did find freedom. But Spoor listed two enslaved in 1800, and one in 1820. Whether these were people connected to Harry is hard to know. Maybe the one in 1820 was still Harry.

In his journal's picture of daily life, Alexander Coventry best illuminated the undeclared war between enslaver and enslaved. The two-thousand-page record of the roving doctor rests, undigitized, in the manuscripts and special collections floor of the New York State Library in Albany. Coventry's attention to detail and blunt honesty makes it one of the most revealing everyday portraits of life in eighteenth-century New York that I've seen. His relationships with two of his enslaved men, named Cuff and Cobus, gave me a sense that this tug-of-war was more complicated than I realized. I thought back to Coventry's comment that hired men "must be humored" so that they will stay. The same apparently applied to the enslaved workers.

Coventry, who had come to America from Scotland to help settle his dead father's estate, hadn't been in the country more than a year when he decided he needed to buy a man to help with work on his farm. He crossed the Hudson in the summer of 1786 "with the intent to buy a negro belonging to Widow Provost." The enslaved man, however, had other ideas. "He is a likely fellow," Coventry wrote, "but not very large, aged about 20, very proud, had a haughty mien, and never was under master. He preferred not to leave his old mistress, and so she would not sell him."[25] Maybe this "haughty fellow" was attached to his female enslaver; maybe he felt his life was marginally better with her. What stood out to me was that the sale was foiled by the enslaved man.

Word must have gotten out that Coventry was looking to purchase someone. Later that year, he was approached by an enslaved man named Jack who wanted Coventry to buy him. Jack told Coventry that his purchase price was forty pounds. His enslaver, however, gave Coventry a different story. He said Jack "had got drunk twice, and in his frolic would have a bill of sale." Was Jack only joking about seeking a new enslaver? The true price turned out to be seventy pounds for Jack and fifty pounds for his wife. "We could not agree on the price," Coventry concluded. "Was invited to stay and had a good supper." Jack's control over the situation could only go so far.[26]

But Coventry kept running into complicated domestic dramas. In 1788 another man named Jack asked Coventry to buy him. Jack was apparently fighting with his mother, Coventry learned, and "had told his master he must have another house to live in." The man's enslaver, though, "did not give much encouragement," so Coventry gave up.[27]

Finally he had some luck. He encountered an enslaved man named Cuff, owned by a man named Cornelius Van Keuren. Cuff said he wanted to be purchased by Alexander Coventry's cousin William, a farmer in the area. But the doctor also wanted Cuff, so he made what sounded like a marriage proposal. "I asked Cuff if he would live with me," he wrote. Cuff turned him down. He wanted William Coventry. But William Coventry and Van Keuren could not agree on a price. Alexander Coventry tried again. "I told him if the negro would agree to live with me, I would buy him." Cuff agreed, and almost immediately began asking for time off.[28] As the months passed, the two men seemed to settle into a steady working relationship. Coventry's journal was filled with errands for Cuff: carrying wagonloads of corn, grain, and wood to market, planting crops, jointing shingles, and helping neighboring farmers with the harvest. While Cuff was carrying out his tasks, Coventry borrowed a Dutch bible to teach himself Dutch, and spent other days reading novels in French or articles in British magazines.

On the first day of June 1789 Coventry noted that Cuff was keeping "Pinkster, a festival or feast among the Dutch." Pinkster, in fact, served as a popular way to push back, reverse the social order, and maybe even escape slavery. Other accounts of the time talk about the enslaved taking extra days off to celebrate Pinkster. The day itself often turned into a celebratory party, with one enslaved man appointed as king.[29] Some enslaved used Pinkster as way to leave completely. In an advertisement for a man named Caesar, who absconded in 1815 from Cobleskill in the Catskill Mountains, Aaron W. Slingerland wrote, "Having got leave of his master to join in the amusements of Pingster Holidays, with a promise that he would come back on the Tuesday following; but he has not yet returned."[30]

As the years passed, Cuff exerted increasing autonomy. The day before Easter, April 3, 1790, Coventry reported that Cuff took a wagonload of wood to Hudson. He was "not home at bedtime, came home very late, and was partly drunk." The next month, Cuff's father showed up, and "Cuff spent most of the day with him." On Christmas of that year, Cuff left the house and "did not come home very soon this morning." The following spring, in 1791, Cuff told Coventry that his wife had had a baby and was sick.[31] He wanted time off as well as some money. When Coventry decided to move west to Fairfield, New York, along the Mohawk River, he bought Cuff's wife (a "whore wench," in Coventry's words), along with their two daughters, Ann and Jean, to accompany him. I suspect he knew that Cuff would not remain with Coventry unless he had his family with him.

As I read the journal, I got a vivid picture of two men, more servant and employer than enslaver and enslaved, or so it seemed from Coventry's equable descriptions. Cuff never held back. Once, after Cuff had treated himself to a few days off, Coventry wrote, "I spoke pretty sharp to him." Cuff responded that he wanted another master. Coventry answered that he should find one for himself, his wife, and children. That never seemed to happen.

The Coventry journal has a gap of about fifteen years, and Cuff disappeared from the journal after 1797. The doctor, however, was not done with enslavement. In 1814 he bought a man he called Cobus. Cobus was even more resistant than Cuff, possibly because he knew emancipation was on the horizon. He ran away in 1818.[32] Coventry went in search of him and sent his son George to look in another direction. He put out advertisements. Cobus was found in Canada a few weeks later and some-how was convinced to return. Coventry put the enslaved man in shackles until he realized he needed to put the man to work. Not cowed by the experience, Cobus said he wanted a new master.

Coventry asked his children what to do, and they gave him an ear-ful: his son George told him he shouldn't tie up Cobus and he shouldn't have struck him. In fact, George said, he shouldn't have bought the man at all. Coventry's other children piled on, as Coventry noted in his jour-nal: "Elizabeth told me that they said they would run away too, if they were slaves." His children told him they didn't "approve of" slavery. They refused to keep an eye on Cobus.[33] With the Revolutionary War long gone and with abolitionists increasingly making the case for emancipation, change was happening on his doorstep.

The next month, Cobus ran off again. Coventry seemed to give up at this point. He bought the indenture of a young woman named Caty, who would serve him until she was twenty-five.[34] The diary ended with Cov-entry's death in 1831.

In November 1793 Albany endured an historic fire that destroyed twenty-six homes. The population of the city of Albany, according to the 1790 census, was 3,498 people. Of that number, 572 people were enslaved, 16 percent of the total population. After the fire, suspicion immediately became focused on the city's enslaved, possibly underscored by the revo-lution in Haiti began just two years earlier. More than ever, white en-slavers were looking over their shoulders. The historical accounts of the event have evolved over time. One fact is that two teenaged, enslaved girls named Bet and Dinah confessed to setting the fire, and they were hung a few months later, on what is known as Pinkster Hill, the site where so many joyous celebrations took place. A third enslaved person, Pomp, was hung a month later. One scholar compared the trial and execution to the witch trials in Salem.[35] Others cast doubt on the motivations of the enslaved, especially since their executions were delayed several times over months.[36]

The fear of revolts and resistance among the enslaved continued. In 1796, just a few years before the start of gradual emancipation, enslav-ers about sixty-five miles south of Coxsackie were nervous enough about runaway slaves that they formed the Slave Apprehending Society of

Shawangunk, with a payment system for those who could capture run-aways and return them to their owners.[37] "A Suspicion seems to prevail among many of the Negro Slaves that the Legislature of the State has liberated them," the men wrote in the society's constitution, aware that slaves were watching abolition measures come and go in the state legislature. The hunters, called Riders, would get fifteen dollars plus expenses for each fugitive they could capture and return. Part of the blame went to white agitators who were encouraging the enslaved to run away, the group said. Whether the group had any luck finding runaways in the state is harder to know.

Those who ran away became bolder. A French expatriate named Honoré Chaurand, who lived in Coxsackie, advertised in September 1798 for a family that had escaped: Dan, Dian, and their children Samuel and Nassey. The children, the advertisement said, were a two-year-old boy and an "unweaned" seven-month-old girl. Chaurand wrote that they could be armed with "guns and pistols."[38] At first, I thought that Chaurand's escaped family were recaptured: on March 25, 1800, two years after the armed escape, I found a woman named Deone registered under Chaurand's name on the Coxsackie Record.[39] But then I discovered something else. Finding himself unfit for the farming life, Chaurand leased his land in 1801 to a farmer named John Wolfe, promising him use of Dan, his wife, and three children. Later, in a lawsuit, Wolfe said that he had been deprived of the services of Dan. My theory is that after Dian (or Deone) had a third baby, they all fled again.[40]

After the gradual abolition statute passed in 1799, newspaper advertisements for runaways doubled.[41] The first ten years of the nineteenth century saw a peak of advertisements, according to *In Defiance: Runaways from Slavery in New York's Hudson River Valley, 1735–1831*. In the years 1791–1800, there were 105 advertisements for runaways. That number nearly doubled to 202 ads in the years 1801–1810.

On November 7, 1799, Jonas Bronk of Coxsackie took out an advertisement in a local newspaper promising a "20 Dollars Reward."[42] Run away from him was "a Negro man named TITUS, about 28 years of age, black complexion, about five feet six inches high, stout built. Had on when he went away a grey homespun sailor's jacket, striped trousers, black knapt hat. Whoever secures the said Negro so that his master may get him again shall receive Ten Dollars Reward, if taken within ten miles of Hudson, or the above reward if taken any greater distance." Bronk added ominously, "All masters of vessels are forbid to take him on board at their peril." Jonas Bronk was the brother of my ancestor Anna, married to Casper Collier.

Casper M. Hallenbeck of Coxsackie, my first cousin six times removed, and his son, John C. Hallenbeck, ran a rather overheated advertisement in 1805 in a newspaper called the *Bee*, based in Hudson, across the river: "ONE HUNDRED AND FIFTY DOLLARS REWARD!" The three men—young, likely healthy, and male—must have been a source of valuable labor. The first two men seemed to have escaped together: Ben, about twenty-two, had gold rings in his ears and was wearing a fur hat. Ben also took an extensive wardrobe with him: a blue broadcloth sailor's coat, a pair of black velvet pantaloons, a striped swansdown waistcoat, and a homemade linen shirt with muslin sleeves. With him was Jack, about twenty-five, who was "stooping in his gait, slow in speech, and parrot-toed." Jack had red silk strings in his ears. The Hallenbecks added in a notice for another man who had run away a year earlier: Mink, a mulatto man who was about thirty-six or thirty-seven years old, a fiddler who was "somewhat addicted to drinking and swearing." Mink had been seen in Utica, they added.[43]

As late as 1807, enslavers such as Isaac Mitchell of Albany were chasing after runaways. Mitchell was especially annoyed that his slave Dine and her six-month-old infant had fled. He speculates that she may have "gone up the Mohawk river, where she said she had children." He fumed: "The conduct of this servant is peculiarly ungrateful; I had owned her about two months, during which time she had never been put to hard service, or ill treated."[44] It didn't matter to him that this sale pulled her from her other little ones. It reminded me of Cadwallader Colden selling his slave to the West Indies so she wouldn't stick around and "spoil" her children.

Legal slavery ended in New York State in 1827. But that fact didn't stop a man named Thomas Williams in tiny Durham in Greene County's mountains. In the May 7, 1829, issue of the *Catskill Recorder, and Greene County Republican*, he took out an advertisement: "ONE CENT REWARD. RAN away from the subscriber, on the 13th inst. a negro slave by the name of Phillip Anders, aged about 23 years.—This is to forbid all persons harboring; trusting, or employing said runaway, as I will not pay any charges whatever contracted on his account, and am determined to prosecute for his wages."[45]

In 1829 Phillip Anders could not have been a "negro slave." He had been born in 1806 and was, by law, a free man in New York. He may have been fleeing his indenture. Announcing that he would only pay a paltry reward showed that Williams was more concerned about the chances that Phillip Anders might create financial liability than he was in recovering the young man. More than that, though, the advertisement was proof that slavery was far from over in New York State.

Elizabeth Freeman died in 1829, two years after anyone who might have remained in her New York family would have been freed. Accounts at the time said that she had a family with a daughter and grandchildren living nearby. Freeman, however, is buried with the Sedgwick family. The first circle after the tall obelisk holds the original Sedgwick family members, next to Freeman's resting place. There, the grave is straight and simple, a somber headstone among the more elaborate ones in this family circle adorned with urns, obelisks, and rounded stones.

At the edge of the cemetery, I picked a bunch of delicate late summer asters as gnats buzzed around my face. I left the flowers tucked in next to the pebbles and pinecones on the tombstone's top ridge and wondered what she might have thought about lying forever with the family that helped her get out of slavery but for whom she continued to work until her final days. Where is her family buried? Elizabeth Freeman rests right next to Catherine Sedgwick, the novelist who fashioned the narrative about her beloved Bett. On her stone are the words: "She was born a slave and remained a slave for nearly thirty years. She could neither read nor write, yet in her own sphere she had no superior or equal. She neither wasted time nor property. She never violated a trust, nor failed to perform a duty. In every situation of domestic trial, she was the most efficient helper, and the tenderest friend. Good mother farewell."

CASPER AND NANCY IN THE TWILIGHT

On a September day in 1823, Colonel Casper Collier was sitting in his farmhouse in Coxsackie.

The War of 1812 veteran was a successful man. Fifty-four years old, the father of seven, the grandfather of two, Collier had been married since he was twenty to Antje (or Anna) Bronk, a daughter of the first family of Coxsackie.

That day, he had a surprise visit. At his doorstep was his former slave, Nancy Jackson. More than twenty years earlier, Casper had sold her off, but today, Nancy had traveled eighteen miles south from her home near the capital of Albany, a good day's journey on foot, to reach out to her former owner for help.

Nancy, now a free woman, was fighting for her daughter, Sarah. She had given birth to Sarah when she was still enslaved in Coxsackie. Casper had sold mother and her two babies off in 1802, launching one of them, young Sarah, into a twilight zone of servitude and confusion that lasted her entire childhood and part of her early adult life.

Casper Collier was my great-great-great-great-grandfather. Although by 1823 he had rid himself of all his slaves, Casper was being pulled back into the vestiges of a bizarre twilight period of slavery in New York that lasted from 1799 to 1827, nearly thirty years of gradual—very gradual—emancipation.

Babies born after July 4, 1799, were technically free. But this was a begrudging and frequently cruel emancipation—a period of virtual enslavement at times as brutal and lasting as full-on slavery. Children born to enslaved mothers in this time were still required to serve until they were young adults. They could end up enmeshed in indentured servitude— almost identical to slavery—for years after the state had legally ended enslavement. This twilight stage was another way New York's enslavers, including my ancestors, held on to slavery for as long as they could, and when they were forced to give it up, found ways to finagle the system to get as much as they could from their human property.

It's true that in the years before the American Revolution, abolitionists, especially Quakers, had advocated for the end of slavery in New York. Even among Quakers, the cause of abolition took hold gradually.[1] But abolitionists in these Hudson Valley towns were rare in those early days. Quaker meetinghouses in Athens and New Baltimore weren't established until well into the nineteenth century. Hudson, across the river, had a Quaker meetinghouse as early as 1784,[2] but any antislavery activities were quiet and hard to pinpoint.

New York's 1777 constitution, which borrowed language from the 1776 Declaration of Independence, makes no mention of manumission, abolition, or slavery. It was not for want of trying from Founding Father Gouverneur Morris, who called slavery "the curse of heaven on the states where it prevailed." Morris, a member of the New York Provincial Congress, wrote the Preamble to the US Constitution. Like many aristocratic men of his time, Gouverneur Morris was born into a slaveholding family. His father Lewis was one of the state's largest enslavers, owning forty-one enslaved men and women.[3]

Gouverneur Morris wanted language inserted in New York's constitution that would commit the new state to emancipation. He failed, though, at convincing his fellow legislators to take even the smallest of steps: a promise of future freedom for the state's enslaved. The best that Morris and other antislavery legislators could do was insert vague language that would ask future legislators to "take the most effective measures consistent with public safety for abolishing domestic slavery." In the villages of Loonenburg, Catskill, and Coxsackie, I found no talk of abolishing slavery, even gradually.

The creation of the New York Manumission Society in 1785 came with its own odd paradox. Founded by enslavers like John Jay, its members continued to keep slaves while they fretted about free Blacks in New York who were being kidnapped and sold south. Instead of an immediate end to slavery, the manumission society wanted a more moderate, gradual manumission.

Why was abolition so stuck in New York while many of the New England states had already abolished slavery? The New York State legislature fell heavily under the influence of slave-owning Dutch farmers throughout the Hudson Valley. Many of them felt no reason to give up their property.[4] Opponents to emancipation threw in further roadblocks, asking: What about citizenship? Should free Blacks have the right to vote? Should they be allowed to marry white people?

A 1788 New York slave act went in the other direction, creating penalties for anyone who helped escaping slaves and affirming that all slaves were slaves for life. The law made one concession to abolitionists: it was now illegal to ship slaves out of state, although even that law was amended to let slaveholders sell unruly and difficult slaves to places where slavery still thrived. If enslavers could prove to a court that their slaves had committed crimes or had been in some other way difficult, they could be sold into harsh slavery in the Caribbean or New Orleans.

When John Jay, one of the principal founders of the New York Manumission Society, ran for governor of the state in 1792, his opponents used his abolitionist beliefs against him. Jay wanted to "rob every Dutchman of the property he possesses most dear to his heart, his slaves," his opponents argued.[5] Jay, meanwhile, promised to manumit his own slaves after they worked off what he considered a "reasonable retribution" for their cost. Jay lost the 1792 campaign but was elected governor in 1795 and helped push forward that 1799 gradual manumission law. To placate slaveholders, the law tacked on a payment system so that enslavers would collect compensation for the cost of raising these gradually emancipated children.

The Hudson Valley was fighting back against slavery's end, both gradual and immediate. This was a place where, in the words of filmmaker

Wendy Harris, slavery died hard. The *History of Greene County* found opposition to slavery so unusual in the eighteenth century that it drew special attention in this short biography of a Catskill man named John Overbagh: "He was an extreme conservative, and took pride in following the ways of his fathers, in food, dress, modes of farming, and all the habits of life. He was slow of thought, silent, of sound judgment, and a firm believer in the tenets of his church. It is remembered of him that he refused to own slaves: such ownership being deemed by him to be sinful."[6] I smiled at the passive construction—"it is remembered of him"—which felt like a good way to keep the whole commentary at arm's length.

The rare references to slavery in Coxsackie and Catskill newspapers were advertisements for runaways. Slaveholders sought men and women, sometimes with their small children, who might go north to Canada, south to New York City, where they could blend in with a larger population of free Blacks, or east to Massachusetts.

The new emancipation law in New York, signed in March 1799, showed just how gradual real freedom could be.[7] Babies born between July 4, 1799, and July 4, 1827, would eventually win their freedom, but it was a freedom they would pay for in years of service. All were trapped as indentured servants for more than twenty years. The law said, "Any Child born of a slave within this State after the fourth day of July next, shall be *deemed* and *adjudged* to be born free: Provided nevertheless that such Child shall be the *servant* of the legal *proprietor* of his or her mother until such servant if a male shall arrive at the age of twenty eight years, and if a female at the age of twenty-five years." Their parents and siblings born before that date were still enslaved. The choice of July 4 was a deliberate nod to American independence, whether the enslaved people embraced the symbolism of that date or not.

This rolling abolition meant that it was not unusual to find households in the Hudson Valley with a mixture of slaves, free Blacks, and white farmers, all living together under one roof. In 1811, for instance, Greene County conducted a census and found 267 slaves, along with 452 "free people not Indian," mostly living in white households.[8] These were the emancipated slaves who continued to live in the homes of their former enslavers.

Since the children were bound to service, their fate was in the hands of those who enslaved their mother, and after that, those who owned their years of service. Children could be sent away from their mothers as young as one, sometimes at four, and most often when they were six or seven—an age that was considered an appropriate time to begin working. Small children could help around the house and farm: serving food, sweeping the chimney, weeding gardens, milking cows, caring for infants, or acting as servant-companions to the white children of the household. This bondage sometimes lasted longer than New York's official end of slavery. If a child was born one day before July 4, 1827, he was stuck for the next twenty-one years. Many indentured twilight children were "bought" and "sold" long after slavery supposedly ended in New York.

The environment also conspired against these indentured children if they imagined they might slip away back to their mothers. The Hudson Valley was an isolated place, with more frontier villages and farms than bustling towns. No trains connected cities, and the roads through pine forests, rolling hills, and mountains could be impassable with snow in the winter and mud in every season. The Hudson River carried the bulk of the traffic north and south, but the river froze solid through the long winter months. If an owner sold a child's indenture to a new boss just twenty miles away, that child could be separated from her mother at the age of six or seven and not see her again for many years, if ever. These lost children truly could be lost forever.

Tracing the stories of the lost children involved a lot of luck and digging. Every so often I found these children and young adults in legal documents, bills of sale, advertisements for runaways, and sometimes even in newspaper accounts of resilient long-lived people, written long after the twilight ended. But what rose to the surface rarely painted a full portrait. Instead, I found myself chasing after the smallest of glimpses. What was the status of these allegedly free Blacks? How much choice did they have in where they lived, what children they might bear, or whom they could marry?

When Casper Collier answered the door to his former enslaved woman, the river community of Coxsackie was evolving from a conservative Dutch-speaking village to an English-speaking town expected to adapt to a new country and a government free from British rule. Most of Coxsackie's residents were farmers, tied to the rhythms of the seasons and to attendance at the Dutch Reformed Church each Sunday.

The Collier family was solidly pro-independence. Casper's father, Isaac Collier, the ancestor I first discovered had been a slaveholder, was one of 225 local men who signed their names to the Coxsackie Declaration. Born in 1769 during the beginning of American colonial unrest, Casper found himself welcomed into a family with comfortable wealth: he was the eighth of eleven children (and the fourth son) of one of Coxsackie's largest landowners.[9] Along with inheriting a large farm in his father's 1796 will, Casper inherited slaves, although it isn't clear how many. Isaac, who listed five slaves in the 1790 census, doled out just three people by name in his will—Marie, Will, and Sansom—and wrote that the rest of his slaves should be divided among his children and grandchildren, "share and share alike."[10]

Some of those slaves are likely part of the six listed by Casper on his 1800 census form, four years after his father's death.[11] Casper married Antje Bronk, a member of Coxsackie's founding family, the area's first white settlers, and the descendant of other prominent families such as the Conines, the Hogebooms, and the Van Vechtens. Antje (later Anglicized to Anna) was the daughter of an American revolutionary hero, Captain Philip Bronk, who fought against the British in the Schoharie valley. Philip Bronk listed seven slaves in the 1790 census.[12] Philip Bronk's wife was Catherina Conine, the granddaughter of Pieter Hogeboom of Claverack, the former enslaver of Mumbet Freeman. The web was large and tangled.

Casper was managing one of the largest farms in town, propelling himself into further prosperity after the hardships of the Revolutionary War years. Everyone knew his place in the town's hierarchy. When families went to the Dutch Reformed Church, they sat in pews according to their standing in the community, with the Bronk family taking up the church's first few rows. Because the churches were not heated, slaves would carry foot warmers—coal or embers of wood in a bucket that women could tuck under their dresses—so that the worshippers could have some semblance of warmth during the hours of wintertime religious services.[13]

By 1810, Casper was down to just one enslaved person, although that early census didn't say whether that person was male or female.[14] The names of the other five who were no longer living with the Colliers are not listed. Casper may have sold, manumitted, or abandoned them. They might have run off or died. Three of them might have been Nancy and her two children, sold off in 1800. It was the same case for the other enslaved people in Coxsackie. Between 1800 and 1820 the town of Coxsackie saw a dramatic drop in the number of enslaved people, from 301 to 29.[15] That sudden decline in numbers proved that official slavery was ending. Indentured slavery lasted far longer.

Each new baby born to an enslaved mother had to be registered with the town within a year. That allowed the owner to technically abandon the child—even if the child still lived with him—to the Overseers of the Poor, an early form of government-run charity funded out of the state coffers, which would take financial responsibility for the infant. Most of the time, those infants remained with the enslaved mother, at least until they were old enough to be productive in some way.

In the beginning, New York State paid owners or whoever had charge of the child a maintenance fee of $3.50 a month per baby, a kind of compensation to enslavers for having to give up their slaves. The program ended up being costly, with the state paying out around $20,000 by 1804, which would be close to half a million dollars in today's money, and a solid 6 percent of the state budget. That's when the state legislature decided to revoke the compensation part while retaining the actual abolition. Even with the financial compensation, some enslavers treated the children as unwelcome dependents who didn't add much in the way of work until they hit puberty. Before gradual emancipation, enslavers might be willing to put up with years of dependence because they knew they'd get free labor once the child was old enough. Now that free labor had a time limit on it. Pregnant enslaved women faced the same issue—those heavy bodies made them less productive, more of a burden. Maybe this was why Casper Collier sold off Nancy and her children.

Whether they were wanted by the owner of the mother or not, the children were still bound to someone's service. Later, as the state began to liberalize the laws bit by bit, owners were required to train the children for some form of service and teach them to read so they would be able to read the Scriptures. After these quasi-servants, quasi-slaves worked until the age of twenty-five for girls and twenty-eight for boys, they were freed. Catskill had enough of these indentures that it created a printed form for enslavers and those holding indentures to fill out. One child, named Gin, born in 1801, for instance, was abandoned by Henry Demarest but also bound to serve him until she was eighteen. In return, Demarest would, according to the form, agree to "instruct her in the art and mystery of

House Keeping and House Work."[16] He also was required to teach her to read and give her "one good new Bible" when her service was done. Gin was six years old when her indenture was signed. An advertisement from the Commissions of Highways published in the *Catskill Recorder* in 1808 said, "Any person wishing to take indentures of negro children, are requested to apply at the above meeting of the overseers of the poor."[17]

How many babies were born in that period is tough to know—the records are sparse and scattered unevenly from town to town. The New York Slavery Records Index—now renamed the Northeast Slavery Records Index, with more than sixty-four thousand records—is an immense project created by the John Jay College of Criminal Justice. The New York site has collected more than thirty-eight thousand individual records of New York slavery, including a hodgepodge database with the assembled records of these twilight births, starting in 1799. Most towns' recordkeeping of these births amounted to a jumble of individual notations, birth by birth, scrap of paper by scrap of paper, mixed in with manumission agreements and other legal notes.

That's why Coxsackie's tidy and complete record became a Rosetta stone for me. It's a carefully inscribed list with columns for slave owner ("proprietor"), slave, sex of baby, baby name, date of birth, time registered, and time recorded, all contained in a long leather-bound ledger. The original volume is carefully preserved at the Franklin D. Roosevelt Presidential Library and Museum in Hyde Park, New York. In 1931 then-governor Roosevelt, just before he became president, bought the volume to add to his history-buff collection of other rare and original New York State records. State historian Alexander Flick wrote a fawning letter to Roosevelt, who had donated a transcribed copy to the state archives. He wrote, "May I suggest that here is an excellent bit of non-political publicity?" Flick also sent Roosevelt a suggested press release that breathlessly said, "Not many of the Chief Executives of the Empire State have shown such an intelligent interest in the preservation and reclamation of the source materials which portray its past civilization."[18] It would have been interesting to see whether Roosevelt, descended from Dutch enslavers himself, had something to say to that.

On the cover of the volume are the words "Record for Slaves." From January 17, 1800, until June 15, 1827, here is the account of the births of eighty-seven babies. Of the forty-six enslavers named there, I counted at least seventeen as my direct ancestors. Its first page reads: "Record of Free Born Slaves in the Town of Coxsackie." The conflation of "freeborn" and "slave" was no mistake. These babies were not truly free, and, given the life expectancy of a Black person in eighteenth-century New York, around thirty to forty years, even if an indentured servant survived childhood and its high mortality rates and achieved her freedom, she might only have a handful of truly free years left. The confusion also showed how interchangeable the words "slave" and "Black" were. Scattered through every document I found in my research were the words "Negro," "slave," "black," "wench," and "boy." Often they meant the same thing. "Servant" was often a euphemism for "slave."

Sometimes the meandering paths of these children showed up beyond the limited records. In the Ulster County town of New Paltz, fifty miles south of Coxsackie, I found the story of Judy Jackson. She was born to an enslaved mother in 1800, the start of the twilight period.[19] When she was about two years old, Judy and her mother were sold to a man named Jeremiah Merritt. After a few years, mother and daughter were split up and sold to different people. The girl went to work for a woman where, according to one account, she faced a life "full of vicissitudes" because her mistress was an alcoholic. Next, a man named Philip LeFevre bought Judy when she was a teenager, and before long he gave her to his son Andries as a wedding gift. She stayed with Andries LeFevre, her obituary said, "until all the slaves in this state were set free about 1827." Even though all the accounts of "Aunt Judy" call her a slave, she was another twilight baby, born free. No one in New Paltz seemed to recognize that or treat her as anything but chattel.

Closer to my home, I found another intriguing story of an abandoned child and her indenture. Molly, along with her twin brother Tom, was born in Coxsackie on February 18, 1801. Her mother Nan was enslaved by a man named Peter Van Slyke. Van Slyke noted the birth of the twins on the Coxsackie Record.[20] Molly lived with her mother in Van Slyke's household for her first years, but when she was nine and a half, Peter Van Slyke sold her into an apprenticeship with John H. Cuyler, another Coxsackie man.[21] Like the language in the Catskill form, this indenture document promised that Cuyler would feed and clothe the child, teach her English, and give her an English-language bible. Molly's sojourn with Cuyler lasted for eight years until he sold Molly (in other words, her indenture) for thirty dollars to Henry Angle of Bern (today spelled Berne), a town thirty miles northwest of Coxsackie, in the hills above Albany. This was a big change for the seventeen-year-old girl. In the early nineteenth century, thirty rural miles was far enough away to feel like forever.

In the three years that Molly lived with Henry Angle, she gave birth to two children. Around the age of twenty, she fled with those little ones, even though she still had five years left on her indenture. Molly ended up back in New Baltimore, the hamlet just north of Coxsackie, where a number of Van Slykes, both white and Black, were living. Henry Angle went after her, enlisting the legal power of Berne's Overseers of the Poor and describing her in a legal document as an "unmarried colored woman."

The year she ran—1824—was just three years before the state's hard-stop end of slavery, so it's possible Molly wanted to jump-start her freedom. But Molly, also called Moll, might have known that the state, in 1817, had changed the law so that indentured servants would be free after the age of twenty-one. To Molly, nearly twenty-one, that could have been as good a reason as any to run off. It's also possible the two babies were a clue. I pictured this young mother and her children fleeing her owner and then being hit with a legal battle to get them all back. Was she escaping a situation in Bern in which she was forced to bear the children of the man who held her indenture? Was she running back to the father of her children in New Baltimore? The only way Molly could advocate for herself was through her flight.

I spent long minutes poring over the legal case on file in Coxsackie's Vedder Library. The faded, spidery ink is tricky to decipher. It looks as though the justices overseeing the case, to their credit, were trying to find a written copy of Molly's indenture and decide if she had served enough time. They wrote, "The question will be whether Moll gained a settlement in the town of Bern." In other words, they were asking if Moll had been told she was done with her service.

For a long time, I thought the outcome of Molly's case was lost to time. Then, many months after I had accepted that I might never know her fate, I found more legal papers, tucked away in a folder for the Overseers of the Poor. There was a legal case: the Overseers of the Poor of the town of Bern versus the Overseers of the Poor of the town of New Baltimore. The justices of Greene County had decided that Molly had gained a settlement by working for Angle for at least two years and was by law free from her indenture. They wrote, "An actual service under such assignment will give a settlement to the apprentice, where he last serves, provided there is a sufficient length of service, to wit two years." In simple terms, Molly won. She may have broken the law by violating the terms of her indenture, but the law in this case sided with her. From the time she was a child of nine to the moment she became a young woman of twenty with two small children, she had been trapped. Now she could live among her family.

In this story, Molly didn't have a last name. Maybe she was Molly Van Slyke, like the other Black Van Slykes I found living in New Baltimore and Coxsackie. Molly's trail disappeared after that, but clusters of Black families with the name Van Slyke lived in New Baltimore through the nineteenth century. Molly's story proved that these twilight children were feeling restless, whether or not they knew that the legal framework of indenture was giving them more ways to slip their bonds. Molly also might have been tired of seeing enslaved people being emancipated everywhere, except in her case, and knowing she had years to go before she was free.

In Catskill I found another example that showed how long slavery could last. Tom, a "Negroe Boy," was born in 1807. In 1814 Samuel Magee of Catskill sold Tom to Jacob Bogardus, also of Catskill.[22] Even though the document called it a sale, Tom couldn't truly be sold—he had been born eight years into the twilight period. Magee wrote that the boy would be emancipated when he turned twenty-eight. Before that, though, Magee explained, Bogardus would "have and to hold the said Negroe Boy" for his term of service. The child was seven years old.

That meant Tom would not be emancipated from his indenture for another twenty-one years, until 1835, eight years after the state legally ended slavery. Magee was also wrong about the years Tom would have to serve, since New York changed its emancipation laws in 1817. Tom would have been free when he was twenty-one, not twenty-eight. The question is whether anyone told Tom.

To be clear, indentures were part of the fabric of the early nineteenth century for impoverished children and teens of all races. For Black children, indentures gave them a place to go and the hope of future employment, at least. Their options were limited. Even free Black parents of young children sometimes secured indentures for their children. I found an 1816 indenture for a child named Nan, the daughter of a free Black man named Dirk Bronk.[23] In her indenture she was "bound" to Daniel Wilcox of Coxsackie, where she "faithfully shall serve, his secrets keep, his lawful commands do and obey, and in all things as a good and faithful servant and apprentice shall and will demean and behave herself towards her said master and all his during the said time," the indenture contract stated. Wilcox agreed to send her to school to learn to read and, at the end of her service, give her a good bed and bedding worth thirty dollars as well as two suits of clothing. If Wilcox moved out of Coxsackie, Nan could leave his service, but she wouldn't get the bed, bedding, or clothes. Nan was eight years old; she would be done with her service when she turned eighteen. Maybe a situation like that for Nan was the only option. Her family may have been so impoverished that it had no choice but to indenture her out, hoping that the servitude would ensure future employment.

With or without indentures, Black children were vulnerable to kidnapping, especially in places like New York City. In fact, there was a so-called Kidnapping Club, named by abolitionists, that employed both slave catchers and corrupt police officers in snatching free children from the streets and their homes to send them south to slavery.[24]

The story of Sojourner Truth's five children, all born between the years of 1815 and 1826, showed just how dangerous that period could be for children. Truth, the abolitionist and suffragist born into slavery just south of these towns in Ulster County, lived through all of this: slavery, the opaque aftermath, and, of course, her own vindication.

Her son Peter's story is especially tragic. Born in 1821, he was "sold"— his indentured years, in other words—to a man who initially wanted the child to accompany him to England. The child, about five or six years old, turned out to be incapable of handling the work that his so-called owner had in mind—although from any perspective, it's hard to grasp just how much any six-year-old could do. Instead of going to England, the boy was sold again and then illegally resold once more to an Alabama planter, who took him south.[25]

Peter spent the next year in Alabama, while his mother, fueled by religious zeal and the help of Quaker abolitionists, sued in court to have him returned. She won. When the child came back, Sojourner Truth realized he had been beaten so badly he was covered with scars. She cried, "Oh, Lord Jesus, look! See my poor child." One small comfort in his ordeal was that because the child had been illegally sold south, he was entitled to his immediate freedom. His slavery, both twilight and real, was over. His sisters—Diana, Elizabeth, and Sophia—still owed years of servitude.[26]

I had one more thread to follow in this twilight period: that of my ancestor, Casper Collier.

Collier's name as "proprietor" showed up twice on the Coxsackie Record of Free Born Slaves.[27] On November 9, 1800, his slave Nan (who later became Nancy) gave birth to a boy named Jack, a fact that was noted in the record. Next to Nan's name on that line was the word "Sold." Further adding to the mystery, the word "sold" was crossed out.

Two years later, on November 15, 1802, Casper's name appeared again on the registry. This time Nan gave birth to the girl Sawr. (Her name later became Sarah.) Enslavers were given up to a year to register the infants born to their enslaved women, so it wasn't until six months later that Casper put Nan's and Sawr's names on the register. Once again, a thin line ran through their names. Why were these lines crossed out? If Casper had just sold Nancy, he was not supposed to collect money for her baby. Selling her also might have meant he was freed from the obligation to record that slave birth, since Nancy was no longer his. Like many slaveholders in New York, Casper may have sold Nancy because he decided that raising a baby from birth—without owning that child fully—was not enough of a return on his investment.

Casper sold Nancy in 1802, right after she gave birth to Sarah, to a man named John LaGrange of Normanskill, a hamlet just south of Albany.[28] It's likely Casper included the two-year-old Jack in this exchange. LaGrange, who recorded no slaves in the 1800 census, listed one in 1810, plus several other free Blacks.[29] That could well have been Nancy, Sarah, and Jack, the baby born in 1800 and listed on the Coxsackie Record.

In the next ten years, a series of events adds to the mystery. Nancy married a free Black man named Jackson. She now had a last name even though she was still enslaved. John LaGrange, Nancy's owner, decided to sell her to his next-door neighbor, Andries Ten Eyck. Ten Eyck said he wanted Nancy but not the child Sarah. (I never found another reference to her son Jack.) Nancy's husband stepped in and found a place for Sarah with Robert Adams, another local man. Sarah was not yet ten.

After a few years, John LaGrange repossessed Nancy. Apparently, Andries Ten Eyck didn't pay Nancy's purchase price. At that point,

Nancy's husband decided he'd had enough. He came up with enough money to buy his wife her freedom. Now Nancy was safe, but Sarah was still bound up in her indentured servitude.

But Robert Adams, the man who now had Sarah, decided to move away without his indentured servant, Sarah. Maybe he simply didn't want to take her. Maybe Sarah, still younger than twelve, announced she didn't want to go with Adams. Instead of moving with Adams, Sarah lined up work with George Ten Eyck, the brother and next-door neighbor of Nancy's former owner.

Sarah's hope to stay close by didn't work for very long. George Ten Eyck moved to a place called Charlotte, which Jonathan Palmer, Greene County historian, told me he figured was Charlotte Creek near Oneonta, New York, high up in the mountains. Sarah went with him. Then George Ten Eyck died. Sarah ended up with yet another owner, a man named Roseboom who lived in Cherry Valley in the northern Catskill Mountains, closer to Albany. We don't know how long Sarah was with this man, but by 1823 Nancy's husband was dead, and the former owner of her husband, John Jackson of Albany, had "purchased" Sarah, or Sarah's service.

It was confoundingly confusing. At this point, Sarah had had seven owners and lived in seven different places. She had barely left her teenage years. She was supposedly free. Maybe Nancy felt her daughter had served enough. During her visit to his Coxsackie house, Nancy asked her one-time slaveholder Casper Collier to file an affidavit, arguing that "neither her said daughter nor the right to her service has been sold at all." It's not clear why she would say this: Sarah couldn't be sold, of course, but the right to her service could bounce around from owner to owner. There is just enough information in the document to see the byzantine confusion of indenture, but not enough for me to fully understand what really happened. In any event, like Sojourner Truth's son Peter, Sarah was lucky she had someone to fight for her rights in a time when the rules were changing, enforcement was uneven, and deception abounded. Sarah was also lucky, of course, to escape Peter's fate of being sold south.

Michael Groth, a scholar of New York State slavery, told me that Nancy's action could have been a legal ploy to exert pressure on whomever was entitled to Sarah's labor and emancipate her before the date he might be required to let her go.[30] The timing would have been crucial: Sarah was

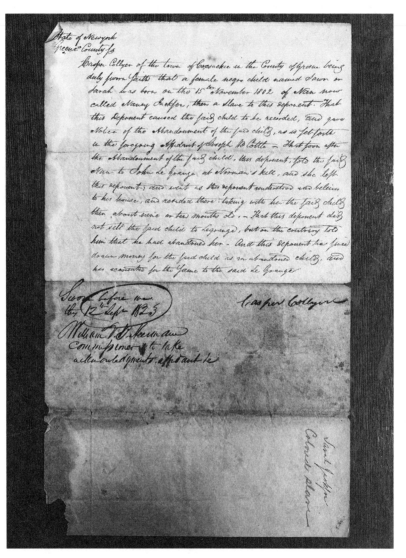

Figure 9. Casper Collier (Collyer) confirms in this 1823 document that he had officially abandoned Sawr, the daughter of his slave Nancy Jackson, in 1802, and then sold Nancy and Sawr to John LaGrange. Photo courtesy Greene County (New York) Historical Society.

about two months shy of her twenty-first birthday, which was the new date of emancipation for the twilight babies.

Nancy's affidavit raised more questions than it answered. By the nineteenth century, Albany and its environs had several free Black households using the family name Jackson. Nancy's husband could have been one of them. Why was Sarah described as Nancy's daughter, but not the child of her husband? Why, at this point more than twenty years after he sold her, was my ancestor Casper getting pulled into the legal process? Casper signed a separate document saying, "This deponent did not sell the said child to LaGrange," and told LaGrange that he had abandoned her, which allowed Collier to collect money from the state to raise her.

Casper admitted that he was still drawing money for the child, even though he was no longer in charge of her. Why would he think he was entitled to collect money for her? Was Casper, who was having his own children at this point, also the father of Sarah?

There is something intriguing about the idea that Nancy Jackson could approach her former enslaver after twenty years, the man who sold her away almost immediately after she had two babies, to ask him to back her up. It might be that her anger at being sold made her feel that she had a right, now as a free woman, to stand up for herself. It might have been that she felt some residue of affection for him. Did Nancy have a hand in her sale? It's possible that she asked to be sold to be closer to the father of her two children, Jack and Sarah.

The Nancy Jackson story also sent me on that deep dive where I tried to find the descendants of the Jackson family in the Albany area. That search ended after I realized that Jackson was too common a name, and that finding any descendant of this scattered family was more guesswork than science.

The examples of Nancy and Molly showed strong-willed women seeking loopholes in the changing laws. In 1810 New York required that owners had to teach their indentured children to read well enough to read the Bible. If they didn't do that, the law dictated, the servant would be entitled to freedom at the age of twenty-one. And by 1817 the law was updated with a rule that children had to have some level of schooling and the ability to read, or they would go free at the age of eighteen.

Even though Casper Collier was a member of the last generation of my ancestors to own slaves, he was far from the only ancestor who was dealing with slavery's aftermath. I will never know what went through his mind as he sold off this young mother, her toddler, and her months-old infant. He rid himself of Nancy as he and his wife had three children of their own born around the same time, during slavery's twilight—Catherine, born in 1801, Jochem in 1804, and my great-great-great-grandfather Jonas, born in 1809. All three of those children, of course, would never have to worry about being sold around to multiple owners. Jonas Collier, born the same year as Abraham Lincoln, went on to have eleven children, nine of whom survived to adulthood, and build one of the largest homes in Coxsackie. He died at the age of seventy-six in 1886.

What about the mysterious Sarah? Did she survive to adulthood? Did she ever marry? Have children of her own? Was she traumatized by being sold and sold again, even though the state called her free? Despite all her efforts, Sojourner Truth's son Peter grew up to become a troubled soul. His mother brought the child with her to New York City, where he cut school, was picked up for petty theft, and was finally sent to work on a whaler out of Nantucket, at the time a common form of discipline for boys and men headed into trouble. His last letter home came in September 1841. He was not heard from again.[31]

New York's supposedly comforting narrative of abolition turned out to be, instead, a history encumbered with so many caveats and lingering restrictions that slavery left its stamp for years beyond its official end.

Just a few years before the end of slavery, in 1820, a man named Harmanus Van Huysen of Bethlehem, just south of Albany, advertised in the *Albany Gazette*:[32] "My servant woman, named Dian, with her son Jack, have left me, in order to seek another home. I understand they are in the village of Coxsackie, and pretend to be free. I do hereby forewarn any person not to harbor or to employ them at their peril. They are my property, and for sale on reasonable terms," he wrote. In a last-ditch effort to try to sell humans no longer under his control, Van Huysen added: "They can be recommended for honesty and industry." Jack was probably not his "property," and Dian was just a few years away from her own freedom. Yet this enslaver wasn't ready to lose his property altogether.

Even antislavery advocates lived in a murkiness shadowed by history. Cadwallader David Colden, the grandson of the Colden who so callously rid himself of his enslaved woman, was president of the New York Manumission Society—and an enslaver. When the 1817 law passed that would free all enslaved by 1827, he wrote that the act "would vindicate and adorn the character of the state." Then again, maybe it was his own vindication he desired. In his 1849 *Civil Disobedience*, Henry David Thoreau wrote, "When the majority shall at length vote for the abolition of slavery, it will be because they are indifferent to slavery, or because there is but little slavery left to be abolished by their vote."

In the final ten years of the twilight period, Coxsackie's Judge Leonard Bronk, one of the most eminent and powerful men in the county and my five times great-uncle, listed three babies born to his enslaved woman named Maria, plus one to his enslaved woman named Mary. The final name on the registry was an infant named Harry, born on May 27, 1826, but not registered until a year later, June 15, 1827. Harry, in other words, was registered just nineteen days before the full emancipation of his mother. The end of slavery didn't mean much in his life. According to the laws of indenture, he was trapped until 1847, only fourteen years before the Civil War, one generation before a fight that tore the country apart over slavery. A scholar named Vivienne Kruger wrote: "The children born owing service between 1799 and 1827 would soon be the only slaves available, particularly after 1827—as such, they were jealously held in bondage by many masters."[33]

That period had a permanent, haunting effect on Black children. They certainly knew they were slaves—their bondage meant they were pulled from their mothers, made to work, sold around, beaten, neglected, and often raped. They faced a changing landscape of laws that limited the kinds of work they would do, and they watched as the specter of slavery in the South meant a perpetual threat to all Blacks in the North. Slavery might have been officially ended in their lives, but its residue pulled them through the rest of the nineteenth century, if they lived that long.

How they persisted, if they did, is a mystery. But every once in a while, serendipity steps in, and one person reveals herself. That was why finding Mary Vanderzee was a gift.

8

THE LAST ENSLAVERS

Sitting in Vedder Library, I pulled the black-and-white photograph out of a thick file marked "Vanderzee." Here was a thin, dignified woman, sitting in a Victorian parlor around the turn of the twentieth century. Wearing a dark dress and leaning slightly forward in a padded Morris chair, she stared out at the camera with an expression close to suspicion, or even fear, but at the same time steely and defiant.

"I look like her," murmured Eleanor, peering over my shoulder.

I glanced at Eleanor, taking in her high cheekbones, slender nose, perfect posture. "You do," I said. "You look like your great-great-great-grandmother."

Mary was raised in the Houghtaling family, beginning as a playmate and evolving into their servant, not quite enslaved but certainly not free. One article wrote that the woman known as "Black Mary" was "brought up as a playmate and companion to the children and children's children" of the Houghtaling family.[1] When she was thirteen, her childhood ended: she gave birth to her first child. By the time she had left her teens and married her first husband, she had borne four children.

Figure 10. Mary Vanderzee, the matriarch of the Black Vanderzee family, poses in 1902 for a portrait on her one hundredth birthday in New Baltimore, New York. Photo courtesy Greene County (New York) Historical Society.

Her truncated childhood and long life came to symbolize for me the messy, confusing, and disturbing ways that slavery both ended and lingered in New York. Her story was like those of so many young men and women born in a period where they might be free, might be enslaved, and might not grasp the difference. For the enslaved and recently enslaved, the rules were still murky and subject to interpretation.

By the numbers, slavery was dwindling. In 1810, there were 369 slaves in Greene County. By 1820, 128 people were still enslaved.[2] Along with that, the twilight period also introduced the slow death of some of the more onerous laws. In the country at large, an 1808 law made engaging in the international slave trade illegal. The outlawing of the slave trade had an unintended consequence of creating a shadowy illegal trade, and it also made those already enslaved in the United States far more valuable. That was one reason kidnappers stole children and tricked free adults into slavery in the South.

New York State was still on its glacially slow route to the end of slavery. An 1817 state law ruled that every enslaved person born before 1799 would be fully free on July 4, 1827.[3] Before that change, their enslavement had no end date. In addition, changes were introduced for the twilight children: they were to be released from their indentured service at the age of twenty-one, instead of the original twenty-five for females and twenty-eight for males.

The changes created a sense of agitation for everyone: white enslavers, enslaved men and women, and Black children in indentures. The dynamic had been altered. How people reacted to the changing world varied enormously. For the enslaved and the indentured, it could be an open invitation to get out of town. Knowing you might be emancipated in eight years or when you turned twenty-one was not enough of an incentive to stop some from running.

Enslavers themselves had one of three reactions: some doubled down on slavery; some freed their slaves with rules and limitations attached to this freedom; and some rare few gave their enslaved total freedom coupled with gifts. Granted, this was wealth derived from lifetimes of free labor, but the enslavers imagined them as gifts.

Those who held on to slavery continued to take out advertisements for runaways and spend money to hunt down those who fled. In 1810 a group of twelve New Paltz enslavers created the Society of Negroes Unsettled.[4] "Unsettled" meant they were fugitives. They would pay four men a fee to search for escaped slaves, with a reward of thirty dollars for each capture.

In February 1811 an Athens man named Abraham Van Buskirk advertised for a runaway slave. He was seeking "a Negro Boy named JIM, not very dark complexion, about 16 years old, and rather tall for his age."[5] Jim, he wrote, ran off wearing a blue jacket and pants, a checked flannel shirt, and a pair of "very large" shoes. He also took another pair of boots, a "small quantity" of money, and a lionskin coat "made for a very large man." This teenage boy running away in a frigid winter month apparently wanted to make sure he didn't freeze to death. Van Buskirk offered a twenty-five-dollar reward for his return.

Van Buskirk held on to slavery to the very end. As late as 1820, he listed one slave in the census: a female between the ages of twenty-six and forty-four.[6] He also named a free Black man, who was between the ages of fourteen and twenty-five. The young man might have been the same Jim who had returned and negotiated his own freedom. Whether Van Buskirk got back his lionskin coat and large boots is a different question.

Van Buskirk may have been stubborn, but he was increasingly rare. For most enslavers, the end of slavery meant there was less reason to resist emancipation or chase after those who left. They also realized that emancipation meant they too would be released from the responsibility of feeding, housing, and caring for slaves. To emancipate them, slaveholders still had to ascertain that their enslaved were younger than fifty and could provide for themselves.[7] Enslavers, at least by law, still were required to provide for those older than fifty who may have been too feeble to earn a living and thus become a burden to the community. For people of working age, emancipation was often the path of least resistance for enslavers. I found records of thirty manumission notices in Catskill, Coxsackie, and New Baltimore, beginning in 1809 and going as late as 1825, just two years before full emancipation.[8] None of the records mentioned any provisions or caveats attached to freedom for their slaves.

Sometimes I found longer contracts for manumission, and in those I saw a far more complicated picture. Many of them coupled their manumissions with rules, warnings, and commitments, as if they sought a way to squeeze as much as they could from their human property before slavery ended completely. The writer Michael Groth explained it well: "Guaranteeing labor for a set period of time, encouraging good behavior, and securing some form of compensation for the eventual loss of the slave was preferable to risking flight and losing the slave altogether."[9]

That was likely the thinking of an Albany woman named Elizabeth Ten Broeck. Her gift of freedom to Susannah in 1810 was coupled with the requirement that she come weekly to do the washing and ironing and help out in the spring with whitewashing and cleaning. She also had to serve during autumn's "killing time," when animals were slaughtered. Susannah could "by no means decline or refuse the same" and had to work "without price, fee, payment, or reward."[10] Perhaps the biggest difference economically for Susannah after her emancipation, then, was she now would have to provide her own housing and food.

Elizabeth Ten Broeck wasn't the only slaveholder who squeezed the last bit of free labor out of her former enslaved workers. Others set a date for eventual freedom, years in the future, dangling emancipation as a reward after years of labor and good behavior. They needed to earn this freedom. In 1806 Constant Abraham Andrews, a miller in the mountain town of Windham, bought a man named Harry Coon, twenty-four, and promised to manumit him "on condition that for eight full years he Behave peaceably Soberly & orderly & runs not away or guilty of any Crime."[11] Being that model of virtue and hard work for eight years would earn him freedom plus a new suit of clothes, Andrews added.

Finally, there was a third type of emancipator, rare but fascinating. These enslavers saw themselves as Santa Claus, handing out gifts to good boys and girls in a paternalistic display of their largess. In their wills they not only freed their enslaved workers but showered them with gifts of cash, land, sheep, and clothing. They must have been imagining a rapturous welcome into heaven after they died.

One of them was a pious German man named John G. Voogd who lived in my hometown of Athens. When he died in 1802, he spread his wealth and generosity through the village, but especially to Mary and Harry, an enslaved couple who lived with him and his wife. In addition to freeing them, he gave Mary forty dollars and ten sheep, and Harry sixty dollars and ten sheep. The charity was nevertheless packaged with rules. Mary and Harry would only get the money "on the condition that . . . they shall behave themselves." Voogd didn't elaborate on what good behavior meant, or who would enforce those rules after his death. He also set out the more complicated future of five other young people under his jurisdiction, who may have been the offspring of Mary and Harry. All five were indentured servants born in the twilight period, required to serve until their early adult years. One of them, a young man named Tom, "shall serve my wife and her only until the day of her death," or until he reached the age of twenty-one, Voogd wrote. A young woman named Elizabeth would be freed at twenty-one, and the other young men freed at twenty-three, he said. Elizabeth and Tom each got thirty dollars when they reached twenty-one. All seven of this group of enslaved and indentured people were given mourning clothes.[12]

When she died four years later in 1806, Voogd's wife Hannah gave away what was left. Elizabeth, who was indentured to a man named John Wager, would receive an ample collection of worldly goods when she was free at twenty-one. The list included a table, a looking glass, eight rush-bottomed chairs, two teaboards, a tea basket, a set of chinaware, six silver teaspoons, a pair of andirons with shovel and tongs, a featherbed, a bedstead, two pillows, a bolster, two pairs of sheets, two blankets, a bedspread, a tablecloth, and whatever else was left of her personal property. To Tom, also not yet twenty-one, she gave all her late husband's clothes and asked that her "good friend" Henry Ritter take charge of the remaining years of his indenture.[13]

The Voogds made a special point of making sure the world saw how they coupled emancipation with philanthropy. At first, the gestures seemed like pure affection and concern for the seven people under their patronage. For a childless couple, the Voogds may have seen Mary, Harry, and the others as family. Even so, it was a paternalistic form of emancipation, gifts mixed in with the assumption that newly free Blacks would not be able to manage their freedom without some boundaries. In addition, this endowment was also a sort of gift to the village of Athens, which would be less likely to have to deal with an indigent, suddenly free couple. While they were smoothing the paths of their former slaves during the end of twilight, they were also creating a legacy and a reputation as benefactors who deserved respect. John Voogd's will left $2,500—close to $60,000 in today's money—for the townspeople to establish an Episcopal church.

Perhaps the best illustration of the ironies embedded in the slow end of slavery showed up most vividly in the relationship between two of Coxsackie's wealthiest enslavers. One of the region's biggest enslaving families used its slaves as pawns in a kind of interfamily drama. The story, I realized, was also evidence that once again emancipation was often a minefield for free Blacks. At first glance, the story of Susannah Bronk looked like an isolated but encouraging sign that some slaveholders were trying to do the right thing.

Susannah Houghtaling Bronk, the daughter of Hendrick Houghtaling, brought her own wealth when she married widower Jan (sometimes called John) Bronk, thanks in part to an inheritance from her father in his 1777 will: money and an enslaved woman named Sarah.[14] Susannah and

Jan Bronk never had children of their own, probably because Susannah was past childbearing age when she became Jan Bronk's second wife. Jan Bronk and his first wife, Elsie Van Buren, had one son, Leonard Bronk, who grew up to become the most important man in town, a judge, informal banker, leader in the church, and state representative.

The Bronks, father and son, lived on the farm in Coxsackie, property that today includes the Vedder Research Library as well as the original Bronk home, considered by some to be the oldest in the state. The cherished son of Jan Bronk and his new wife at first all lived together in two conjoining houses on the Bronk property. Jan and Susannah had the older section of the home, built in 1663, while Leonard, his wife Catherine, and his growing brood took the newer section, built in 1738. The enslaved also lived there too, possibly in the cellar, or maybe in the tiny building called the "kitchen dependency," a detached summer kitchen behind the main buildings. In the 1790 census Leonard Bronk listed six slaves.[15]

When her husband died in 1794, Susannah continued living on the property. Eventually she must have felt cramped in the home of her stepson, so she bought a separate farm nearby and lived there with an increasing number of slaves: Sarah, Sarah's sons Pomp and Jacob, a woman named Maria, and another enslaved woman named Phillis whom she had purchased in 1806.[16]

Like many stepmothers and stepsons, Susannah and Leonard likely had different ideas about many things. In their case, those differences included property, freedom, the end of slavery, and wealth. One intriguing document offered a hint at that fluctuating dynamic. In 1809 Susannah decided to write out her will.[17] After appointing her brother-in-law and two nephews to be the executors, she got to the first item: "It is my Will and desire, and I do hereby manumit and give freedom to my Slaves Sarah, Jacob, Pomp, Maria and Phillis respectively at the time of my decease." After giving money to her brothers Thomas and Coenradt Houghtaling and her nephews and nieces, as well as the children and grandchildren of her stepson Leonard Bronk, she moved on to the third item.

This was the biggest gift in her will, and it didn't go to the obvious recipient, her stepson. Instead, it went to Sarah, her enslaved woman. "I give devise and bequeath unto my trusty Slave or Servant Sarah a Farm, Containing Fifty five acres of land," including a house and barn. After Sarah died, the property would go to Jacob and Pomp "to have and to

Hold to them their Heirs and assigns forever." She also made sure that Maria would always have a home with Sarah, Jacob, and Pomp. She was careful to refer to Sarah, Jacob, Pomp, Maria, and Phillis as "slaves or servants," so there would be no confusion. She also gave them her bedding, clothing, furniture, soap, and candles. She gave Jacob a horse "which I am entitled to by the Will of my late husband," currently in the possession of her stepson. She gave her former slaves a pig, four cows, two oxen, and five sheep, which were "in the possession" of the farmer from whom she had bought her fifty-five acres. None of the generosity to her slaves and her extended family went to Leonard. She also didn't name him as one of her executors. In fact, making a special point that the horse in Leonard's possession was to go to Jacob seemed like a deliberate dig. Rather than giving him control of her estate or even leaving him her wealth, Susannah was undermining her stepson's significant power in property of all sorts.

Susannah lived another five years after that first will. In 1814, just a few weeks before her death, she bought an enslaved woman named Mary from Leonard. One day after she bought Mary, she revised her will.[18] This time Mary was included in the emancipation of every slave. Susannah described Mary as "the wife of a negro belonging to Leonard Bronk" and gave her the right to live on the premises with her other former slaves. Her enslaved woman named Sarah doesn't appear in this codicil to her will. She must have died. When Susannah wrote her first will in 1809, she had enslaved Sarah for thirty-one years. Despite Susannah's seemingly generous efforts, Sarah ended her life enslaved.

Susannah Bronk may have seen herself as exemplary for buying slaves expressly to free them, but she was far from an abolitionist. Another document from 1804 showed her hiring out her "negro wench named Bet" to a Coxsackie man named Rullif Ryan, after which she would become the property of Ryan. She may have imagined herself superior to her father Hendrick, the man who had sought the Spanish-speaking runaway Anthony in 1761, but she had her limits. Enslaving people right up to the moment of her death, Susannah used her wealth as a reward for good service and loyalty. The bonds of affection between Susannah and Sarah were on Susannah's terms. The gifts were both generous and narrow, beneficent and self-serving. Her actions were also easy in another way: like John and Hannah Voogd, Susannah Bronk had no children of her own to claim the inheritance.

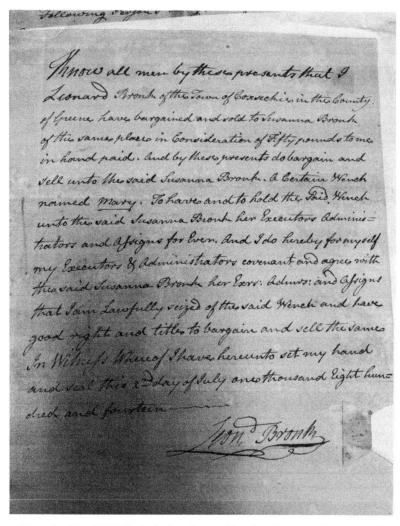

Figure 11. The 1814 bill of sale from Leonard Bronk to his stepmother Susannah Bronk for an enslaved woman named Mary. Susannah subsequently freed Mary in her 1814 will. Photo courtesy Greene County (New York) Historical Society.

The codicil to her first will made it even more evident that she was again chipping away at Leonard's position as the county's largest enslaver. In the files of Vedder Library, his role is clear: he was buying human beings in 1803, 1808, 1815, 1820, and 1821. In December 1815 Leonard bought a twenty-year-old man named Baus from John R. Vandenburgh for $260. In the bill of sale Vandenburgh wrote, "I do hearby covenant and agree with the said Leonard that the said negro is a slave for life."[19]

Not every detail makes sense, however. Why would Susannah buy Mary and not Mary's husband? Maybe Leonard had plans to split up the couple. Or possibly she could only afford to buy one person, and Mary needed greater protection. When I told Eleanor about Susannah's efforts to free and care for her slaves, she wondered what her family might have had to say about that. Were they angry? I scoured the letters of the Bronk family from that period and found nothing on the matter. Maybe her brothers, nephews, nieces, and step-grandchildren were satisfied with the hundreds of pounds she left them.

In the end Leonard Bronk, by outliving Susannah, almost certainly won this tug of war. He may have been willing to sell one of his slaves to his stepmother, but Susannah's actions didn't seem to have that much effect on her stepson's accumulation of slaves, right up to the end of slavery in New York. In the Coxsackie Record of Free-Born Slaves, Leonard Bronk recorded six babies born to his enslaved woman named Maria, in 1811, 1813, 1816, 1818, 1820, and 1823. I wondered if this was the same Maria who was promised a life on Susannah Bronk's property under the guardianship of Sarah, Jacob, and Pomp. Leonard Bronk also recorded that his slave named Mary had that boy named Harry born on May 27, 1826, at the tail end of slavery. If this was the same woman that Susannah bought and emancipated a few weeks before her death, Mary may have fallen into the gray area of servitude and obligation that lasted through those years. It also raised another question: if Leonard Bronk still considered Maria and Mary enslaved, what happened to their property?

In 1911, almost a hundred years after Leonard Bronk's death, a family member wrote a hagiographic ode to Bronk. Lewis Lampman, the husband of Leonard Bronk's granddaughter, wanted to describe Bronk for posterity. "During all his life he was a slave-holder, and for the last twenty years of his life quite a larger owner of slaves," Lampman wrote. "When any of these slaves ran away Judge Bronk refused to go after them. When his friends remonstrated with him he would answer, 'If they are not satisfied with my treatment of them I will not force them to live with me.' "[20] That may have been true, or it may have been the rosy perspective created by the distance of many years. I suspect that Bronk simply fell into a final category of slaveholder: not one who was obstinate in pursuit of runaways nor one who would manumit with or without limitations or gifts, but simply a lawyer who was waiting for the changes in the law to make the decision for him. He was one of the last big enslavers in Greene County.

It was a lot easier to find the perspectives of white enslavers than it was to find the thoughts of Black men and women during this fading twilight. Their words and their preferences were not carefully written out in wills, their descendants didn't write glowing tributes, and their names were mostly left out of official records. But every so often, I found glimpses of larger stories.

One of the most intriguing stories upended my thinking about power dynamics and what slavery meant to Black Americans. Cuff Smith was in many ways another symbol of all that was contradictory about those chaotic last years of New York slavery. Smith, a free Black man, showed up in the village of Catskill sometime around 1811. He had grown up in nearby Connecticut, the grandson of a formerly enslaved African-born prince named Venture Smith.

Why Cuff Smith chose to move to a Dutch-speaking village in a state known to be hostile to abolitionists was a mystery, until writer and genealogist Sylvia Hasenkopf found clues in the records.[21] She discovered a man named Thomas B. Cooke manumitted Smith's daughter Rebecca in 1818, roughly ten years after he had moved to Catskill from Wallingford, Connecticut. Cuff must have followed the Cookes to Catskill. Whether he purchased his daughter's freedom or convinced Cooke to manumit her without cost or conditions is unclear. It's possible that Cuff saved enough money by working as a laborer around Catskill, then came up with the cash to buy his daughter.

It was a powerful story, the perfect parallel to the stories I had read about his grandfather Venture Smith. In 1798 Venture Smith published *A Narrative of the Life and Adventures of Venture, a Native of Africa: But Resident above Sixty Years in the United States of America*, describing how, through hard work and perseverance, he had purchased his own freedom, followed by that of his wife and children, and ended his life a well-off landowner in Connecticut. When Venture Smith lived in Connecticut, an enslaved man convinced Venture to buy him for sixty pounds.

The man promised to pay him back for his purchase price. Instead, he ran off after reimbursing Venture Smith just twenty pounds.[22]

Cuff, it turned out, also owned a slave. The census records for 1817 in Catskill showed him living with three free Black family members—and one slave, a man named Diego.[23] Then, in 1819, one year after the manumission of his own daughter, Cuff Smith signed Diego's manumission papers.[24] How a free Black man could countenance the enslavement of a fellow Black man baffled me. Maybe this was a transactional relationship, and Cuff was working the system. Maybe Cuff Smith saw himself as Diego's protector and teacher, training him in a trade until he was old enough to support himself. Maybe Diego, like the man enslaved by Venture Smith, negotiated a deal to earn his freedom. If Cuff's main purpose was to use any means necessary to win his daughter's freedom, maybe Diego was part of that equation.

It could also represent a certain practicality. Black men and women had to engage with the very system they resisted. I found another example of that during the endless searching and conjecture that Eleanor and I did on her family. We knew that Mary Vanderzee and her parents Cesar and Rebecca lived with the family of Conraedt Houghtaling. While Conraedt's sister Susannah Houghtaling Bronk was freeing her slaves, Conraedt was running a household in which a young girl of thirteen or fourteen, "raised to be a companion and playmate to the children and the children's children," was bearing her first babies, offspring whose skin was light.

That detail was part of an oral history. A friend of Eleanor interviewed Vera Randolph, Eleanor's grandmother, for a school project in the 1960s. Writing in the voice of Eleanor's grandmother, she wrote, "My mother's father was Dutch. He had blue eyes and blond hair."[25] Thomas Vanderzee was born around 1815, which would have made Mary just thirteen years old when she gave birth to him. It was hard to find more information about those early years of Mary's life—until we came upon a slip of paper that offered a partial answer. We know that Mary had her first children when she was a teenager. We also know she had a six-year hiatus in childbearing before she married her first husband. What changed?

The clue came from a document connected to Cesar Egberts. In 1819 Conraedt Houghtaling sold Cesar to a Coxsackie man named Richard McCarty. Egberts immediately bought his freedom from McCarty for $130, a substantial amount in the early nineteenth century, close to the annual wages of farm workers.[26] Cesar must have seen emancipation happening all around him in Catskill, Coxsackie, and New Baltimore, while Conraedt Houghtaling was resisting. In 1820 he still reported three slaves and one free Black man in his census records.[27] In 1823 he finally emancipated a man named Sam.[28] I wondered if Sam, like Cesar, had to pay for his own emancipation.

Eleanor had a theory about Cesar's pricey bid for freedom. The year 1819 was not just when Mary's father became free. It was also the year when she stopped having children. She didn't have another child until after she married John Van Bergen in 1825. "I think that Cesar took Mary out of the Houghtaling household to put a stop to her pregnancies," Eleanor said. Like Cuff Smith, Cesar Egberts may have used his leverage as a free man to extract his daughter from a household—and the white man who was impregnating her. Freedom, to many Black women, meant some control over childbearing.

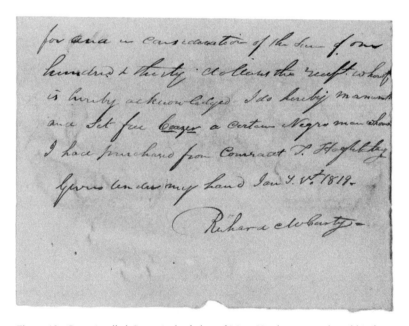

Figure 12. Cesar (spelled Ceazer), the father of Mary Vanderzee, purchased his freedom for $130 in 1819 from Richard McCarty, who had purchased him from Conradt T. Houghtaling (spelled Hoghtaling). Photo courtesy Greene County (New York) Historical Society.

We had one more clue that Mary's first babies came from a white father. Eleanor told me that when she did her DNA testing, the name Houghtaling came up frequently. Which Houghtaling might have been responsible was one of the infuriating mysteries we encountered again and again. But we had also realized something else: the stories showed how both Cesar Egberts and Cuff Smith found ways to work the system and create avenues for Black families to get on their feet after an enslaved past. Now they could begin to establish themselves in the community.

There was another way for enslaved and free Black people to build status in the community. In 1816 and 1817 Coxsackie's First Reformed Church started registering the marriages of slaves and free Blacks, five years after state law made slave marriages legal.[29] I found an intriguing collection of the marriages of enslaved men and free Black women, free Black men and women, and enslaved men and women owned by different people all marrying in the church. Two of them had the last name Van Bergen. One was Tone Van Bergen, an enslaved man owned by Anthony Van Bergen, who married a free woman named Gin in 1817. Another name that showed up added one more detail to Mary's story. On April 9, 1825, John Van Bergen and Mary Hoghtaling, "People of Colour" who were living in New Baltimore, were married. That was Eleanor's ancestor Mary Vanderzee, and this was proof of Mary's first marriage.

Mary's use of the last name Hogtaling was an example of the confounding nature of research in slavery. Last names were fluid: whoever kept the records could decide to give the enslaved and formerly enslaved the last name of their enslaver or the family they lived with, rather than the name of a parent. For instance, when Cesar Egberts bought his freedom, he was listed with the name Cesar McCarty, probably because for a brief time he was owned by Richard McCarty. That was how Mary could be listed as a Hoghtaling and not as Mary Egberts, which was her father's last name. Names changed without warning or explanation, and those keeping the records had little motivation to be accurate. Before they were fully free, many Blacks were simply listed with a first name and a dash in the place where a family name might have been.

Baptisms in the church surged, particularly on one momentous day. May 31, 1822, was a big day for Coxsackie's Black community: twenty-five babies and children were baptized at once. Some of the parents were described as "belonging to" Leonard Bronk or Leonard Conine, and others were recorded as "free." They ranged in age from weeks-old babies to nine-year-old children. First Reformed might have had a revival, since over the course of that same year the church baptized sixty-eight white babies and children and four other Black children. That avalanche coincided with the Second Great Awakening period of religious revival in Protestant churches in New York. *History of Greene County* credits the church's fifth minister, Gilbert R. Livingston, pastor from 1811 to 1826. During a revival in 1821, "373 persons were brought into the church."[30] The church, on its website, noted that there were "great revivals" during Livingston's years as pastor, and as many as five hundred people joined the flock during that time.[31] It certainly looked like the beginning of progress, possibly even for those "belonging to" enslavers at the very end of the twilight period.

Tone Van Bergen was one of the parents baptizing his four children that day in May. Born from 1815 to 1822, the children were probably not the offspring of his second wife Cris, whom he had married in the church after that, in 1823. His first wife Gin must have died.

At the height of the Second Great Awakening, another event rolled through the Hudson Valley like a shock wave. It offered Catskill a moment of glory unlike almost anything it had ever seen, and it gave me a glimpse into the mindset of both Blacks and whites in this period of change. Gilbert du Motier, Marquis de Lafayette, the Revolutionary War hero and close aide to George Washington, came through the area. Without the support of France and the personal involvement of Lafayette, the American Revolution might have gone a different way. His visit was a symbolic vindication that the American experiment had worked. Lafayette, invited by President James Monroe, was making his first visit to the United States in forty-one years. For thirteen months in 1824 and 1825, Lafayette, an older man at sixty-seven, traveled more than six thousand miles around the country, making it a point to visit all twenty-four states of the union. In September 1824 he traveled from New York City up the Hudson to Albany, stopping at as many places in the Hudson Valley as he could manage.

His reception everywhere was rapturous. One description of Lafayette from a stop he made in Poughkeepsie just south of Catskill noted that though he had some "physical infirmities," he was "intellectually strong, in manners and feeling cheerful, elastic and accomplished."[32] There were parades. There were dinners and dances. There were rocket shows. Any community that managed to get on his whirlwind schedule decided to pull out all the stops. For tiny Catskill, it was a chance to be part of history.

According to the book *Historic Catskill*, enormous preparations were made. What townspeople really wanted was the ultimate symbol of liberty—a bald eagle. First, they prepared a "triumphal arch" for the procession to pass under. "Fortunately," the author writes, an eagle "chose that day to alight on a big tree" in town. A hunter brought the poor bird down with a gun, "and the eagle to the delight of everybody was mounted on top of the arch."[33]

The arch—a garland made of flowers, evergreens, and the unlucky bird—was set up over the entrance to town and adorned with the words "Welcome, Lafayette." Starting at 5:00 a.m. on Friday, September 17, the planned day of arrival, hundreds of people lined the streets and a military band played. They waited. What the folks in Catskill and the surrounding villages didn't realize was that Lafayette and his party had been feted late into the night at the Clermont estate, twenty miles south on the eastern shore of the Hudson River. A ball in his honor at the Livingston family home didn't wrap up until 3:00 a.m., and his boat got underway at sunrise.

Finally, around 10:00 a.m., the steamer carrying Lafayette arrived at Catskill Landing.[34] Newspaper reports didn't detail how many people were still waiting after five hours, but the crowd at the wharf let loose a thirteen-gun salute. Some reports said Lafayette at first didn't even want to get off the ship because he was late for his next stop in the far more important city of Albany. Other smaller towns along the Hudson, which had waited with bonfires all night to see the great man, had to satisfy themselves with waving to his boat as it passed. Lafayette was eventually convinced to come ashore at Catskill, and the men let fly another salute, this time with twenty-four guns. Lafayette was led to a carriage drawn by four white horses. He traveled into the village and bowed to the throngs lining the streets. The people of Catskill had planned an address and had raised money to make him a life director of the American Bible Society. But Lafayette had no time for such formalities.

Today, a red, white, and blue historic plaque marks the spot in Catskill where Lafayette was received at Croswell's Hotel. Catskill still retains its rural, bucolic nature, so I can picture the hundreds who stayed up all night to wait for Lafayette. Maybe even Mary Vanderzee made her way to Catskill with her small children. For many Black people Lafayette may have represented an even larger symbol. As he fought for American independence, Lafayette hated the idea that this new country would continue to enslave humans. Later, he wrote to George Washington, his mentor and father figure, "I never would have drawn my sword in the cause of America if I could have conceived that thereby I was founding a land of slavery."[35]

The year after Lafayette's visit, Tone and Cris Van Bergen baptized one final child in Coxsackie's Reformed Church. On April 26, 1825, Marquis Lafayette Van Bergen was born. The child named after a Revolutionary War hero was lucky to have been born to a free woman. He wouldn't have to serve any kind of indenture. His name was also a symbol of the kind of liberty his own father had achieved just a few years before. I wonder if Tone Van Bergen had any idea that Lafayette despised slavery, or whether he simply chose a name that carried a sense of dignity and gravity. Another enslaved man—Lewis Hayden of Lexington, Kentucky, who had escaped to the North—recalled the same visit of Lafayette through Kentucky. Lafayette bowed to the young boy, an act that "burnt his image upon my heart," he later wrote.[36]

Marquis Lafayette Van Bergen lived his life as a free man. But for the last child listed on Coxsackie's Record of Free Born Slaves, life was far more encumbered. For Harry, the baby born on May 27, 1826, a little over a year before the full end of slavery, the terms of indenture still applied. He was registered as the child of an enslaved woman named Mary owned by Leonard Bronk—likely the Mary who was supposed to have been freed in 1814. I found the baby baptized in the Coxsackie Reformed Church on October 22 of that year. His name is recorded as Henry, and his parents are described this way: "Tom, living with Judge Bronk," and Maria.

Every time I visit Vedder Library, I try to stroll back behind the seventeenth-century house and barns to visit the plot of land where Leonard Bronk is buried, along with other family members. Leonard Bronk died at the age of seventy-six in 1828, one year after the state decreed full emancipation. On Bronk's gravestone are the words, "In Memory of Leonard Bronk, who died April 22nd 1828, aged 76 years. 'I am the resurrection and the Life. John XI. 25.' "

About a hundred feet behind those gravestones is a burial place that is much harder to make out. A few weathered stones jut out of the ground. Some people call it the "slave cemetery," although it's hard to tell whether they were free or enslaved when they left this world. A description of the cemetery from the book *Dear Old Greene County* describes the graveyard like this: "And beyond the inclosure, crowding all the rest of the knoll, are the graves of the faithful servants who trusted him [Leonard Bronk] while he was alive and wanted to be buried near him when they were dead."[37]

I've stood there many times. I brought Eleanor back there, and we read the sign just before visitors reach the cemetery. Part of it said, "Pieter Bronck, the original settler on this site, and his wife were buried in Albany in a much moved and now lost burying ground. Pieter's son and some of his grandchildren may have been buried here in unmarked graves side by side with the graves of family slaves and their freeborn descendants."

Most of the stones in both the white and Black sections of the tiny cemetery are weathered and nearly unreadable. The cemetery rests on a knoll leading down to a creek where birds flit back and forth and a family of beavers has started forming a modest dam. As we strolled back to look at the grounds, we saw just how separated the marked and unmarked graves were. In the far back section, most of the stones are just jagged pieces breaking the ground and reaching up into the sunlight. Only one, for a Black man named Ezra Bronk, is clearly marked.

9

"Roots of Poison and Bitterness"

The end of slavery in 1827 was heralded with parades and speeches by New York's Black communities. While many of the white-owned newspapers barely commented on the date, one New York City paper devoted columns of coverage to it. *Freedom's Journal*, the first American newspaper owned and operated by Blacks, also underscored the need for caution.

"We cannot but express our satisfaction, at the great degree of order observed throughout the day," the editors wrote. The paper recounted celebrations in Albany ("the proceedings were conducted with a degree of order and propriety highly credible") and in Cooperstown ("everything was conducted decently, and in order"). An observance in nearby New Haven, Connecticut, went too far. One orator, wrote the newspaper correspondent, "exhibited a factitious zeal without any substantial knowledge. Such a one does more injury to a good cause than a dozen sensible men can repair with twice the labour."[1]

The *Greene County Republican*, writing two days before emancipation, quoted from the Black-run *Freedom's Journal*: "It is very important, if possible, to prevent [freed slaves] from flocking into our large cities where there is very little for them to do and where every thing is calculated to draw their uncultivated minds from the line of duty."[2]

In 1828, a year after emancipation, *Freedom's Journal* again positioned itself as the champion of propriety. There were celebrations in New York City ("in the most orderly manner," one correspondent noted, "everything passed off without the least riot or confusion") and upstate, just across the river from Greene County in Chatham ("the proceedings of the day were conducted with the utmost order and decorum"). But once more, outliers had taken the rejoicing too far. A celebration in Brooklyn a few days after the Manhattan observance had crossed the line. "Nothing serves more to keep us in our present degraded condition, than these foolish exhibitions of ourselves," the paper noted. Whatever happened was too awful to spell out, apparently, but may have involved alcohol. "We have heard of officers high in authority scarcely able to bear their standards—of the insolence of certain Coloured females, and of the debasing excesses committed on that ever memorable day."[3]

Most of the celebrations throughout the state and the Northeast took place on July 5—to avoid competing with America's Independence Day, or possibly to underline the truth that Black independence would always be a thing apart, a reminder that the first Independence Day did not apply to them. Frederick Douglass, twenty-five years after New York's emancipation, voiced that sentiment in his speech, "What to the Slave Is the Fourth of July?"

Gradual emancipation was over, and Blacks in New York State might have been free from slavery, but they weren't free from the obligation to demonstrate that they deserved independence, if not full citizenship. Flaunting freedom too, well, freely could backfire. The paper wrote, "Placed as we are in society, propriety of conduct, never was more essential to any people than to us."[4] Freedom came with rules. And restrictions.

Freedom's Journal may have been right to advise caution. Almost every time I found evidence of progress in the Black community, problems pushed the clock back. One undeniable obstacle was that freedom was also coupled with limited employment options. In farming communities, the occupations of newly freed Blacks were hardly different from the work they had done before, as household servants, farmworkers, and sailors. They may have been paid for their labor, but they had to worry about housing, food, and care for their children. In fact, after emancipation some of the more indigent ended up in Greene County's poorhouse, a place first established in 1826 and so horrendous that those considered insane were restrained with chains in their cells "without air, except from a small hole in the door," according to a report from 1857.[5] The records from those early years are sparse, so I couldn't find how many people sent to the Greene County poorhouse were former slaves. But I did find one Black woman in 1880, twenty-two-year-old Hannah Brandow of Athens, who was sent to the poorhouse for "debauchery."[6] It meant she was an unmarried mother, who gave birth to her son Samuel there.

At first, I assumed that challenging conditions meant that many in the Black community kept their heads low and worked on farms and as servants in homes, while others headed to better jobs in the cities and along the Erie Canal, which was completed in 1825. But the more I dug, the more I saw a different story about Black activism. In the beginning just a few men were involved, but the feeling of community clearly grew with time.

One of the men who was instrumental was a Black man named Martin Cross. Beginning in 1822, he began advertising his services as a barber in Catskill. At the time the villages of the region included a mixture of white families, enslaved men and women, and free Blacks. Cross, who had moved forty miles north from Poughkeepsie, must have seen Catskill's growth, from lumber mills and tanneries in the mountains to brickyards along the river, and figured all those workers would need a shave and a haircut. The brickyards of the area supplied the construction boom in New York City, and sloops regularly carried their loads to the city.

Cross may have been the push behind the opening of a school for "colored children" in 1832. The *Catskill Recorder* described the need: "It is well known that there are in this village, a large number of these children, who have been heretofore excluded from the advantages of common school education, by the inability and negligence of their parents, or by the prejudices of those who have had the direction and management of the schools." A new school served thirty children, who received "room, books, and instruction by the charity of individuals." The *Recorder* blamed the Black parents in part for the earlier neglect: "For the most part, their parents are too poor or too careless of the advantages of education, to procure it for them." The paper called for donations. "We owe it to them, as the children of an oppressed race; we owe it to ourselves, as the guardians of public virtue, and the almoners of Heaven's bounty."[7]

That sentiment—that free Blacks were both "oppressed" and prone to threaten "public virtue"—was part of the reason many of the white inhabitants of the area became proponents of colonization. Beginning in 1816, the American Colonization Society had advocated for transporting freed slaves to Africa, particularly to the newfound country of Liberia. This, they argued, was the solution to the problem they imagined would develop post-emancipation: free Blacks would not easily integrate into white society. Free Blacks might also become activists and cause insurrections among the South's enslaved populations.

Most abolitionists and Blacks saw through this solution as a racist ploy to get rid of people of color. This was not progress; this was regression. The debate roiled Greene County. Jim Planck, Greene County Historical Society vice president, discovered that the topic had made its way to the lecture halls of the villages and was covered both in the white-run Catskill newspapers and in two abolitionist newspapers: the *Liberator*, founded in Boston by William Lloyd Garrison, and the *Emancipator*, the New York City–based newspaper of the American Anti-Slavery Society.[8]

A Quaker abolitionist from Rhode Island became one of the leading voices against colonization. Arnold Buffum, who also was president of the New England Anti-Slavery Society, traveled through upstate New York in 1833, giving lectures in any church, lecture hall, or meetinghouse that would have him. He described his experience in the pages of the *Liberator*, bitterly calling out the number of New York towns that greeted him with apathy, if they greeted him at all. The idea of colonization "has had a strong hold in Albany," he wrote, while Hudson, a Quaker town, gave him a rare enthusiastic welcome. Buffum was able to gather a small group at the Quaker meetinghouse in Athens, but when he got to Catskill, a huge rainstorm prevented many people from showing up. He had a date to speak elsewhere, so rather than reschedule his talk, he gave it to the small group who had braved the rain.[9]

A month later, the Black community of Catskill held its own conference on colonization, led by Martin Cross as well as Robert Jackson, a second Black man who had set up a barbershop in town. The group adopted—and published in the *Liberator*—five resolutions that left no doubt of their sentiment. One said, "The scheme of the American Colonization Society is one of the wildest ever devised by human beings." Another resolution declared that "we are determined not to forsake or leave this our home, the country of our birth." The colonization society was "THE AMERI-CAN DEATH SOCIETY," they wrote in a final flourish. This was not a community keeping its head down or seeing itself as victims.[10]

Meanwhile, those same members of the community pushed their activism beyond Catskill. Beginning in 1830, "colored conventions" were forming to advocate for a cornucopia of rights: comprehensive equal rights for Blacks, the end of slavery in the South, universal suffrage, and resistance to colonization.[11] The second annual convention, held in Philadelphia in 1832, reported that Catskill had formed an auxiliary society of the convention. The Catskill society came up again in minutes from the 1833 convention. By 1834, Robert Jackson's name showed up as a delegate to the convention in New York City.[12]

While some pockets of activism were increasing, many cities upstate rejected the ideas of universal suffrage or rights for Black people. Albany was an especially racist city, according to Frederick Douglass. Within ten years of his escaping slavery, he spoke at an 1847 National Colored Convention there. He had just returned from England, where he had fled to escape slave catchers and where English friends had purchased his freedom. Perhaps the contrast to England made Albany even more unattractive to him. In a letter to fellow abolitionist Sydney Gay, he wrote: "I believe that many of its wealthiest and most influential families have either been slaveholders, or are connected with slaveholders by family ties, and it is not too much to presume that they have not been entirely purified and cleansed of the old leaven. Their influence is yet visible on the face of this community." Douglass added that while slavery had been ended for nearly twenty years at that point, "its roots of poison and bitterness may yet be felt in the moral soil of this community." Abolitionists were not welcome. "So hard and so dead are its community considered to be, our lecturers pass through it from year to year without dreaming of the utility of holding a meeting in it; all are disposed to think Slavery may be abolished in the United States without the aid of Albany," said Douglass.[13]

Even so, Albany hosted another colored convention a few years later, in 1851. Included among the thirty-two men who attended were two from Catskill: the barber Martin Cross and a man named Rev. Henry Hicks, who was appointed secretary of the group and led prayers on the convention's second day.[14] At that convention, the men had to worry about the recently passed Fugitive Slave Act of 1850, which required that slaves be returned to their enslavers. No fugitive slave was safe from recapture.

The 1855 colored convention in Troy, just north of Albany, once again hosted the increasingly famous Frederick Douglass. I saw a new name on the list of participants.[15] Listening to Douglass speak on "equity, honor, and human brotherhood" and rail against the complicity of the North in slaveholding was Peter Vanderzee. Mary Vanderzee's stepson was thirty-two, already married to Mary's daughter and his half sister, Julia Ann Van Bergen. Peter Vanderzee didn't take a leadership role among the forty men at the convention, but the words of Douglass must have resonated with him. Douglass was a mesmerizing speaker, who had just published his second autobiography, *My Bondage and My Freedom*. He condemned the Fugitive Slave Act and warned that the country was headed for a "grand conflict" over slavery.

The speech must have marked a powerful and memorable moment for the young boatman from New Baltimore. Douglass was discouraged and near despondent in his words, blaming the North for not doing more to end slavery. Even so, seeing and hearing the most famous Black man in America must have allowed Vanderzee to envision a different sort of future for himself and his children. Vanderzee, like several other men in his family, worked on the Hudson River steamers that sailed out of New Baltimore. Was there a connection between his work on the river and his involvement, however brief, in the colored convention? Perhaps having access to the world passing by this hamlet on the Hudson opened his eyes.

Eleanor, who was perpetually looking for connections within her family tree, thought that Peter Vanderzee's work offered a clue to another possibility. New Baltimore also was home to more Quaker meetinghouses than many other towns on the west side of the Hudson. In 1855 the Quaker meetinghouses welcomed nearly half of the village's churchgoers.[16] Maybe Peter Vanderzee, influenced by his Quaker neighbors and the buzz about activist organizations, was involved in the Underground Railroad. Maybe a few encounters at the convention with the well-known Underground Railroad agent Stephen Myers of Albany were enough to encourage Peter Vanderzee.

At first I thought that was just another romantic story. I assumed that the conservatism of the region and its proximity to cities like Albany meant that fugitive slaves didn't need to risk making a stop in Athens or New Baltimore. Scholars backed me up. Most steamboats with people fleeing slavery in the South likely sailed directly from New York City to Albany, where Myers could help them get to Canada through the western segments of the state, said Fergus Bordewich, author of *Bound for Canaan: The Underground Railroad and the War for the Soul of America*. I told Bordewich that several people, hearing that I was writing on slavery in the Hudson Valley, made sure that I knew about the houses and tunnels in Athens and New Baltimore that they said had been hiding spots on the Underground Railroad.

That was very unlikely, he said. "As often as not, sadly, such vague lore is attached to the houses of early slave-OWNING families," he wrote in an email. That lore "morphed over time into flattering associations with ANTI-slavery." Coxsackie and New Baltimore were both river ports, he acknowledged, but proving evidence of the Underground Railroad was next to impossible.[17] The tendency to label basements, root cellars, odd shafts, or tunnels as hiding places for slaves was "pure fantasy so far north. There was close to no danger to fugitives once they had gotten that far north," he added. They were also not hiking along the roads from village to village. The Dutch were the least friendly to abolitionism outside of New York City.

While that was true, I started to find intriguing hints that were harder to dismiss. Maybe this time the rumors had some basis in fact. From the book *The Underground Railroad Conductor*, I learned that the famed abolitionist and Underground Railroad promoter David Ruggles spoke in Catskill in 1836.[18] His topic was celebration of Britain's 1833 emancipation in its colonies. But Ruggles's purpose might also have been linked to work for the Underground Railroad, since Martin Cross of Catskill and William Thompson of Athens were listed as agents (or sellers) of the *Northern Star and Freeman's Advocate*, the newspaper founded by Myers. Besides his newspaper, Myers was also important in the Albany Committee of Vigilance, which Ruggles had described as "the most efficient organization in the State of New York, in the business of aiding the way-worn and weather-beaten refugee" from slavery.

Another book, *Underground Railroad in New York and New Jersey*, added more detail: "In Catskill, a site was operated by the local agent there, Martin Cross. In addition, the town had a large population of free blacks who could have given aid to runaways. A few miles north of Catskill, the town of Athens, right across the river from Hudson, had a site in the home of William Thompson. Both Cross and Thompson were members of the Northern Star Association."[19] These were all intriguing hints. Paul Stewart of Albany's Underground Railroad Education Center explained that the purpose of the Northern Star Association was to help publish and distribute the *Northern Star and Freeman's Advocate*.[20]

I now had at least some idea that there was activism, however small in scope. Whether they hosted safe houses or whether they simply contributed financially, it certainly looked as though there were men near my hometown who played a part in the Underground Railroad. Stewart added that since Martin Cross was an ally of Stephen Myers, by definition he was a "supporter of Underground Railroad work." Even when we couldn't find concrete proof that supporters harbored people in their homes, they nevertheless were part of the system. "People have different roles," he wrote. Maybe this time the rumors added up to something.

Then I came across another rumor. Mary Vanderzee worked as a servant in the home of the Rev. James A. H. Cornell, a Dutch Reformed minister who had supposedly been "instrumental" in helping Blacks escape on the Underground Railroad, according to a local legend repeated in the book, *Heritage of New Baltimore*. One of the women Cornell supposedly helped was Emily Campbell, who then went to work for Cornell's brother Theodore, a doctor in town. Emily had been born a slave. "In the 1890s Emily's home was a favorite visiting place for the little girls in the hamlet. The attraction was Emily's dolls. As a slave, all her children had been taken from her and sold. In her mature years she compensated by making beautiful dolls, some of which she named for her lost children," the book said.[21] That wrenching detail and her connection to the Cornell brothers connected more dots. It also reminded me that the horrors of slavery might be slipped inside a seemingly charming tale about an old woman making dolls. Did the little girls who played with the dolls realize what those dolls represented? What were their names, those dolls and those lost children?

Reverend Cornell's name never appeared on any lists of men on the Albany Vigilance Committee or in other records about the Underground Railroad, so I don't know if he or Peter Vanderzee—or anyone in New Baltimore—had a role. If they did, they kept it well hidden. Helping also might have meant something as simple as looking the other way as a steamship with fugitives made its way north to Albany.

A large poster on display at the Stephen and Harriet Myers residence in Albany, today the home of the Underground Railroad Education Center, is a framed copy of an 1856 advertisement for the Vigilance Committee. It blasted the news that from September 1855 to July 1856, the committee had proudly paid for the passage of 287 fugitives through Albany to Canada. It called for more funds and cast-off clothing to "help the poor, unfortunate Fugitives who come to us daily—in many cases destitute of clothing, weary of traveling and hungry." As Stewart of Albany's Underground Railroad Education Center said when I visited, "If the Underground Railroad was so hidden, how could they have made so blatant a poster?"

A different but related activist movement appeared in broad daylight. It was legal, it was socially approved, and it was, in short, a safe way for Black men and women to gather in large groups without the white community looking askance.

The temperance movement in the Black community was based in part on the idea that alcohol handicapped Black men. A love for the bottle could lead them to lose jobs, hurt their families, and remain stuck in their "degraded" condition.[22] But temperance also took on loftier goals, a way for Blacks to prove that they deserved an equal role in society. Leaders like Frederick Douglass, Sojourner Truth, W. E. B. Du Bois, and William Lloyd Garrison endorsed temperance and abolition in the same breath.

Some of them added another argument. Temperance would emancipate Black communities from the sort of capitalism that preyed on the vulnerable. In other words, alcohol was less about booze and more about how the stupor it produced, in the name of making a buck, controlled weaker people who were struggling for a foothold. Despite its societal acceptability, many white temperance organizations refused admission to Black members. Black communities created their own organizations—including many in the Hudson Valley. An 1843 rally in Kinderhook drew about twelve hundred participants, with a hundred people from Catskill and Hudson, according to the *New-York Tribune*.[23]

That same year, Stephen Myers of Albany spoke in Catskill. According to the *New-York Tribune*, his topic was temperance, and his newspaper, the *Northern Star*, was the "only temperance paper for the colored people in the United States." Depicting the abolitionist, anti-colonization, pro-suffrage newspaper as a "temperance paper" made it respectable and showed how combining temperance with equal rights served a purpose.[24]

In 1843 Catskill apparently hosted an even more massive rally that attracted three thousand people. A rally in Hudson in 1845 created a parade nearly two miles long.[25] In 1846 the Delavan Temperance Union "of colored people of the United States" met in Poughkeepsie, according to the *Poughkeepsie Journal*. "We counted no less than six bands" and fourteen banners in a parade with about five thousand participants, the paper wrote. "We may say without extravagance, that a body of people more respectable in manners, appearance and orderly behavior, have never visited us," the *Journal* opined.[26]

Myers and other abolitionists were threading a needle—taking the lesson about dignified celebrations from the earliest days of emancipation and coupling it with an approved message—that made other messages possible. By celebrating temperance, Black communities could simultaneously endorse freedom, suffrage, and resistance to colonization. While thousands felt comfortable marching en masse through village streets proclaiming their vow of temperance, I wonder how that kind of activism would have been received if the parades had been championing equal rights or collecting funds to support the Underground Railroad. Myers, who was openly active in his role in the Underground Railroad from the 1830s through the 1850s, undoubtedly knew what he was doing.

Perhaps the white community was beginning to be more receptive to abolition. As early as April 1834, Charles W. Denison, the first full-time agent of the American Anti-Slavery Society, lectured in Catskill, Athens, and Hudson. Later that year William Goodell, a white abolitionist and the new editor of the *Emancipator*, held conferences in Catskill, Athens, and Hudson to collect donations and subscriptions to the newspaper. He apparently told some correspondents that the people of Dutch descent in the area lacked any racism against Blacks.[27]

Maybe Goodell was picking up on a slowly expanding acceptance for abolition. I found that a Greene County Anti-Slavery Society was formed in 1838 with twenty-seven members. "We have been able to form a respectable society without any opposition," wrote P. Gould, an agent of the antislavery society. By 1839, according to *Friend of Man*, a short-lived abolitionist newspaper, the county had two hundred members.[28]

Even with that kind of progress, the idea of immediate abolition was far from being universally accepted. At first, Cairo's Presbyterian church allowed the group to meet, but then they were forced to meet elsewhere, at the village's Baptist church.[29] Elsewhere in the state, that same tension surfaced. Some pockets of the state had abolitionist sentiments, and other areas were staunchly proslavery. In western parts of New York, abolitionists were hung in effigy and prevented from holding lectures.

Suffrage for Black men became more difficult. In 1821 New York passed a law requiring free Black men to own $250 of real property to be able to vote, roughly $10,000 in today's money. In the 1840s Gerrit Smith, a wealthy landowner and antislavery advocate, came up with a solution. He donated 120,000 acres of his land to three thousand urban Black men.[30] The idea was that they would simultaneously win the right to vote while they cleared the land, high up in the Adirondacks, and create a kind of Black utopia away from the diseases and racist prohibitions of New York City. The community later called Timbuctoo drew fewer than two hundred Black families brave enough to come north and try to chisel a livelihood out of rocky land that faced a short growing season, land that was sometimes under water or situated on mountaintops. According to Amy Godine, author of *The Black Woods: Pursuing Racial Justice on the Adirondack Frontier*, the effort was also hampered by the inexperience of urban men who knew next to nothing about farming.[31]

Gerrit Smith never mapped out the land he gave away, and many men swapped out the land they were given for other plots. Today, the utopian project lingers in some place-names, such as Freeman's Home, near North Elba. The only visible part of the community is the land that abolitionist John Brown and his family took nearby. At the John Brown Farm State Historic Site, visitors can read about the experiment that was Timbuctoo.

Mary Vanderzee and her family had those kinds of ups and downs as well: hope mixed with disappointment; progress offset by loss.

Her son Thomas—Eleanor's great-great-grandfather and Peter Vanderzee's half brother—worked as a boatman on the Hudson River, starting in New Baltimore and eventually moving farther south to the river towns of Saugherties and Kingston. Over time, he became captain of a sailing sloop called the *Albert Richards*, taking quarried slabs of bluestone down the river to help build the sidewalks of New York City. Steamboats had begun carrying passengers on the Hudson, but the slower sailboats still carried heavy freight such as bluestone. It could take a sloop a week to sail from Albany to New York, and another week to get back.[32]

His role running the ship caused trouble for Thomas Vanderzee one day in August 1859. A man described as Captain McClain, the policeman who headed New York City's Eighth Precinct, was alerted that someone had spotted a stolen sloop steering north from Brooklyn up the Hudson River. Quickly chartering a steamer, the captain "went in pursuit of the pirates."[33]

McClain finally caught up with the "runaway" sloop some miles up the river. "They found a crew of a half dozen negroes on board," a breathless newspaper account related.[34] The police captain thought he had captured a slave ship. Other newspapers imagined that the sloop had been stolen from its white owner. The *New York Daily Tribune* elaborated in an article called "Stealing a Sloop" that "a party of negroes took possession of the sloop" but the police "arrested all on board." Capt. Thomas Vanderzee, his crew, and the ship were towed back to the city and the men thrown in jail.[35]

There was only one problem. Vanderzee was doing nothing more than piloting a ship under his watch. The ship's owner, John Field, was forced to come to New York to bail out the crew and retrieve his ship. Field wrote a long and outraged letter to the *New York Express*, one of the papers that had covered the incident. The letter was dripping with irony: "I will hereby trouble you to insert a correction, which is justly due to me, as well as to the Captain and crew of the sloop Albert Richards, although it may detract somewhat from the high fame of the praiseworthy Captain McClain in his courageous conduct on the capture of a seeming slaver." The sloop, he said, was "performing her regular and lawful business of freighting from Saugerties to New York under the charge of Captain Van Dezee." Field explained that he had hired Vanderzee to run the ship, "and although a black man, for honor and honesty he stands much higher than some of lighter color." In a postscript, Field added, "Instead of the deck of the sloop being covered with colored men, as stated, all that were on board was the Captain, his son, a boy, and daughter, a young girl, and one other man—being four, all told."[36]

I didn't find additional articles on the incident or its aftermath, so I don't know whether any of the newspapers did trouble themselves to correct the record. In truth, Thomas Vanderzee was guilty only of sailing while Black. The story represented the mountain of obstacles free Black men and women in New York faced as they fought to manage life after emancipation.

The advent of the Civil War signaled a brutal time of loss for white and Black citizens of Greene County, but it also offered many of those men a way to prove themselves. Whatever the Confederates might have believed, the men of the North knew they were fighting to preserve the Union. How they felt about making that sacrifice and how much they cared about ending slavery were as varied as the soldiers themselves.

The white men of Greene County enlisted by the dozens. One of them was an Athens man named Isaac Van Loan, descended from the same Van Loon family that had founded the village. He enrolled with the Ninety-Fifth Infantry and later recounted his story in a diary that was transcribed for the Athens Bicentennial celebration in 1976.[37]

In 1864 Van Loan was captured with other members of his regiment near Petersburg, Virginia, and marched to Richmond. For five weeks the men were held at the Belle Isle Prison on an island in the James River, and then shipped by train to another prison, in Salisbury, North Carolina. Van Loan described men dying by the dozens in freezing weather, tormented with lice infestations, having barely enough to eat, and living in conditions so crowded that the men had to sleep "spoon fashion" and turn simultaneously to rest on the other hip. If a man died but the Confederate guards didn't realize it, the prisoners kept the fact quiet so that the other starving men could take his rations. At its peak Salisbury held about seven thousand men. "Many of the prisoners who arrived here first were not little better than skeletons," Van Loan wrote. Their bread was made up of corn and the cob ground together, and the sandy water they drew from wells brought on dysentery.

When they were finally released toward the end of the war, Van Loan and some of the other men decided that they preferred to head north without being watched over by Confederate soldiers, so they broke away and headed north on their own. Somewhere in Virginia, the small group of men encountered a former slave who offered to feed the starving men in exchange for Van Loan's blanket. Van Loan made a point of noting that he trusted a Black man more than any southerner. "If he had been a white man I would have been more cautious about going with him alone," Van Loan wrote. For his blanket, Van Loan received two loaves of bread, a pair of pork chops, a lump of salt, a dozen round molasses cakes, and some dried apples. That night, the men "enjoyed a right good supper before the blazing fire," he wrote.

Eventually they encountered troops from the North. They saw "two open ranks of colored U.S. soldiers, waiting to receive us," he wrote. "Oh, how good the stars and stripes looked, and how good the colored soldiers looked, too!"

He finally made his way back home "as one alive from the dead." His friends and family in Athens hadn't heard from him in seven months. They had assumed he was dead but that his body hadn't been recovered. Another Athens man named Caleb Brady had been imprisoned with Van Loan. Brady said that if he ever got home, he was going to ask his mother to make him a chicken pot pie. "He got his pie," Van Loan noted in his diary. Van Loan never commented directly on his overall feelings about the war, other than that the southerners called him and his comrades "blue bellied Yankees and other vile names."

Isaac Van Loan died in 1905 at the age of seventy-two and is buried in Athens Rural Cemetery, a peaceful place where I hope to be buried myself one day, not far from my grandparents, parents, aunts and uncles, former teachers, and fourth and fifth cousins. Isaac Van Loan, it turns out, was my first cousin five times removed. His grandfather Albert Van Loon, one of the village's first residents and enslavers, was my five times great-grandfather. My family, who had enslaved men, women, and children, ended up fighting in the war that ended slavery. It may have taken two hundred years, but the thought that this branch of the family ultimately made enormous sacrifices for the Union side was nevertheless comforting.

I knew that Isaac Van Loan was not the only man in my family tree who had enlisted in the Civil War. I counted ten men with my mother's family name, Van Valkenburg or Van Valkenburgh, in the enlistment registration records for Greene County. My second great-granduncle, Arthur Tappan Van Valkenburgh, served and fought at Petersburg, Virginia. Not all of them survived the war. Monroe Henry Van Valkenburgh, Arthur's cousin and the nephew of my ancestors Jacob and Permelia Van Valkenburgh, died on April 4, 1862.[38] His records said he died of a sickness he acquired in service. One of the Greene County ancestry sites posted a portrait of Monroe. He sports a thick black beard, a pocket watch, and a bowler hat.[39] In the background is a white tent and an American flag. His elbow rests against another man. They both look at the camera solemnly.

Greene County also saw more than a hundred Black men signing up to serve in the Colored Troops, starting in 1863. They served in the Massachusetts Fifty-Fourth as well as in the New York Eighth, Twentieth, Twenty-First, Twenty-Sixth, Thirty-First, Fifty-First, and Eightieth. Their names are often the same familiar Dutch names of their former enslavers: Van Slyke, Van Allen, Van Loan, Ten Eyck, Brandow, and Bronk.[40]

To these troops, the Civil War was undoubtedly a war against slavery. Even so, it's hard to imagine the bravery of the men serving in the Colored Troops. Like the white soldiers, they were at enormous risk of injury and disease. They also knew that if they were captured by the Confederates, they were far more likely to be slaughtered on the spot. Many of them were fighting for a country that had enslaved their parents and grandparents and generations before that, and they returned to a nation that did its best to prevent them from voting, getting good jobs or an education, and, most especially, mixing with its white citizens.

A Black man named Samuel Van Slyke of New Baltimore, the son of Phillis and Prince Van Slyke, enlisted in 1864 in the Twentieth Regiment. Van Slyke was a coachman for some of the ship magnates on the Hudson. He was discharged in June 1865 after spending time with an injury at the Corps d'Afrique hospital in New Orleans.[41]

Cato Vanderzee, Mary's son, who had by then moved to New York City where he too worked on boats, joined Company H of the US Colored Troops Eighth Regiment as a musician.[42] He was forty-four when he enlisted. Out of that regiment, which counted about a thousand men, 251 troops and officers died from war injuries and disease in two years of engagement. But Cato Vanderzee was a witness to history: he was at Appomattox Court House on April 9, 1865, when Confederate general Robert E. Lee surrendered to Union general Ulysses S. Grant.

Also at that fateful courthouse in Virginia that day was a man named Ezra Bronk.[43] He was a company cook and with Cato Vanderzee saw some of the most horrific battles of the war, including the battle of Olustee in Florida, where 34 percent of the Eighth Colored Regiment were killed,

Figure 13. The gravesite of Ezra Bronk, who served in the Eighth US Colored Troops during the Civil War. After he died in 1898, he was buried in the so-called slave section of the Bronk cemetery in Coxsackie. Photo by author.

wounded, or missing. Some historians considered it the second bloodiest battle of the Civil War for Union soldiers. Ezra Bronk survived the war and died on September 3, 1898, at the age of sixty-one. His grave rests in the far back section of the Bronk family cemetery.

The barber Martin Cross's son Martin served in the Fifty-Fourth Massachusetts Regiment, the regiment made famous by the bronze relief sculpture by Augustus Saint-Gaudens in the Boston Common, and by the movie *Glory*.[44] Although the movie got some details wrong, the valor of the regiment during the infamous assault on South Carolina's Fort Wagner, with 270 men killed, wounded, or captured out of a regiment of six hundred, inspired many other Black men to enlist. I wondered how Cross managed to join a Massachusetts group, but then I learned that the Albany abolitionist Stephen Myers had tried to organize a company of Black soldiers. New York's governor, Edwin D. Morgan, refused to accept a company organized by a Black man, so they joined the Massachusetts Fifty-Fourth. It proved once again the strong connection between Albany's famed Underground Railroad conductor and Catskill's Cross family. Cross was wounded in the right leg during that battle and hospitalized for nearly a year. After the war, he returned home to Catskill and resumed his life as a barber.

As I searched through the records, I found one more name. I'd always been curious about the fate of the very last child registered on the Coxsackie Record. Harry was born to Leonard Bronk's slave named Mary, and unlucky enough to be born on May 27, 1826, just before the end of the twilight period. That meant he likely owed Bronk at least twenty-one years of service. It was the same child as Henry in the baptismal records of Coxsackie's First Reformed Church.

Could I find out more about Henry? A search of Ancestry gave me a name. There was a man named Private Henry Bronk of Company C in the Twentieth US Colored Infantry Regiment. He enlisted on January 4, 1864, and served in battles throughout the South. In a hospital near Camp Parapet outside of New Orleans, Henry Bronk died on July 16, 1865.[45] The last "freeborn slave" in Coxsackie had lost his life fighting for his country.

Confederates in the Family

All but one of the ten Van Valkenburg men from Greene County who went south to fight in the Civil War returned home and resumed their lives as farmers, mill workers, and storekeepers. Greene County was where most of these men and their children's children remained well into the twenty-first century. Or so I thought. It turned out that I missed one branch of the tree.

As I poked around for other stories about the Civil War, I stumbled upon a name I recognized: James Dunbar Van Valkenburg. He was my three times great-granduncle, the brother of my great-great-great-grandfather Jacob Van Valkenburg. My attention was also drawn to the name for another reason: Mary Vanderzee's mother was named Rebecca Dunbar. It's possible that some earlier branch of that tree, the Dunbars, had enslaved Rebecca. These Van Valkenburgs lived the tiny hamlet of Lexington high up in the Catskills.

The story of James Dunbar Van Valkenburg is fascinating. The first mention I found of him was in a 2016 newsletter of the National Association of the Van Valkenburg Family.[1] Titled "My Great-Great-Great Grandfather Was Lieutenant Colonel James Dunbar Van Valkenburg," the article was written by someone mysteriously described as "LTJG Van Valkenburg of the USS Laboon (DDG-58)." The man who was the focus of the article was apparently the eldest son and namesake of my ancestral uncle, who had moved south from the Catskills.

I was transfixed by all the details, including a romantic story about how this upstart Yankee with a Dutch name eloped with Molly Morgan, "daughter of a middle-class family whose father had left for the gold rush and left a $20,000 inheritance to his daughter." The couple then "built a quaint home just outside of Macon, Georgia, and freed the nine slaves her father had owned. Both were against the institution and drew fire for their views," the author wrote.

How fantastic. I had an ancestor who moved south and was nevertheless an antislavery southerner who freed his slaves. What a great story, I thought. At that point, I had no sense of how many southerners could have been unabashed abolitionists. Perhaps, I thought, this was just another sign of that old Dutch stubbornness in the face of peer pressure. As the nation approached the Civil War, James and Molly apparently became "avid secessionists." That piece of information gave me pause: they were antislavery secessionists? James enlisted in Georgia's Sixty-first Infantry Regiment in 1861. He also recruited local men who served at the fire station he founded. His exploits in one battle earned him the title "the Hero of the Wilderness." Van Valkenburg was killed at the battle of Monocacy in 1864.

Along with the article was a picture of James, a slight young man with thick black hair, looking determined, jaw set, his right hand resting on a sword by his side. That picture is on the walls of the Cannonball House in Macon, a history museum that houses Civil War memorabilia and other historic artifacts. His clean-shaven face looked so young I wondered if he could even grow a beard. His dark eyes stared ahead with a stern expression. Who was this young abolitionist who also felt it was important to fight for the South? I had no idea how a southern man could be against the "institution" of slavery but nevertheless become a Confederate officer and battlefield hero, but I was pleased by the story. I wondered if there were elements of the South I hadn't known about. It had the feel of the romance surrounding the Underground Railroad: uplifting and compelling. I wanted to know more.

Figure 14. The portrait of James Dunbar Van Valkenburgh, the Confederate officer who was killed at Monocacy, is displayed on the walls of the Cannonball House Museum in Macon, Georgia. Photo courtesy Cannonball House Museum.

The newsletter article included a link to a site called Rally Point, a digital platform like Facebook or LinkedIn for members of the military. That's where LTJG Van Valkenburg first posted the article in 2014.[2] In one of the responses to the post, another writer wrote that he owned the gold-plated trumpet used by Van Valkenburg in his role with the Young America Fire Company. There was a photo of the shiny instrument. The Rally Point article had been reprinted verbatim in the pages of the Van Valkenburg newsletter in 2016. I tried, without success, to track down LTJG Van Valkenburg. I later learned that LTJG was a navy term for "lieutenant junior grade" and that the USS *Laboon* is a naval destroyer.

Then two years after the Van Valkenburg newsletter article, the identical article was picked up in a newsletter called the *Howling Dawg*. The heading for the article was "On the Altar of the Confederacy," and there again was the picture of the young Lt. Col. James D. Van Valkenburg in uniform. Uh oh, I thought. Anything on an "altar" of the Confederacy had the feeling of the Lost Cause about it. The newsletter seemed to be connected to the Sidney Lanier Chapter of the United Daughters of the Confederacy of Macon, Georgia. Sidney Lanier was the "poet of the Confederacy," I learned. I scrolled through the newsletter and found other items written about men from Macon who fought for the Confederacy, followed by this quotation: "To you, Sons of Confederate Veterans, we submit the vindication of the Cause for which we fought; to your strength will be given the defense of the Confederate soldier's good name, the guardianship of his history, the emulation of his virtues, the perpetuation of those principles he loved and which made him glorious and which you also cherish. Remember, it is your duty to see that the true history of the South is presented to future generations."[3]

Further on in the newsletter, a reader had submitted a photograph of his granddaughter alongside a Confederate flag, saying, "I follow LEE." A book review of a biography of Confederate Nathan Bedford Forrest said it was the real story, "as opposed to the one dimension cardboard villain fabricated by Liberals." This review, the writer wrote, lacked "the bigoted intrusions of Yankee editorializing, Southhating mythology, and absurd Left-wing lies." Another article, "Fixing Blame for African Slaves," noted that British merchants and New England traders were responsible for the institution, and that Black tribes in Africa had also been enslavers.

I was beginning to get a picture of the *Howling Dawg*, and I didn't like what I saw. No author was listed, but the portrait of James Dunbar Van Valkenburg haunted me. I had found so few nineteenth-century images of anyone in my extended family. I kept coming back to the one picture I had. Maybe tracking down someone at the Cannonball House, its home, would help fill in some gaps. I reached out to the museum, which connected me by email to Wayne Dobson, the museum's archivist. Dobson was polite and helpful, emailing: "We have collected all the information we can because we are working on a book. Would love to share what we have and would be interested in anything you might have learned." I was hoping he had some new documentation. I wanted to make sense of the man who freed his slaves and fought for the South. I told Dobson I was writing a book about the Dutch enslavers in the Hudson Valley who were connected to my family. "This branch of the family is an important part of the narrative," I said.[4]

Dobson sent me the same issue of the *Howling Dawg* newsletter I had already found. "I had a hard time seeing that it cited any sources," I wrote. "I have yet to find any evidence that James Dunbar VV did free his slaves, other than on this site, which seems to be connected to the United Daughters of the Confederacy."

Dobson responded: "From what I gather they never were his slaves but—as noted—came from his deceased father-in-law's estate. I am trying to find my citation for that." He added, "The *Howling Dawg* is my newsletter that I publish monthly."

Whoops. My implication that the United Daughters of the Confederacy would not be impartial went right to the author of the report. Even so, our exchanges remained civil. Dobson offered to find any articles he could that might support the details. Every few weeks I would write him and ask if he had uncovered the documentation showing Van Valkenburg had freed his slaves. Each time, he answered promptly but didn't come through with proof. Admittedly, seeing the original Van Valkenburg article picked up by a neo-Confederate group made me more certain that I needed to get to the bottom of the story. Was it fake? What was I missing?

Then I found a gold mine. *Sam Richards's Civil War Diary* was written by a man who had married James Van Valkenburg's sister Sarah. Large portions of the diary were transcribed, annotated, and published by Wendy Hamand Venet, professor emeritus at the University of Georgia. Samuel Richards kept the diary for more than sixty-seven years. Born in England, Richards had settled in Macon to start a bookstore with his brother. He joined its Baptist church, which was where he met the senior James Dunbar Van Valkenburg, who had moved to Macon around 1846 or 1847. Besides being a vivid picture of southern life in Georgia before, during, and after the Civil War, the diary was an intimate glimpse into the lives of my distant cousins.[5]

Van Valkenburg moved to Macon for dual purposes: business opportunities coupled with a warmer climate, which he hoped would improve the health of his fragile wife, Mary Eastwood Church. Macon in the 1840s was a thriving commercial and financial center, with iron and brass foundries; factories that made furniture, horse carriages, and coaches; and a hub for cotton brokers. Steamboats on the Ocmulgee River flowing through town would connect the cotton trade with cities like Savannah.[6]

Van Valkenburg brought along his family of eight children. They ranged in age from toddlers to teenagers, including two daughters of marriageable age. A budding entrepreneur, he built a steam-powered mill in the heart of the city, became a deacon at the church, and organized its choir. The climate didn't do much for his first wife. After giving birth to one more child, Mary died at the age of forty. Her daguerreotype on Ancestry showed a woman with piercing dark eyes, wearing a large white bonnet and looking thin and ethereal. In 1854 James married again, to a woman named Mary Wealthy Bradley, who was more than twenty years his junior. He opened a mill outside of Macon.

Sam Richards fell in love with James Van Valkenburg's second-oldest daughter, Sarah, called Sallie. Before their marriage, Richards asked Sallie to start keeping a diary. I realized that meant I had access to two diaries that could allow me to time travel to that very different world. They also brought me closer to the truth: some of the entries confirmed details in the original article, including the made-for-Hollywood elopement of the younger James and Mary (also called Molly) Morgan. Sallie's diary, whose original pages were posted online at the Atlanta History Center, lingered on the details of Molly's dramatic escape from her childhood home. I lost an afternoon peering at Sallie's feathery, faded script as I followed the unfolding story.[7]

Mary's widowed mother was firmly against the courtship, possibly because he was a northerner. James didn't give up. He told his sister that "he would marry [Mary] if he had to wait till she was 60 years old." To prevent the couple from eloping, Mary's brother slept in her bedroom, and another man, armed with a gun, sat outside the house all night. Mary's mother tried a different tactic. She sent James a fake letter saying

Mary didn't love him. James realized the letter was not written in Mary's handwriting. No luck.

James outwitted his future mother-in-law. On July 17, 1852, Sallie wrote: "This morning I was awakened before day by a knock at my door, and James saying 'open the door, I've got something to tell you.'" James told her he had married Mary Morgan. "A young man came with them who helped *steal* her," she wrote. Mary got out of the house by telling her mother she wanted to visit the sisters of a family friend, where she would stay overnight. This family was apparently not as vigilant as those in the Morgan household. "After the family had gone to bed Charlie—the young man—let J. inside and as soon as they could manage affairs, which was not till half past twelve, they started for Macon." It was a tumultuous night. James's horse threw him off and ran off with the buggy, which broke into pieces. The couple borrowed fresh horses and rode fifteen miles through the rainy night, finding a judge to marry them "somewhere on the road" and arriving in Macon at 4:30 in the morning. The newlyweds were drenched and muddy. Mary had no other clothes with her, so she sent back to ask her mother for clothes. Her mother responded: "If James wished her to have some, he could go to town and buy them."

The marriage was a done deal. At first, Sallie didn't much like her new sister-in-law. Her snobby northern bias came through in her descriptions: "This is a perfect specimen of a *southern lady*, or girl, for there is nothing ladylike about her." She went on, "One is very likely to conclude that she has been raised on *Bacon, greens and cornbread*." She was only sixteen, so "Pa"—James Sr.—figured she would mature, Sallie wrote. But the "southern lady" didn't make her bed, keep her room tidy, or even pick up a handkerchief that had fallen to the floor.

The handkerchiefs, the cornbread, the galloping horses: it all felt like scenes out of *Gone with the Wind*. The one thing that seemed to be missing, though, was a reference to slave emancipations, the assertion that loomed over the modern accounts and stuck in my mind as the single most important fact. The Richardses were certainly slaveholders. In the diaries the Richardses mentioned various enslaved workers, whom they rented at first. After the war started, the couple moved to Atlanta and purchased one young woman, whom they treated with a harsh callousness. In May 1862 Sam Richards wrote, "The first thing I did this morning was to give our girl Ellen a good whipping." Her offense? She had used Sallie's toiletries.[8]

Where, I asked myself, was the part where James "drew fire" for his antislavery views? Then I put the pieces together. The Van Valkenburg family was deeply divided over slavery. James Sr.'s unmarried sister Huldah, who had moved to Macon to help her widower brother care for the younger children after his first wife died, was a fervent abolitionist. Huldah was reading Harriet Beecher Stowe's new novel, *Uncle Tom's Cabin*, even on the Sabbath, Sallie commented with disdain. In fact, both Sallie and Sam Richards admitted they had read the book, but Aunt Huldah "is so much interested in it that she cannot let it alone." Huldah's reaction to the book irritated Sallie. "Aunt H is crying over the wrongs and hardships of the poor negroes. They have easier lives than *we* poor white folks—don't they?"[9]

It probably didn't help matters that Aunt Huldah was also a bit of a pill. Sallie wrote in her diary, "I don't think Aunt Huldah has got one bit of sociability about her." Then again, maybe Aunt Huldah, finding herself living in the midst of a family and a community that supported slavery, was horrified by what she saw.[10]

The other unabashed abolitionist was James Sr. In 1863 Sam Richards made an offhand comment about his father-in-law: "Sallie got a note from her father today but he is such a tory that it is no pleasure to hear from him."[11] Secessionist southerners called pro-Union people in the South by various names: tory, black abolitionist, and phrases too racist and crude to repeat.

What about Sallie's brother, the Confederate hero? I found the damning evidence. The 1860 slave schedule for Macon, Georgia, finally gave me incontrovertible proof that neither James nor his wife Mary had opposed the institution of slavery. On a page dated July 2, 1860, there was Mary E. Van Valkenburg (Mary Elizabeth, the wife of the younger James), listing six slaves.[12] A seventh enslaved man, twenty-four, was checked off in the column for fugitives. The law of coverture said that when she married, a wife's property automatically belonged to her husband, although Mollie Van Valkenburg's father may have stipulated in his will that the slaves belonged to her. There were other female slaveholders named on the slave schedules for 1850 and 1860. Then I found additional evidence that the couple had slaves. On September 5, 1860, James Van Valkenburg listed two slaves, a fifty-year-old female and a thirteen-year-old female.[13] Both were checked off in the fugitive column. The column for "number manumitted" was empty. In short, James and Mary Van Valkenburg enslaved six people in 1860. Another three had escaped. At that point, James and Mary had been married, and holding slaves, for eight years.

I stared at the list of the people enslaved by Mary. There was a man, thirty-two years old, a woman, thirty, plus two boys, nine and twelve, and two girls, four and eight. It was a little sickening to see these columns describing people only known by their color (B for Black), age, and gender. The group enslaved by the Van Valkenburgs certainly looked like a family, and it also looked like a pretty good reason why they didn't try running off. Even in the tumult and chaos of the year before the war, it would have been hard for this young couple to escape with four children. What were their names?

As I scoured the 1860 slave schedule for Macon, I saw that a small number of enslaved people did escape. One dramatic story out of Macon in the years just before James Dunbar Van Valkenburg's move to Georgia was that of Ellen and William Craft, the enslaved couple who disguised themselves as a white man and his enslaved servant. The Crafts used Ellen's very light skin and her ability to sew a suit of clothes for a small man to create her disguise. Both used intelligence and a vigilant calm to take trains and boats as far as Boston in the 1840s and 1850s.[14] They didn't have children until they were free.

As for the Van Valkenburgs, it's possible that earlier researchers who credited James with freeing his slaves were conflating the two men with the same name—one antislavery, one proslavery. To add to the confusion, James Sr. twice married women named Mary—Mary Eastwood Church, the native of Troy, New York, who died in 1851, and Mary Wealthy Bradley.[15] James Jr.'s wife was also named Mary. Even so, there was not a shred of evidence that James Sr. had ever owned humans or emancipated them. I did find people in the Macon area with the last name Bradley who listed slaves on the 1850 slave schedule, but I couldn't connect them to Mary Bradley.[16]

The father was an abolitionist. The son was anything but. Unlike his father, James fit comfortably into the prevailing ethos of Georgians at the time: slavery was part of the human condition, and slavery was what allowed white Georgians to live comfortable and profitable lives. He was eighteen years old when his father moved the family south, and twenty-three when he eloped with Mollie. If Sallie's brother James had manumitted any slaves, that fact would have been a subject of enormous discussion and snark in the pages of the Richards diaries, in the same way they discussed his father.

The repetition of "facts" does not make them truer if they are untrue to start. People who build a family tree on a genealogical site often base their "facts" on items that others have posited first. It's the crowdsourcing of information. But sometimes that means that a very confident falsehood, knowingly or not, develops a certain legitimacy through sheer repetition. The repetition can extend over many years, as in the case of Caesar, the "oldest slave" in New York whose details were falsely described in 1951 and then repeated in the 1970s. A succession of writers assumed the original source was accurate. In the case of the Georgia Van Valkenburgs, a piece of information based on a partial truth obscured the actual truth.

I knew I needed to go visit Macon and see if there was more that I could find of the byzantine Van Valkenburg saga. I also wanted to look at the Confederate Van Valkenburg portrait face to face. On a blustery spring day my husband and I flew into Macon's Middle Georgia Regional Airport. The walls of the tiny airport, host to just one commercial carrier named Contour, welcomed visitors with a colorful sign that said, "We're glad y'all are in Macon."

Macon turned out to be a quiet city that wanted tourists to savor its two-hundred-year heritage, dozens of enormous antebellum homes, and tradition of southern hospitality. Our visit coincided with the city's cherry blossom festival. There were no blossoms: global warming had hurried the timing of the blossoms, and the city's cherry trees showed only the remnants of petals. Macon made up for the absence by decorating every lamppost, storefront, and restaurant with fake blossoms so pink they nearly glowed. Tourists strolled the city and lined up at food trucks for beer, ice cream, and kettle corn.

We may have missed the blossoms, but we did get to experience a living history day at the Cannonball House, home of James Dunbar Van Valkenburg's portrait. Roaming around the house and grounds were women wearing hoop skirts and men in woolen Confederate uniforms sporting scraggly beards and goatees. Wayne Dobson, my correspondent, was dressed as Judge Asa Holt, the former owner of the house. He wore a black satin string tie and a wary expression. While he was talking to other visitors, Dobson introduced me to a young man named Brick Nelson, a twenty-five-year-old Confederate reenactor who also was a reporter for the NBC news affiliate in Macon. Brick showed us around the museum: uniforms, flags, old coins, rosters, swords, pistols, paintings, maps. Finally, on the second floor, I came upon the portrait I wanted to see.

The Confederate war hero, James Dunbar Van Valkenburg, was tucked into a corner like an afterthought. I had to slip into a narrow nook to view the portrait head-on. We were face to face through several layers of glass and glare, and he refused to meet my eyes. It looked as though someone had touched up the original daguerreotype or copied an earlier portrait in charcoal. James Dunbar Van Valkenburg looked disappointingly like a stiff doll, wooden and lifeless.

I kept poking around the museum, peering at moth-eaten uniforms, rifles, revolvers, swords, and framed newspaper clippings, waiting for a chance to get Dobson's attention. I was anxious about showing him my evidence about slavery, so first I gave him information I had picked up at the Monocacy National Battlefield Visitors' Center, the site where James Dunbar Van Valkenburg had been killed. I showed him a copy of a hand-written letter by Gen. John B. Gordon, talking about the death of Van Valkenburg.[17] Then I pulled out my copies of the 1860 slave schedule for Macon.

"Here's what I found. You can see that both James and Mary enslaved people," I said. I pointed to the blank column for manumission. Dobson peered at the documents. He nodded, made copies, and thanked me, still cordial. I told him my theory that the names of the father and son had been conflated. He nodded again. That was, at least for that moment, the end of the conversation. It occurred to me that I was the only one on earth who cared whether the young Confederate freed his slaves or not.

Dobson showed us the yard behind the Cannonball House, where slave cabins had stood into the 1950s. He said that the home's most well-known owner was Asa Holt, who had kept hundreds of slaves on a plantation outside of town. He brought in select young men and women from the plantation so he could rent them out and, according to Dobson's interpretation, train them for a trade so that they would be ready to earn a living when they might be freed. The yard also held a collection of items donated over time, Confederate bric-a-brac. One was an iron fence with a plaque: "Jefferson Davis, presidency of the Confederate States, stood within this rail on the balcony of the old Union depot when he visited Macon Oct 25 1887." Another plaque marked a hotel where Davis was held prisoner in May 1865. It included a quote from Davis: "When time shall have softened passion and prejudice, when reason shall have stripped the mask from misrepresentation, then justice, holding evenly her scales, will require much of past censure and praise to change places."

Davis was figuring that praise for the South would come, someday. Then I realized that the feeling of being misrepresented and unfairly censured was also the tone of the Confederate reenactors and of the contributors to the *Howling Dawg*. As we sat on folding chairs and chatted, Dobson asked me, "Were you surprised at how pro-Black we are?" I was stunned into silence. Where was the pro-Black part? I mumbled something about how polite everyone was, and then asked him why some of the comments in his newsletter talked about liberal Yankees who hate the South. "I'm a liberal Yankee, and I don't hate the South," I said. What I didn't say was that I thought the whole idea the Civil War had been a huge "misrepresentation" was absurd. Dobson looked embarrassed. He said he'd have to check to see if he wrote that or someone else did.

It was as close as I could get to a face-to-face reckoning that day. In Macon the Lost Cause is kept alive by those who want to think of themselves and their ancestors as good people who fought a war because the North was destroying their rights. Rude northerners who showed up at the Cannonball House challenging that narrative were like folks who showed up at Great-Aunt Millie's afternoon tea and picked a fight with her. I wanted a reckoning, but I suppose I found it easier to feel confrontational from afar. They wanted to imagine living in a genteel past. Dobson told me that when some northerners had come through on tours, one told him he planned to challenge everything he said. Dobson described this as an unpleasant moment, a rarity in a sea of acquiescent visitors to the house. He didn't elaborate on the challenges the tour guest posed to him. It was more he thought the man wasn't visiting with an open mind. I squirmed, because I realized he was giving me a small opportunity to throw down a few challenges myself.

I missed the chance. Later, I asked myself if revisiting the topic would have done much more than underline our positions. As we wandered through the dining room, we came upon one man dressed as a Civil War surgeon, with red streaks of fake blood splashed across his apron. Somehow our conversation, which started with the horror of Civil War amputations and disease, shifted to topics like weather and storms. When he started talking about the "end times" and California's punishment at the hand of God, I had a feeling that the next question was going to have to do with salvation and repentance. We swiftly made our retreat. The gift shop of the Cannonball House was filled to the ceiling with Confederate items: mugs and pens adorned with the Confederate flag, "Southern States Paper Money," miniature Confederate flags, and several dolls, including one boy doll wearing a gray crocheted Confederate uniform and crocheted hat, next to a crocheted bald eagle. I texted a photo of the Confederate dolls to Eleanor. "Oh my Jesus . . ." she wrote. "Breathe deep . . . serenity now."

We walked to Rose Hill Cemetery to try to find the grave site of James Dunbar Van Valkenburg. Its fifty acres are dotted with large trees, rolling hills, terraces, and obelisks, plus the graves of around six hundred Confederate officers and troops, the unmarked resting places of slaves, and the graves of two of the Allman brothers, Duane and Gregg.

We spent an hour wandering up and down the hills, peering at faded lettering and getting lost in the meandering pathways. Eventually Bob resorted to a combination of the site Findagrave.com and GPS. He called me over, just as I was reading a large plaque dedicated to the Confederate colonel John Basil Lamar, who died after being wounded at Crampton's Gap, Maryland. The plaque, dedicated by the Athens (Georgia) Historical Society in 1994, was inscribed: "He is remembered as a loyal son of the South, which he defended with sword, voice and pen."

The Van Valkenburg site had no historic plaque. Its only marking was a brick at the foot of the small family plot, etched simply with VAN VALKENBURGH. (The family has always spelled the name both ways.) The plot was halfway up a small hill starting to erode, with red dirt running in a narrow gulley. Inside the modest square surrounded by tumbling bricks were James and his family, four of their children who had died young, plus James's brother, Charles Wheelock, and Charles's son Edward. The stones, flat to the ground and dark with mold and moss, were nearly impossible to read. Everything was green and sunken.

"Was it worth it?" I asked James Dunbar. His tiny children lost their father, and this Hero of the Wilderness had no glorifying sign, no Civil War plaque. The only mention of his service is "Colonel 61st G. REGT

Figure 15. The cemetery plot of the James Dunbar Van Valkenburgh family at Rose
Hill Cemetery in Macon, Georgia. Photo by author.

CSA"—the Sixty-First Georgia Regiment of the Confederate States of
America. His death date is marked as "July 9, 1864 at Monocacy, MD."
Underneath those words are written: "Buried in this lot are 4 of the children of J. D. & Mary Van Valkenburg." One died in infancy, one at age
three, one at age twelve, and one at twenty-three. Only one of their children, James Edward Van Valkenburg, lived to adulthood. His wife is not
buried with him. A separate stone reads, "In loving memory of my dear
mother who is buried in the churchyard at Lapile, Arkansas."

Many children didn't make it past childhood. I had read the diary of
one Macon boy, LeRoy Wiley Gresham, in *The War Outside My Window.*

Gresham, afflicted with a form of spinal tuberculosis, was confined to his home, but his detailed account of life in Macon during the war, the enslaved men and women who cared for him, and his zeal for news of the war made the diary invaluable. We stayed in the boy's home in Macon, today called the 1842 Inn.

On October 17, 1862, Gresham wrote about a family slave who tried to flee and was caught. "'Dave' is in jail, been run away 2 weeks." On Friday, May 7, 1863, he tallied the war's costs: "List of killed + wounded in the Macon Volunteers. 1700 nasty, stinkin' Yankee raiders have arrived in Atlanta."[18] As we ate french toast and eggs in the home's parlor, I tried to imagine the sickly boy who coughed incessantly, read Dickens before the fireplace, and plied himself with whiskey, morphine, and other painkillers to dull his pain. He was only seventeen when he died in 1865.

In the cemetery, I came upon LeRoy Gresham's grave, an elaborate white marble rectangle topped with an urn draped in marble cloth. "In life, this dear child was the light of the home circle. Lovely and endearing by nature, he was purified by suffering, sanctified by grace and rests now in the bosom of his savior," the inscription said. "Blessed are the pure in heart, for they shall see God."

Just outside the gates of the cemetery, facing Riverside Drive, is a small park. In the summer of 2022, two Confederate monuments that had been placed in the center of the city were moved to the entrance of the cemetery along the Ocmulgee River. The Confederate Memorial to Men of Bibb County at one time had stared down at Cotton Avenue, the historically Black business district of Macon. The monument had been defaced during the 2020 Black Lives Matter protests, then surrounded by plywood scaffolding. While cities like Charlottesville and Richmond have either put their monuments in storage or delayed the decision about where to put them, Macon has given them a new location, away from downtown but still visible. C. Jack Ellis, the city's first Black mayor, had argued for the removal. "This era is dead, dead and gone. Put it in the cemetery where it belongs."[19]

On the side of the Confederate memorial are the words, "Erected A.D. 1879 by the Ladies Memorial Association of Macon in HONOR of the Men of Bibb County, And of all who gave their lives in the South to establish the Independence of the CONFEDERATE STATES 1861–1865." Below are the words, "With pride in their Patriotism, With love for their

memory, This silent stone is raised, A perpetual witness of our Gratitude."
We had just missed the rededication of the monuments by two weeks.

Later, I felt like a coward for not confronting the neo-Confederates.
I didn't accept their interpretation of the war, and I felt like an imposter
as I sat there on the folding chairs alongside the men dressed in Confederate gray uniforms. Maybe I should have pushed harder. Not long after
I got home from Macon, Dobson sent out another one of his *Howling
Dawg* newsletters. The content was mostly chatty posts about Civil War
reenactment events and an obituary for a fellow reenactor who had died
suddenly. But one of the other people on the email chain decided to do
a "reply all" response to the newsletter. He wrote, "We who are holding
the line will surely outlast the latest fads of the wacky left wing. We now
have a new Lee-Jackson Park on Interstate 81 near Lexington, Virginia.
It opened this past Saturday. I always say that everytime the Left takes
down one of our Honored Symbols, we should put at least two or three
of them back up. We are winning the Second Civil War, by being true
to our values and our ancestors."[20] Then he signed the email "Deo Vin-
dice," or "with God as our defender," which I learned was the motto of
the Confederacy.

When I looked for the site and location of this new park, I read, "The
park is not open at this time." I also couldn't find an exact location. But
that gave me a better answer about whether it would have done any good
to try to start an argument in Macon. I don't know if there will be a second Civil War over monuments, but I do think the first Civil War lives on.

His grave site didn't say it, but James Dunbar Van Valkenburg was a
Confederate hero. His exploits in the battle of the Wilderness south of
Fredericksburg, Virginia, in May 1864, explain how he was dubbed "the
Hero of the Wilderness."[21] During that battle, with thick woods making it
nearly impossible to see soldiers or horses, Van Valkenburg and his small
group of ten to fifteen men came upon a regiment of Union soldiers. He
decided to bluff. In a letter he later wrote home to his wife and published
in the *Macon Telegraph*, he said, "My first impulse was to turn back," but
he realized that would show weakness and make him and his men targets.
Instead, he called back as if several regiments of Confederates were just
behind him. Then he announced to the Union's commanding colonel that
"he and his party were prisoners to General Gordon's brigade."[22]

It worked. The colonel surrendered, and Van Valkenburg demanded his sword and pistol. So many Union men then started surrendering their swords and pistols that Van Valkenburg was forced to allow the soldiers to hold on to their swords as he brought them in. As he marched his prisoners back to Confederate lines, southern soldiers "opened a heavy fire of musketry on us"—all they could see was Union soldiers. In all, Van Valkenburg had bluffed his way into capturing 433 men, a colonel, three majors, and another forty staff officers. Confederate private G. W. Nichols wrote, "When we got them out and they found that they had been captured by Major Van's stratagem they were the worst set of mortified officers and men I have ever seen."[23] I'll admit I'd have liked to see that moment.

Over the next few months, the Confederates made their way north, hoping to capture Washington. On a hot July day, they approached Frederick, Maryland, a bustling city forty-five miles northwest of the capital. As they got closer to the city, the soldiers appealed to residents to join the South, since the slaveholding state of Maryland was very much divided and had supplied soldiers to both sides of the war. It was also a city that had become jaded about the war. As the skirmishes began, crowds of men, women, and children came out to the farmland just south of Frederick to perch on fences and watch the fighting. Horrified, Union major general Lew Wallace told his soldiers to order the people back to the safety of Frederick. The spectators refused.

On the morning of July 9, 1864, the battle began. On the farms belonging to John T. Worthington and Christian Keefer Thomas, both slaveholders who probably had southern sympathies, the wheat had been harvested but stood in tall shocks on the fields like pointed tents.

A five-year-old boy who had watched the battle from a window in the cellar of the family home later described the last moments of Van Valkenburg's life. In his 1932 history, *Fighting for Time: The Battle of Monocacy*, Glenn Worthington wrote, "As the gray-clad boys climbed the post and rail fence, running along the top of the hill, and dividing the Thomas and Worthington farms, they gave the rebel yell and moved resolutely forward."[24] They ran down a hill into a ravine and then back up the hill. Concealed inside the Thomas farmhouse were Union sharpshooters from the Eighty-Seventh Pennsylvania and Fourteenth New Jersey Regiments. As they took aim at the Confederate soldiers, one of them picked off Van

Valkenburg. He died on the spot. Private Nichols wrote: "The Sixty-first Georgia Regiment went into the battle with nearly one hundred and fifty men, and after the battle was over we could not stack but fifty-two guns by actual count. Our beloved Colonel J. H. Lamar and Lieutenant Colonel J. D. Van Valkinburg [*sic*] (the hero of the wilderness) were both killed on the field."[25]

Because Union forces were forced to retreat toward Baltimore, some historians say the Confederacy won Monocacy. In actuality, the battle slowed Confederate forces and forced the South to miss its chance to seize Washington. The "battle that saved Washington" was, in hindsight, far more significant than anyone realized at the time.

Monocacy, a national site run by the National Park Service, today is split in two by Interstate 270, where the noise of traffic gets louder by the day as the DC suburbs reach farther into rural areas. Small brick ranch houses with pickup trucks in the driveways line up next to fields marking the park. The low rumble of airplanes overhead competes with the dull drone of cars passing through. The battlefield itself is an empty expanse of grass, and the insects buzz by on a hot summer morning. I walked past the Thomas house and looked out over the fields where the rebels charged. The calm of the place made it harder to imagine the rebel yell or picture soldiers dying as they fought over this quiet farmland a short drive from the seat of power. One writer later said the losses were so great that the stream running through the ravine was red with the blood of soldiers.

In the visitors' center at Monocacy, I asked National Park Service staff members whether they had any information on Van Valkenburg. I said, with some chagrin, that he was an ancestor who fought for the Confederacy. "We all have ancestors who fought for the South," one ranger said. They plied me with the details that filled in Van Valkenburg's story.

Later I went back to observe a living history day at Monocacy. Volunteers in blue Union uniforms shot their rifles off to the distant nothing, a northern counterpoint to the volunteers in gray firing off a cannon in the backyard of Macon's Cannonball House. And like the living history day in Macon, the women wore hoop skirts, the men wore moth-eaten woolen uniforms, and no one looked as underfed as the nineteenth-century Americans who lived through years of privation and loss. Inside the Thomas house, I peered out the windows and wondered which man from the Pennsylvania or New Jersey regiments took down the thirtysomething

Confederate from Georgia. It could have been a man with a Dutch name like Van Valkenburg.

James Dunbar Van Valkenburg's large family served the Confederacy and the cause of the South in other ways. A second Van Valkenburg son, George Seymour Van Valkenburg, ten years younger than James, enlisted in May 1862 and was wounded a year later at Chancellorsville. The elder Van Valkenburg daughters—Harriet, Mary, and Martha—all married southern slaveholders. Harriet's husband, Seth K. Taylor of Americus, Georgia, owned a large plantation with hundreds of enslaved men and women.[26]

As for Aunt Huldah, she eventually married a Pennsylvania lawyer and pro-Union politician named William J. Turrell. The Macon Van Valkenburgs didn't see her until the last days of the war, when Sam and Sallie Richards took temporary refuge in New York City. Even then, Sam Richards harbored resentment toward Aunt Huldah. In March 1865 he wrote, "She was quite affectionate and I could not refuse her proffered kiss.—They did not talk any *war*." In April 1865, just before Lee's surrender at Appomattox, Richards continued to be vexed by his Yankee relatives. "Miss Cornish and Mrs. Turrell [Aunt Huldah] called on us Tuesday night. The latter is such a black Abolitionist that I don't care much to see her. It is just fanatics as she that brought all this desolation and misery upon our country." Mary Smillie, first cousin to both Sallie Richards and James Jr., "is just such another only more of a *squirt*—a black, loud-mouthed Abolitionist, I wish she could be *drafted* and made to fight!—Aunt Huldah was glorying in the news that Lincoln was occupying Pres Davis' house in Richmond and I *riled* her somewhat by remarking that *he* was not the only Yankee that was in a place that did not belong to him."[27]

I thought back to the other Van Valkenburg who died in the Civil War. Monroe Henry Van Valkenburg, first cousin to the Confederate James Dunbar Van Valkenburg, served with Company G, Twentieth New York State Militia.[28] He died of injuries received during battle, which may have been gangrene after a limb had been sawed off or typhoid picked up in dirty water. Monroe Van Valkenburg was treated at Columbia College Hospital not far from President Lincoln's Summer Cottage, four miles northeast of the White House. The treatment failed, and he died on April 4, 1862, leaving his wife Alice and two young children in Lexington, New York.

Figure 16. The grave of Monroe Henry Van Valkenburg, who died in 1862 fighting for the Union in the Civil War, rests at US Soldier's and Airmen's Home National Cemetery in northeastern Washington, DC. Photo by author.

He is buried at the US Soldiers' and Airmen's Home National Cemetery, peaceful rolling acres that abut both the hospital and the summer cottage.

I decided to pay him a visit on a quiet and cool Sunday morning in the spring. If I had stared at the stone of a Confederate ancestor who died in the Civil War, it was fitting that I should pay my respects to a Union soldier who had made his sacrifice to a greater cause, the Van Valkenburg who did not die in vain. Some fourteen thousand soldiers are buried at this cemetery, which was a predecessor to Arlington National Cemetery.[29] About 5,200 Civil War dead lie here. The cemetery had been open less than a year when Van Valkenburg was killed, and his grave rests in one of the oldest sections. The day I visited was almost exactly 161 years after his death. I was the only living soul in the cemetery that morning. I sank down into the grass, deep green and cushioned, next to his stone. It was hard to make out the raised letters on the soft marble stone.

I would like to imagine that as he fought for his life in the hospital, he was visited by President Lincoln. The president and his wife sometimes walked through the soldiers' hospital, greeting soldiers, since their summer cottage was a five-minute walk from the grounds of both the hospital and the cemetery. Lincoln didn't begin spending his summers on the outskirts of Washington until June 1862, so he may not have offered comfort to the young man from New York, but he certainly looked over his fresh grave later that year. Mortality was very real to the Lincoln family in those early days of 1862; their beloved son Willie had died just two months before Van Valkenburg's death.

Two days before Monroe Van Valkenburg died, Richmond fell to Union troops. As Richmond burned, some of the Black infantry marched through the former capital of the Confederacy. According to diarist Mary Fontaine, the Black troops played the song "Dixie" as they paraded through the streets. She observed, "Then our Richmond servants were completely crazed, they danced and shouted, men hugged each other, and women kissed, and such a scene of confusion you have never seen."[30] Eleanor told me she figured there was a good chance that her ancestor Cato Vanderzee was one of those men marching in. She said, "Cato was a musician. As a musician in the Colored Troops, he would have been at the front of the first soldiers who marched into Richmond. . . .. I love that f'n story."

While I'm not sure whether the Eighth US Colored Infantry made it all the way to Richmond, I do know they were witness to another event. On April 9, 1865, Gen. Robert E. Lee surrendered to Gen. Ulysses S. Grant at the Appomattox Court House in Virginia. Cato Vanderzee and Ezra Bronk, both members of the Eighth US Colored Infantry, watched that day.

The Confederate James Dunbar Van Valkenburg had been killed the year before. Of Georgia's Sixty-First Regiment, just eighty-one men survived, none of them officers.[31] That remaining ragtag group of Confederates was also watching the day Lee surrendered. Less than a week later, Lincoln would be assassinated at Ford's Theatre in Washington.

Vanderzee by Vanderzee, Filling in the Puzzle

I wonder if Cato Vanderzee made his way back home to New Baltimore to tell his mother about that day in Appomattox. She must have been worried about her son. A bugler would have been on the front lines of a war that killed so many. After the war, Cato landed work as a boatman in New York City, living in Lower Manhattan just a few blocks from the piers of the Hudson River.[1] He died in 1894 and was buried in Brooklyn.[2]

Eleanor and I kept coming back to the photo of Mary Vanderzee. She haunted us as if she wanted us to tell her story. Because we could return to her face again and again, she wasn't just an abstract name on a family tree. That photo was a portal into our investigation of Mary, her family, and how my own family intersected with Eleanor's.

Just as I've done with the unwinding tales of the Van Valkenburgs and the Colliers, Eleanor and I hoped to bring life to what was hidden. The old Dutch families—the Bradts, the Hallenbecks, the Houghtalings, the Van Slykes—have family associations with six-hundred-page genealogical books that trace the patriarchs back to the seventeenth century. We knew we wouldn't be able to do that for most Black families, where any search for material evidence before the nineteenth century runs into the erasure that slavery created. It means that those who are hungry to know more often stay hungry. The only thing we could do was connect as many pieces as possible.

Mary Vanderzee came to symbolize all that was frustrating and fascinating about research into Black families. A matriarch who founded a family that thrives to this day was, judging from that single photograph, thin and frail. We knew, though, that she had combined faith and grit to persevere. Her story needed to be told. She was born in the same year as the social reformer Dorothea Dix, the Civil War nurse who changed the way the mentally ill were treated. I wondered what feats Mary Vanderzee might have accomplished if she had been given access to schooling and freedom of movement.

Tracing the white Vanderzees, in contrast, was simple. We already knew so much about that family, the enslavers and descendants of enslavers whose name carried through centuries and generations. In my family tree, it lingers like a ghostly shadow. I lost count of the Vanderzee names I came across with a kaleidoscope of spellings: Vanderzee, Van Der Zee, Vander Zee, Van Derzee. The original Storm—my nine times great-grandfather who was born on a ship and decided he would rather be a Vanderzee than a Bradt—had descendants who moved to Greene County and intermarried with the Houghtalings, the Colliers, and more names in my family tree than I could track.

Hannah Van Der Zee Collier, for instance, was the daughter of my three times great-grandfather. Her father Jonas Collier and his wife, Hannah Sager, had nine children and had accumulated some wealth from farming. In the 1855 state census, Jonas and Hannah were living in a brick home valued at $1,500 at a time when most people lived in wooden frame houses worth about $500.[3] His son, Casper Jonas Collier, my second great-grandfather, and his wife, Rachel Armstrong, had fourteen children. In 1870, when Casper Collier was sixty, his farm was worth $20,000 and he listed $5,000 in personal estate.[4] Living next door to the Colliers was a Black man named John E. Vanderzee, thirty-seven, a carpenter, and his wife, Mary. Eleanor and I couldn't figure out just how this John Vanderzee was related to her family, or to mine, for that matter. There were so many mysteries.

Another white Vanderzee tracked me down after I appeared in a TV interview talking about my enslaving ancestors in New York. In an email with the subject line "My last name is VanDerzee," Sandy VanDerzee told me that her family had owned a two-thousand-acre farm in the Hudson Valley until the 1990s.[5] The family was proud of its name. Even if she married, she said, she would keep the name VanDerzee. Her brother gave his son the middle name Storm so that he could include the "origin story" about the first Storm Vanderzee in his heritage.

Sandy VanDerzee had never heard a thing about slaveholders in the North. She grew up on the Upper East Side of Manhattan, and for years people would call her family's apartment, asking to speak to the Harlem Renaissance photographer James Van Der Zee. She had laughed off what she saw as an odd coincidence. Was he a member of her family? When she found out that James Van Der Zee was Black, she would say, "Hmmmm. I don't think so."

She remembered someone in her family telling her that Black Vanderzees had borrowed the name, possibly from a tombstone, when they escaped north on the Underground Railroad. "It made sense to me," she said. As for the idea that the Vanderzees were themselves enslavers, she said, "I don't even know if my father was aware of it." She wondered when the oral history about Vanderzees as slaveholders had died out. "Who would have been the last generation in my family to know?" she asked.

The idea of borrowing a name off a tombstone was intriguing, I thought. Confronted with the unsettling fact of Black Vanderzees, some white families ignored the most obvious answer or deliberately created a fanciful version of the story. The idea of a man casting off a past and landing on the name Vanderzee because he saw it on a tombstone while he fled slave catchers also played into the romanticized image of the Underground Railroad.

VanDerzee said that she knew her father and grandfather had treated the workers on the family farm well, so she hoped that treatment applied to earlier centuries and their enslaved men and women. When we initially corresponded, she was just beginning to come to terms with the truth. But that reaction, however well meaning, made me think of earlier comments. Were those Vanderzee slaves "devotedly attached" to the family?

I assumed that the Black Vanderzees knew their name hadn't been borrowed from a tombstone. Fitting in more pieces of the puzzle turned out to be an exercise combining exasperation with occasional insight. Eleanor and I spent more hours expanding this family tree than I could tally. We wanted to create a giant network that made the rest of the family as real as Mary was to us. We wanted to understand her children and her children's children. We wanted to pinpoint where they lived, what they did, and how they negotiated a life after slavery in a world that sometimes hated them, sometimes ignored them, and often used them to their own purposes.

Instead of a tidy family tree, we found a motley assortment of ghostly passion, blizzards, freak shows, and picnics. Even the story of Mary Vanderzee, the daughter of an enslaved couple named Cesar Egberts and Rebecca Dunbar, was an example of more things hidden than revealed. Eleanor's genealogical work had begun despite her family's denial of the past. Her grandmother told her that her Hudson Valley ancestors had never been enslaved. Her grandmother might not have known the truth, or she might have been shying away from a terrible period of history.

I thought of what another Vanderzee descendant had told me. Cheryl Rollins said that when she first started studying her family's history, her mother had warned her to be careful. She might not like what she found. Focusing on slavery meant directing attention to the past, long gone and good riddance. Refusing to acknowledge some shameful facts or rejecting the ugliness were both ways to exist in a country still grappling with its messy history. After World War II, many of the survivors of the Holocaust chose a similar response to trauma: they simply did not talk about it.

Increasingly, though, I kept meeting members of the Vanderzee family who wanted to know. For me, fleshing out this story became part of the reckoning. We might not be able to produce an enormous book crammed with begats like the 776-page *Descendants of Albert and Arent Andriessen Bradt*,[6] but we could create, instead, a scrapbook. For Eleanor, the search was a way to celebrate and honor her ancestors.

Mary Vanderzee was our keystone, our Founding Mother whose face opened the door for us to continue to ask questions. She was born in 1802 when Thomas Jefferson was president and many of this country's Founding Fathers—John Adams, James Madison, James Monroe—were alive. The Revolutionary War was a recent memory.

We know that Mary Vanderzee spent her childhood as a playmate to the Conraedt Houghtaling family. What else could we discover? Newspapers in Greene County had begun publishing a few years before her birth, but the only evidence of Black people in those early columns were advertisements for runaway slaves. Nevertheless, we parsed every detail, scoured every newspaper article for clues and hints of clues that might lead us to understand something of the narrative arc of her life. In the way that Mary became symbolic to me, so did the hours of paging through old newspapers and peering at census records, as if through the search itself I could find some redemption.

One essay written on Mary's hundredth birthday gave some details of her earliest days. "Her life is a romance," wrote Lillie S. Jones Baldwin.

> A few years ago she never tired telling of the changes she had witnessed, then the children, aye, and the parents, would gather around to listen to the tales of long ago, of the soldiers in the war of 1812 passing the farm, her fear of the strange artillery, and of deserters from the army, who hid in the barn. Wolves were numerous and fierce, fire was borrowed from neighbors, and many a bitter winter morning Aunt Mary, sometimes accompanied by one of the older children, ran with heart in mouth to the frozen brook for water, or across to Grandpa's house for fire.[7]

When Mary was coming of age, the village of New Baltimore was coming of age as well. Carved from the northern tip of Coxsackie in 1811, the hamlet, like so many other Hudson Valley towns, sloped down to the river on steep hills, jagged with rocky slate. Its abundant streams flowing into the Hudson powered local mills. In 1829 New Baltimore boasted ten schools, four gristmills, nineteen sawmills, and 425 farms. Anthony Van Bergen, formerly one of the largest enslavers in town, owned a seven-hundred-acre farm. By the middle of the century, river commerce began to increase. Shipbuilding and ice harvesting boomed.[8]

Well into her eighties and nineties, Mary worked as a servant and a cook at the tables of local families. On Sundays she attended services at the New Baltimore Reformed Church, which she had joined almost at the beginning of its establishment in 1833. Her children and stepchildren worked nearby: Cato Vanderzee was a farmer until the Civil War began; William Vanderzee was a carpenter. Others took jobs as boatmen, possibly because the white Vanderzee family had been shipping goods from New Baltimore as early as the 1790s in their sloop called *Friendship*.

By her hundredth birthday in 1902, she had outlived two husbands and all her children and stepchildren except her daughter Julia. The *Coeymans Herald* marked the occasion of her birthday. "The old lady is remarkably well preserved and has nearly full use of her faculties. Some of the old residents claim that she is really over a hundred years old, and insist that her correct age is 103 years."[9]

After I read that line for the third or fourth time, I stopped. If she was 103 in 1902, she would have been born around 1799. She might have been born on the wrong side of the gradual emancipation law. Was she born enslaved? Eleanor thought it was a plausible theory. "It's possible that she was born earlier, but that they hid her birth date so that she could be born free," she said. What didn't add up, though, was the secrecy. Hiding a baby's birth, even one born to a Black woman, would have been nearly impossible in a small town of just a few hundred people.

Newspaper stories loved to exaggerate the ages of the elderly. But then I realized an earlier birth could resolve another mystery. If she was really 103 and born in 1799, I texted Eleanor, "*that* could be the reason the name Mary does not show up in the Coxsackie Register." We had already entertained the idea that Mary's mother was not enslaved, but we hadn't thought about the fact that if Mary herself was born earlier, she wouldn't appear in the record. The Coxsackie Register of Free Born Slaves was strictly limited to babies born in the twilight period between July 4, 1799, and July 4, 1827. In New York a person's destiny could be determined by the accident of birth: if Mary had been born in May or June 1799, she was born a slave. If she was born after the magical date of July 4, she was not.

There was one major flaw with that theory, however. According to her death certificate, Mary had been very specific about the day of her birth: May 27, 1802. There was a birth registered one day off from that day, even if the names were not a match. "Her birth date was too much of a coincidence," Eleanor said. She had to be baby Nan, whose mother was enslaved by Peter Van Bergen. We will never know, without a séance or a miraculous discovery, why her first name was changed from Nan to Mary, if that theory holds. And besides the obsessive curiosity of the two of us, we started to wonder whether sending each other GIFs of Alice falling down the rabbit hole was just a sign that we were staring into an abyss that had no end and no answers.

Mary's childhood and her all-too-brief years as a companion and playmate to the Houghtaling children ended when she had her first baby. She was about fourteen years old. Piecing together clues from census records and genealogical work her cousin's wife had done, Eleanor and I knew that Mary had three or four children in her teens: we found records for Sarah, Thomas, and Cato. Then she married John Van Bergen and had two more, Julia Ann and Caesar. We haven't been able to figure out what happened to her first husband, but next Mary married John Vanderzee and gave birth to Anthony. In the meantime, her firstborn sons Thomas and Cato were given—or took—the name Vanderzee, even though when they were born, Mary was not married to anyone named Vanderzee.

When her second husband John Vanderzee died in 1860, he named his beneficiaries: his wife Mary, his sons Peter, William, and John from his first marriage and Anthony from his marriage to Mary, and his stepchildren Sarah, Thomas, and Cato.[10] He doesn't mention two other stepchildren, Julia Ann and Caesar Van Bergen. The names in John Vanderzee's will helped us work out who was included in the family. But these clues also raised questions. One complication was that John's son Peter Vanderzee had married Mary's daughter, Julia Ann Van Bergen, his half sister. Then there were more mysteries that turned up in the census records: Sometime between the 1850 federal census and the 1855 state census, Caesar Van Bergen changed his name to Caesar Vanderzee.[11] Even the name of Cato, one of Mary's earliest-born children, sometimes appeared as Cato Van Bergen and sometimes as Cato Vanderzee.

These sorts of name evolutions made genealogical research headache-inducing. It also showed us, to our frustration, the fluidity of Black family names. Even the Vanderzee name raised endless questions. Mary's family name could as well have been Houghtaling (where she was raised and first gave birth), Van Bergen (the name of her first husband), or Egberts (her father's name). We understood why Mary Vanderzee would retain the family name of her second husband, but the mystery of her children's names eluded us. There was an additional complication with names: the children's first names were often identical to the first names in the white families, like Anthony Van Bergen or John Vanderzee. To do genealogical research on Black families, we had to engage in a form of reverse whitewashing.

The brick walls didn't stop us, but they made the research harder. Every time we'd look for a "Thomas Vanderzee" or a "Maria Hallenbeck" on the genealogical sites, we would stumble over white men and women with the same name. It was easy to conflate names or birth dates, easy to lose the trail of a woman who died in childbirth, perhaps even long before she chose a family name. When some slaves and free Blacks were baptized in churches, they occasionally marked the occasion by dropping earlier names and taking on a first name, a Christian name from the Bible. Even then, they were not always given surnames. How, we wondered, could we research people like those in the Coxsackie Reformed Church registry: "Samuel; parents are slaves of Ab'm Hallenbeek," or "Ben, belongs to Leonard Bronk." It was infuriating to gaze into the chasm that removed Samuel's and Ben's personhood by depriving them of full names.

Occasionally I would come across a name that was unmistakably non-white. In 1822 a Black man named Quash Osterhout, along with Caty Brown, described as "free," registered the baptism of their baby David in Coxsackie's First Reformed Church.[12] Quash was a West African name, so it's possible that Quash or his father had been born in Africa. The white Osterhout family were enslavers in Greene County. Quash Osterhout was a rarity, but his son David was given a name that could have fallen on either side of the racial divide.

Vanderzee by Vanderzee, we collected pieces of the puzzle. As we gathered specific facts about each person, we were also painting in what had been a shadowy picture of life for Blacks in nineteenth-century Greene County. Mary's child Sarah, for instance, gave us a new way to look at the lives of Black families in the area, and how they managed in the face of racism, genetic anomalies, and economic struggle. Sarah married a Black man named Thomas Van Allen.[13]

Eleanor uncovered a brief, unsettling item about an albino baby born in Coxsackie in 1837. According to the *Albany Argus*, the child was being "held" at the Albany Museum.[14] The museum, founded in 1808, was more like a Coney Island sideshow. Exhibits included a stuffed rhinoceros; the original Siamese twins, Chang and Eng Bunker; and a woman who claimed she had been enslaved by George Washington's father and was 161 years old. Along with those displays the museum announced a new exhibit. "The museum has recently received a rare accession in the live way," a "white negro child" from Coxsackie. "Its parents are African, of the ordinary depth of color for the Africo-American race, and irreproachable in character." Calling the family "irreproachable" preempted any talk that the child might have had a white father.

Another article from the same year described a baby about seven or eight months old, who was probably the same child. The child's parents were Black, but he had whiter skin than most white people. "This is no hoax," the paper reported. "We have seen the child, ourself, and the character of the mother is stainless."[15] A doctor examined the child and pronounced him "the most remarkable incident of this character he ever met with, and most probably that has ever occurred." A few weeks later the *Albany Argus* provided its readers with an update: "This child is now at the Museum in this city, and is certainly a rare curiosity."[16] The Philadelphia-based *United States Gazette* wrote: "The youngster is alive and kicking, and no doubt will greatly add to the attractions of the place. He is perfectly tame and quite contented with his situation among the wild

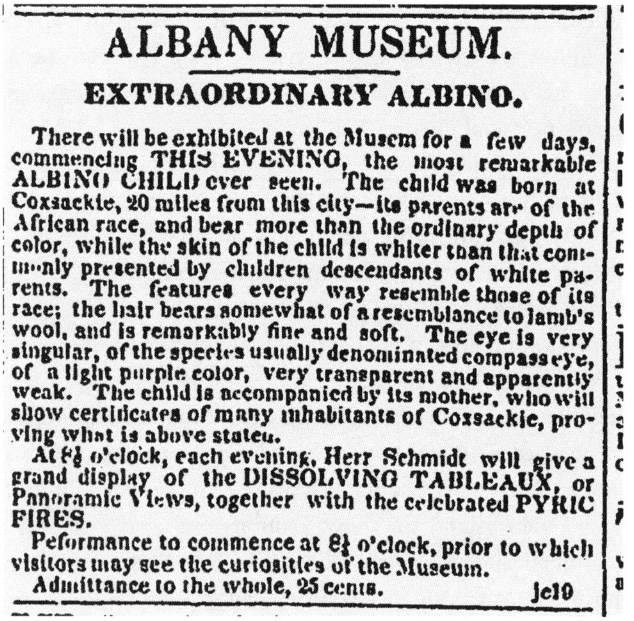

ALBANY MUSEUM.
EXTRAORDINARY ALBINO.

There will be exhibited at the Musem for a few days, commencing THIS EVENING, the most remarkable ALBINO CHILD ever seen. The child was born at Coxsackie, 20 miles from this city—its parents are of the African race, and bear more than the ordinary depth of color, while the skin of the child is whiter than that commonly presented by children descendants of white parents. The features every way resemble those of its race; the hair bears somewhat of a resemblance to lamb's wool, and is remarkably fine and soft. The eye is very singular, of the species usually denominated compass eye, of a light purple color, very transparent and apparently weak. The child is accompanied by its mother, who will show certificates of many inhabitants of Coxsackie, proving what is above stated.

At 8¼ o'clock, each evening, Herr Schmidt will give a grand display of the DISSOLVING TABLEAUX, or Panoramic Views, together with the celebrated PYRIC FIRES.

Performance to commence at 8¼ o'clock, prior to which visitors may see the curiosities of the Museum.
Admittance to the whole, 25 cents.   Je19

Figure 17. An advertisement in the *Albany Argus* from June 1837 describes an "extraordinary albino" of the African race, on display for a few days at the Albany Museum.

beasts."[17] The *Albany Argus* explained that the child, accompanied by his mother, would be "exhibited at the Museum for a few days."[18]

After that mysterious series of articles, we couldn't find another mention of the Coxsackie albinos for almost fifty years. But our curiosity compelled us. Then, in the 1860 federal census for Coxsackie, I found them: Sylvanus Van Allen, a laborer and boatman on the Hudson, his wife Jane—both listed as B for Black—and three of their children—Theron, twenty, as well as daughters Josephine and Lavinia.[19] Next to their names, the word "albino" had been written in the column for race. Two other children were recorded as M for "mulatto." Theron had to be the infant on display at the Albany Museum. I lost track of Theron after that, so I don't know what happened to the infant who was "perfectly tame and contented among the wild beasts." But I did find Theron's sisters.

Two of them showed up later. They had turned the sideshow nature of their skin color into profit. In 1874 the *Hudson Evening Register* wrote, "There is to be a new feature in connection with the fair of the St. John's M.E. Church, to be held at City Hall." The "Albino Sisters" are "natural curiosities, besides being good singers, and it will more than pay the price of admission to see them and hear them sing."[20] In the state census from the next year, 1875, Sylvanus's two albino daughters, seventeen and nineteen, list their professions as "on exhibition." An article in 1877 described the Coxsackie Albino singers playing four- and three-handed duets on the piano. "The parents of these Albinos have always resided in Coxsackie and although themselves coal black every alternate child the wife has borne has been an Albino."[21]

As late as 1893, the *Catskill Recorder* advertised an upcoming show that would include "plantation songs." In addition, "the Albino sisters (formerly with P. T. Barnum) will give a concert, singing a number of popular melodies."[22] Barnum's American Museum in New York City had been, from 1841 to 1865, an expanded version of the Albany Museum, with beluga whales, a bearded lady, and Tom Thumb, on Broadway and Ann Street.

Mary's daughter Sarah and her husband Thomas Van Allen undoubtedly knew the albino Van Allens. Working out the biological or familial connection between the families was another one of those moments that made us want to pull out our hair. History has erased so much. We had also heard from a man named Joe Brevard, who was descended from the

Black Van Allens and Van Hoesens in Greene and Columbia Counties, and we were never able to link up his family line either.

The Van Allens had done something remarkable. They had transformed a genetic aberration that made them a "natural curiosity" into a profit-making enterprise. It was a sign of resourcefulness that marked many of the area's Black families. Operating within a system that treated them more like animals than humans, the Van Allens turned it to their advantage. Sarah and Thomas Van Allen, like the other Van Allens, established themselves throughout the Hudson Valley. They went on to have nine children.

Thomas, Mary's second child, was another symbol of resilience, transcending the debacle of his false arrest in 1859 and establishing an enormous family in the Hudson Valley. He continued to work as a boatman on the Hudson, moving first to Saugerties, thirty miles south of New Baltimore, and finally another twelve miles south to Kingston. On September 1, 1874, Thomas Vanderzee's death made the newspaper. "Sudden death," wrote a Kingston paper. In somewhat gory detail, the item described Captain Thomas Vanderzee's final conversation with a friend when suddenly "blood gushed from his mouth" and he couldn't speak. Before the friend could help him, "the captain fell to the ground and expired." He was about sixty-two, the paper said. "He has for many years sailed vessels in the stone trade from Wilbur, and was not only considered, one of the best boatmen on the river but he was universally respected as a citizen," the paper opined. "Being a man of frugal habits it is supposed he has left his family in comfortable circumstances." Thomas and his wife Sarah left many children: named were Sylvester, Thomas, William Franklin, Sarah Louisa, Charlotte, Ella May, Melissa Jane, Victoria, and Martha.[23]

Thomas's children continued to establish themselves in Kingston well into the twentieth century. In September 1937 the *Kingston Daily Freeman* covered a family reunion of Thomas's son Sylvester. The picnic supper included fried chicken, baked beans, potato salad, sliced tomatoes, rolls, pickles, olives, iced tea, fruit punch, mints, nuts, ice cream, and cake. The group celebrated the birthday of "Miss Anna Van Der Zee," who "expressed the opinion of the entire group when she said that a reunion such as this should be an annual affair."[24] Even though newspapers of the time often covered the most insignificant of events—I recall one from 1911 that announced that six-year-old Edna Collier, my grandmother, "is confined to the house with a very hard cold"[25]—the Vanderzee news item showed just how eminent the family had become in Kingston.

Apparently, Miss Anna's wish was fulfilled for some time, because on Labor Day in 1948, the paper reported that "members of the original Van Der Zee family" met at a family picnic. Descendants of Sylvester, Melissa, and Ella Vanderzee were there.[26]

There was one more fascinating link to history through the Vanderzee family. It was a connection to the eighteenth president, Ulysses S. Grant. John J. Vanderzee, a man we believe was the grandson of Thomas, moved to New York City after the Civil War. John and his wife Susan worked as butler and maid for the former president in Upper Manhattan. Grant, struggling with financial ruin and throat cancer, was encouraged by the author Mark Twain to write his memoirs. When Grant's money ran out, John and Susan returned to their home village of Lenox in western Massachusetts, where a growing community of free Blacks had settled to work. It was fast becoming a summer refuge for the wealthy.

Eleanor had mentioned the Vanderzee link to Grant when we first connected. The idea that her ancestors had worked for the eighteenth president was one of the reasons she was stopping people on the street to talk about her family, she told me. Every year she takes her son Jake to Manhattan on his birthday, and they visit Grant's tomb. The president who led the Union army to win the Civil War and employed her ancestors is a hero, she told me.

We know about this connection to Grant thanks to a biography of John and Susan's son, James Van Der Zee, arguably the most famous Vanderzee of all.[27] James Augustus Van Der Zee (his choice of capitalization) is known today as the man who captured images of the Harlem Renaissance in the 1920s and 1930s. For most of his career, Van Der Zee was far more obscure, a successful small businessman who eventually slipped into poverty. His inclusion in the 1969 exhibition "Harlem on My Mind" at the Metropolitan Museum of Art gave him national prominence toward the end of his life and brought acclaim to the man who used the camera lens to interpret New York's middle-class Blacks in both their successes and aspirations to success.[28]

Being rediscovered in his eighties, decades after the photographs were first taken, was both gratifying and overwhelming for Van Der Zee. He told his biographer, "It was too much, too late."[29] Van Der Zee died in 1983 at the age of ninety-six. In 2021 and 2022 the National Gallery of Art in Washington, DC, mounted a forty-photograph retrospective based on its collection of Van Der Zee photographs. "James Van Der Zee's Photographs: A Portrait of Harlem" called his work "an extraordinary chronicle of life" in Harlem. The beauty of those photographs entranced me: a slender bride holding a spray of flowers, the Vanderzee sons with their father John, a small girl with her hands in the pockets of a shearling trimmed coat, a handsome young man, leaning on one knee with a fedora in his hand.

Then we discovered that there was another member of the Harlem Renaissance we had never known. James's older sister Jane Louise Vanderzee, known as Jennie, was one of the country's first Black filmmakers.[30] She married a man named Earnest Touissant Welcome, and the couple ran the Toussaint Conservatory of Art in Harlem and Queens for more than forty years. The woman known as Madame Touissant Welcome called herself the "foremost female artist of the race." Over the years of their marriage, she and her husband had numerous business ventures, including the Touissant Motion Picture Exchange. One of her early silent films was a World War I recruiting film called "Doing Their Bit." Sadly, that film is lost today, as is almost all her work. Just one tangible piece of history remains: one of the posters she created to recruit Black soldiers to enlist in World War I was used by the US government's War Savings Stamp and Liberty Loan drives.[31] It was the only painting accepted from a Black artist. Jennie died of cancer in 1956.

Besides the connection to Mary, Eleanor and I realized that the Egberts and Osterhout families of Lenox had also come from New Baltimore. They had all moved east to Massachusetts sometime after the end of slavery in New York. Even though he was not his biological grandfather, James Vanderzee considered David Osterhout, his grandmother Josephine's second husband, his grandfather. He told his biographer that he had been raised by his unmarried Osterhout aunts. David Osterhout was probably the son of that baby baptized in Coxsackie Reformed Church in 1818, whose parents were Quash Osterhout and Caty Brown. There were so many overlapping family trees.

In the community of Glen Wild in a section of the Catskill Mountains known as the Borscht Belt for its historic connection to bungalow colonies, hotels, and supermarkets attracting Jewish families from New York, conceptual artist Mike Osterhout lives next door to a former church that he has transformed into what he calls a forty-year performance art project. He calls it the Church of the Little Green Man.[32] When he learned that his ancestors had enslaved humans and that generations of Black families took the Osterhout family name, he responded the way any good artist would: with an outburst of art, writing, and a barbaric yawp that he detailed in a 184-page self-published book.

It is his brilliant and messy way of acknowledging, understanding, and expressing horror at the thirteen generations of Osterhout ancestors and slaveholders who have lived in New York's Catskill Mountains and Hudson Valley. For the last six years, part of that response has been an art project, called (F)ancestor, to make what he has found real and palpable. The project, commissioned by a gallery in San Francisco, was later cancelled. The plan, he told me, was to create a long piece of art that incorporated objects, paintings, collage, photographs, and drawings that, as he said, "dealt with Indian removal, disenfranchisement and genocide, enslavement of Africans and the eventual discovery of African American Osterhouts photographed by their nephew Harlem Renaissance photographer James VanDerZee." This could have been an artistic reckoning unlike anything I had ever seen. Osterhout told me that he felt it was crucial for people in the art world to shine a light on this history. I would have loved to see it. Osterhout visited Lenox, Massachusetts, where many of the Black members of the Osterhout family moved in the early twentieth century. When he met some of the Osterhouts' former neighbors, they reacted with surprise. "I never met a *white* Osterhout," they told him.

As for the Vanderzee family, it turned out that even the Black branches of the family drew on imaginary theories for the origin of the name. James Van Der Zee told his biographer that he had received a letter from a white Vanderzee woman in Canada. She had heard that a shipwreck off the coast of Holland left as its only survivors a group of children who were too young to recall the names of their parents. Someone gave them the name Vanderzee—of the sea. Van Der Zee, his biographer wrote, "wondered if one of his ancestors might have been the 'black diamond' . . . in that group of children."[33] I realized that it wasn't just the white families who concocted theories about the origins of the name. Even descendants of the Black Vanderzee family skipped over the obvious link to slavery and went for the romantic tale, one more whimsical narrative. It was almost as if the name itself cast a spell on its descendants.

The puzzle continued to fill. I always wondered if Mary's stepson Peter Vanderzee, who had attended a Colored Convention and heard Frederick Douglass speak, had ever become actively involved in antislavery work. All I could find, instead, was his death. Peter died of pneumonia at the age of seventy in February 1895, on a day the thermometer registered –22°, according to the *Coeymans Herald*.[34] After a blizzard the next day made roads impassable, his funeral was postponed for three days.

Mary Jane Vanderzee, Peter and Julia's daughter, never married. Janey's two brothers, Anthony and Edward, died young. Although Janey worked as a servant in New York City for a few years, she moved back to New Baltimore, where she lived with her grandmother Mary and mother Julia. She was a dressmaker. New Baltimore's 1976 bicentennial book described her this way: "Many New Baltimorians still recall Miss Janey who occupied the Mill Street home as long as she lived. She was a tiny, immaculately neat woman who always firmly declined invitations to eat at the tables of any families for whom she might be working."[35] Miss Janey, the message appeared to say, knew her place.

I thought that was all we could find for a meek woman who had not married and lived with her mother and grandmother. But she wasn't done with us. Maybe there was something to our hunch that these ancestors were finding ways to make themselves known.

Cornelia Read is a mystery novelist who sometimes uses historical figures in her plots. As she read census records for a character she had based on an ancestor, she came across the name of Mary Jane Vanderzee in New York City, listed in his household. Mary Jane Vanderzee, she imagined, worked as a dressmaker. Then she learned that after living in Manhattan, Vanderzee had returned upstate. In the census she had listed her occupation as dressmaker. "Well, I started to cry when I read that, as you might imagine, because I had already imagined her as this fierce and brave young woman who fought to become an artist in the only way available to her, and she HAD ACTUALLY DONE IT," she wrote in a long email.[36]

Then she saw my article about Mary Vanderzee, Eleanor, and our complex kindredship. "When I read the caption below the first photo," she added, "I shrieked so loud I scared the cat and woke up my husband in bed beside me." She had been thinking about slavery in New York ever since she had visited her mother's family graveyard in Oyster Bay. "I asked whom the slate headstones with no names on them were for, and was told, 'Oh, those were just the slaves' by my grandfather. It enraged me as a child, and still does," she said.

This was another bizarre coincidence: Janey was tapping us on the shoulder. Maybe she was not a woman who refused to sit at the tables of the white families. Maybe Miss Janey was as fierce and brave as Cornelia had imagined. We thought of her the day Eleanor and I visited that Mill Street home in New Baltimore, where Mary Vanderzee and her daughter and granddaughter last lived. The home's current owner, Debra Sottolano, welcomed us to visit. We walked through the rooms, gazing out at the peaceful river flowing by and imagining this small family of women sewing dresses, cooking, and walking to the nearby church.

When we first connected, Eleanor told me, "I knew Mary's ghost would touch people." What neither of us knew was the number of ways in which that would turn out to be true. Cornelia, hearing Eleanor's comment, put it best: "Eleanor is correct about the charisma and power and luminous wonder of Mary's ghost, and no less Mary's ghostly passion and fortitude manifesting in all her progeny." We were going to have to add more pages to our expanding family scrapbook.

It turned out that Eleanor even had a connection to Frederick Douglass. Mary's stepson William moved west and established a life in Kansas and Nebraska. William's son, also named William, became a pastor of the Ninth Street Christian Church in Lincoln. That man married Matilda Adams, who was the daughter of Ruth Cox. Ruth Cox had escaped from slavery in Maryland and believed she was the sister of Frederick Douglass.[37] Douglass claimed Ruth as his sister, and even renamed her Harriet, in honor of his mother.

Eleanor's grandmother must have known these stories, she said. "My family is unbelievable," she said to me. "And it's all from my grandmother's side, who never told us anything."

As we continued to fill in missing pages, the modern-day progeny also started tapping us on the shoulder. Cheryl Rollins, the college administrator, contacted me after my article ran. She descended from Thomas's daughter Melissa. In fact, Rollins's family had lived for many years in

Poughkeepsie, not far from the Kingston family. Rollins came to the DC area for college and never left. "I majored in history at Howard University in part because of the family stories I had heard," she told me when we talked on the phone.[38]

Then I found another person, thanks to a moving photograph I had seen in a *Washington Post* feature called "Historically Black," which posted artifacts from family collections.[39] Angela Barnes, who was an executive assistant at the paper, descended from Thomas's son, also named Thomas. She had shared a photograph and the story of her great-grandparents' wedding rings from 1895. Along with a photograph of two tarnished, bronze-colored wedding rings was her family story.

Bertha and Thomas Vanderzee had lived on South Pine Street in Kingston. "When my last remaining uncle passed away, in 2006, my mother, sisters and I went to Kingston to the little house, to clean it out and prepare to sell it," Angela wrote. She found the rings from the great-grandparents she had never met and took them as keepsakes. "To me they represent the perseverance of a family and what lasting love can mean," she wrote. "Someone put those two rings together in that jewelry box, so that the commitment they made back in 1895 would allow them to be together."

We decided it was time for some of us to start getting to know each other. Eleanor, Angela, and I got together on a video chat. Eleanor told Angela that since she is descended from Thomas's daughter Ella, "We're cousins!" Angela got tears in her eyes. She said to Eleanor, "I can hear my family's voice."

The more people we gathered, the more it seemed that connections were stirred. I received a note through Ancestry. "Hello! I'm reaching out because I'm pretty sure we are cousins!!!" Kitt Potter wrote.[40] She descended from Melissa, another of Thomas's daughters. Calling me "cousin" was an imperfect interpretation of our family relationship. In truth, I said gently, it's more likely that one of my Vanderzee ancestors had enslaved hers. Of course, I thought to myself, we could be cousins linked by DNA through the Houghtaling family. We were also cousins through shared names and shared history.

It didn't dissuade Kitt from calling me "Cuz." We set up another virtual meeting so all the Vanderzees we had found so far could see each other face to face. Angela told us about cousin Geraldine on the West Coast, who was approaching a hundred years old. We talked about Vanderzee names on the wall of Kingston's AME Church.

Just before Christmas, Angela invited Kitt and me to a tree-trimming party at her house. When the other guests started to arrive, Angela kept introducing us this way: "This is my cousin Kitt and this is Debra—well, I'll let her explain herself." Each time, I took a deep breath and explained, as well as I could, about my discovery, my article, my book, and the fact that my ancestors enslaved the ancestors of these women who were Vanderzees. It wasn't a topic that normally came up around the mulled wine. I was the awkward white guest feeling something like an interloper, invited for the strangest and most American of reasons.

Kitt and Angela, on the other hand, had an easier link: Their great-great-grandparents were siblings. "It was love at first hug, like we've known each other all our lives and just took up where we left off," Kitt later said.

At the party, Kitt said, "I've been praying and praying for a long time to find family and this year my prayers are finally being answered." We also knew we now had a small army of Vanderzees keen to fill in more missing pieces.

12

WHAT REMAINS

When we first met, Kitt Potter wanted me to know about a place that almost got turned into a parking lot: the Pine Street African Burial Ground in Kingston.

Kingston, at one time the state capital, is one of the oldest towns in New York. Maps from the eighteenth and nineteenth centuries marked a "Negro cemetery" not far from Old Dutch Church, which dated to 1659. Churches prohibited enslaved people from being buried in their churchyards, so their burial places often showed up outside city boundaries. In 1990 Joseph Diamond, an archeologist and associate professor of anthropology at the State University of New Paltz, was intrigued by the maps. He decided to survey the area.

As he and his colleagues began looking around Pine Street, a man came out of his house and asked them what they were doing. They were looking for a graveyard. "And he said, 'Hold on a second,'" Diamond said. He handed them a box of "human remains," which he had found beneath his bathroom floor years earlier when during repairs. The remains turned out to be African American. Besides the notations on the maps, this was the first real proof that a burial place was nearby.

Even with the maps and the box of bones, Diamond said, Kingston officials were skeptical. They asked him, where were the gravestones? The property in the area they had pinpointed had long been used for other purposes: a lumberyard in 1878, a home in 1915, a concrete garage in 1928.

Diamond finally got permission to use ground-penetrating radar on land he suspected might have burials. The GPR found "anomalies" in the soil—likely evidence of graves. In his 2006 report, "Owned in Life, Owned in Death: The Pine Street African and African-American Burial Ground in Kingston, New York,"[1] Diamond estimated that the cemetery was huge. It is, he wrote, "one of the few cemeteries for enslaved individuals currently known that is almost as large as the African Burial Ground in New York City." That 1991 discovery in the heart of Wall Street in Manhattan revealed a site that could hold the remains of as many as fifteen thousand former slaves.

The Kingston property probably extended a full city block and held the remains of most of the enslaved and free Blacks who lived in Kingston between 1750 and 1878. It was "inconceivable," Diamond wrote in his report, that the 1915-era house and 1928-era garage "could have been constructed without intruding upon the remains of at least 25 to 50 individuals." Recent research has revealed that the cemetery was known for some time, then the information was lost.

Even with this convincing evidence, the city slated the property, heading into foreclosure, to be developed into a parking lot. After years of wrangling and fundraising, enough money was raised to purchase the site, which went first to the Kingston Land Trust, a nonprofit, and then finally to Harambee, a nonprofit coalition named for the Swahili word for "all pull together," which would be stewards of the site.

While the land had been secured, no one yet knew who was buried at the Pine Street African Burial Grounds. The cemetery could hold the remains of her ancestors, Kitt told me. Maybe someone would even find Mary Vanderzee's eldest son Thomas, the patriarch of the Kingston Vanderzees, who died in 1874.

Armed with the "anomalies" gleaned from ground-penetrating radar, archeologists planned to do a summertime dig. I wanted to see the site.

Kitt wanted to show me that as well as Mount Zion Cemetery, where later generations were buried, so we met up in the spring of 2022.

We began at Mount Zion, owned by AME Zion Church and opened in 1853. Since some of Thomas's children are buried here, it could also be where Thomas rests, without a headstone. It's a wooded refuge, set on a high ridge on the outskirts of the city. That day it was covered with several inches of melting snow and the fallen branches of pine trees. We picked our way through the slush, reading the Dutch and Huguenot names I kept finding in my research: Van Allen, Van Deusen, Deyo, DeWitt, Hasbrouck, Dubois, Ten Broeck, Van Dyke. We found Thomas Vanderzee's sons, Thomas and Sylvester.

We stopped by Old Dutch Church in downtown Kingston. Lydia Newcomb, a white woman who is an elder at the church, met us. She told us she knew Black people with Dutch names when she was growing up, including a woman named April Vanderzee. "It never occurred to me as a kid to ask why April had a Dutch name," she said. Then she saw, with horror and surprise, a will of her ancestor Sarah Kiersted: she had bequeathed six slaves to her children. "It was a dose of reality," she told me. "I decided it had come around to me."

She started asking questions about Black membership in Old Dutch Church and was told there was none. But as she dug back through the records, she found Black members with names like Hasbrouck and Ten Broeck. How had no one known they were there? It was a deliberate omission, she said. "As soon as I discovered this, I thought, 'I've got to find out more. Where do I join?'" The church had records going back to 1659. Newcomb gave me a file that included census records of Black households in Kingston in 1840 and 1855. She found baptismal and marriage records of Black families in Old Dutch Church, including those known or believed to be slaves. There were ten baptisms of enslaved infants from 1703 up to 1802, along with baptisms of twelve free Blacks.[2]

That day, Kitt Potter also told me a little bit about herself.[3] She had grown up in the Hudson Valley. Her grandfather had been a civil rights leader and led the Newburgh, New York, chapter of the NAACP for fifteen years. On her father's side she was a Vanderzee: Ellsworth Smith Potter, her great-great-grandfather, had married Thomas's daughter Melissa. Her mother's family came from Virginia, and that branch of the family knew its ancestors had been enslaved. "But the Vanderzees never talked about slavery," she said. Potter had joined New York's Twentieth Regiment of the US Colored Troops and served with them during the Civil War.[4] Maybe he knew Samuel Van Slyke and Henry Bronk from Greene County, also serving in the Twentieth.

We didn't get to the Pine Street burial ground that day. The *Daily Freeman* had heard we were meeting and wrote an article: "Descendants of slaves, slave owner to meet in Kingston."[5] That premature publicity turned out to be both clumsy and ill timed. A member of the Harambee board announced that we did not have permission to visit the site. I realized that the appearance of a descendant of enslavers, especially without clearing it with everyone involved with the burial ground ahead of time, was an insensitive move. I felt like the interloper.

Part of the reason could have been that disturbing the burial ground had become controversial. Some Black community members, I was told, worried that an archeological dig could turn a sacred space into a scientific experiment where, once more, the bodies of Black people were treated disrespectfully. I tried, without success, to get through to Harambee, the group that oversaw the site. Later that year, the dig got underway. Ken Nystrom, a bioarcheologist working with Diamond at the site, told the *Daily Freeman* that anyone was welcome to come by and see the work. I decided that was enough of an invitation to visit.

Most people would drive by. On a street lined with modest older homes, the burial grounds are tucked away behind the green Harambee headquarters. I parked my car and walked into the back. In a long and narrow yard, a handful of sweaty college students worked in three pits, shoveling sandy brown dirt into buckets, then pouring the dirt over grates to sift out larger objects. Nystrom said they had found a small stone bearing the initials "BT." Inside the pits, a few stones jutted out, and in one pit a long bone extended horizontally from the dirt into the air. Nystrom said he thought it was an animal bone.

A few blocks away, a simultaneous dig was taking place in a graveyard adjoining Old Dutch Church. This one was focused on the ancestors of the white DeWitt family of Kingston. Here were more sweaty laborers, many of them members of the DeWitt family, tossing shovelfuls of dirt onto a blue tarp and sifting through to pull out pieces of glass and stone. In a video the DeWitt family made about their history and the reasons for the Kingston dig, descendant Gage DeWitt said that the plot probably held four generations of their earliest American ancestors. Many markers had been lost to time. With extraction of some of the bones and the potential for facial reconstruction based on the skulls and bones, he said, "We will be able to see the faces of our ancestors."[6]

It was not hard to see the irony of the two simultaneous digs: one, an old Dutch family buried just outside the doors of Old Dutch Church, and the other, the people who had undoubtedly been enslaved by them, pushed to a place that had been almost lost to history.

On a hot and humid day in August later that summer, a small group of what I had begun calling the Vanderzee diaspora gathered in Kingston. It was time to walk the same streets and see the parks, houses, and trees the Vanderzee kin had seen. It was also time to connect Kitt with Eleanor Mire, her sister Bev, and Eleanor's son Jake. But in terms of seeing anything meaningful to the Vanderzee family, the day was a letdown. We started with Mount Zion Cemetery since we knew we could find Vanderzees there. It had been rededicated in 2011, after volunteers helped clear the land and apply for historic preservation status after years of neglect.[7] But more than ten years after that revival, the cemetery had once again fallen into some disrepair and was covered with poison ivy. Finding the headstones of ancestors wasn't worth the skin rash. The unkempt Black cemetery, managed by AME Zion Church, had struggled with the financial wherewithal that could keep it manicured and mown. In 2021 the cemetery received renewed recognition as a historic site, and that attention might draw funds for further restoration.[8]

We headed over to Old Dutch Church and met up with Pastor Rob Sweeney. He told us that Old Dutch had owned a separate cemetery for the white Houghtaling family. It had sold that land in 1963 because the church found it too expensive to keep up. The bodies were exhumed and reburied at Old Dutch, and the church gave the proceeds from the sale of that land toward the work at the Pine Street burial grounds.[9] Again, I saw the contrast: care taken to reinter bones in a white cemetery as bones in a Black cemetery were ignored.

That day, we left the church and headed to a coffee shop for a cold drink, passing what is touted as the "oldest four corners" in the country. The houses facing the intersection of John and Crown Streets had been built between 1663 and 1775. One of them was the Matthewis Persen

House Museum. We peeked inside and met Ulster County historian Taylor Bruck, who told us that up until recently, the acknowledgment of slavery had been absent from its historic placards. The reason, he later told me, was twofold: no one knew much about slavery in Kingston, and what information earlier historians did have was not seen as "kid friendly" for the school groups that came through.

But the Persen house is undergoing its own reckoning. New signs and updates to its website will "include a comprehensive history of *everybody* who lived in the house since the 1600s," Bruck told me a few months later.[10] Four enslaved people who are listed in the 1790 census records as owned by Matthewis Persen probably worked at his public house. During an earlier dig, archeologists found an ivory ring or bracelet, an item that had originated in Africa. "It is likely that the item belonged to one of the enslaved people who lived at the house," Bruck said. That small piece of jewelry could tie Kingston to the transatlantic slave trade.

One sign will mention Baltus, who in 1674 was the earliest enslaved man on record for the house. What is not on display—but is available on the Persen house website—is his gruesome story. In 1676 he was accused of murdering one woman and severely wounding another. His punishment was horrific: "Baltus' right hand shall be cut off, his legs and arms shall be broken and directly thereafter he shall be hung to the gallows as an example for others."[11] The document is too graphic to display, said Barbara Carlson, administrative assistant at the Ulster County Records Center. Even so, the expansion of the story at one of the oldest historic sites in America proved that Kingston is taking steps, however careful, to move beyond anodyne storytelling.

We passed by Pine Street that day, but the archeological work had wrapped up for the year. There was nothing to see but dirt and grass. Later in the year the project's archeologists and students reported their findings.[12] They had found evidence of seven human burials: teeth, leg bones, a jawbone, a skull, collarbones, and parts of torsos. Two of the humans were very small, one a baby less than six months old and one a five-year-old child.

Earlier, when a gas line was being dug between two houses, workers found an intact headstone in a sewer trench, Nystrom said. Carved on the marble tablet was the name Ceazar Smith, who died in 1849. Alongside the human remains were coffin nails, evidence of rotted wood, fragments of stones that might have been grave markers, and shroud pins. The archeologists took small DNA samples from bones and teeth, which they hoped would help determine where these dead were born and where they lived, Nystrom said. Some of the findings were bizarre, such as the discovery of the remains of a Capuchin monkey in a collar—an animal who could have been someone's pet. A second dig in the summer of 2023 discovered the remains of another seventeen people, several of them young children.[13]

While the samples might allow archeologists to determine more about the people who were buried there, they could also lead to living descendants. If modern Kingstonians take DNA tests, they might be able to match with their ancestors who were buried in this spot. Kitt Potter was hoping to be one of them.

At the end of the summer, the human remains were blessed, draped with colorful African fabrics in yellow, green, and red, and reburied. On Facebook one of the participants posted the pictures of the tiny bundles, one for the infant and one for the young child, lying at the bottom of a deep pit. He wrote, "You can't imagine the emotion that hits you. We own the land now, our ancestors can sleep in peace."

It took Kingston years of struggle and advocacy to reach the point where part of an ancient burial ground is preserved, and where a historic home begins a reckoning with its past involvement in slavery. Now Kingston seems to be making up for lost time. In 2023 the Sojourner Truth State Park was opened to honor the abolitionist and suffragist who lived nearby.[14] The park, reclaimed from land that had once been used for cement production, is marked with trails and views of the Hudson River. Port Ewen, a village just south of Kingston where Sojourner Truth spent her early years, has a bronze statue of her as a child. The child, barefoot and carrying two water jugs, looks over Broadway, the main street through the town.

I didn't realize her statue was there until we rented an Airbnb nearby for a wedding. Serendipitous wanderings were often the way I stumbled upon the footprints of slavery in New York. On the next corner was an eighteenth-century stone building that turned out to be the tavern where Truth worked and lived for two years when she was a child. A marker had been on the spot, just off Route 9W as it intersects the village, since 2013.[15] It reads, "SOJOURNER TRUTH 1797–1883 A SLAVE HERE AT MARTINUS SCHRYVER'S TAVERN: 1808–1810. SPEAKER-ACTIVIST ON ABOLITION, WOMEN'S RIGHTS & TEMPERANCE." While it's true that Sojourner Truth was all these things in her life, the marker diminishes the events that happened there and emphasizes the redemptive parts. After her emancipation, Sojourner Truth never again lived in Ulster County.

I set out to investigate what else remained. I especially wanted to find the places in New York that figured in Eleanor's and my families. I kept coming back to the very first question I had when I read the will of Isaac Collier. Why did no one tell me? Did I *miss* something?

I started with my little hometown of Athens. Athens is too small for a museum, a statue, or even much in the way of historical markers. The main street through town—Washington Street—is also Route 385, and trucks, school buses, and cars whiz by on their way north to Coxsackie or south to Catskill. From that road, village streets rise away from the river, and many of the homes offer a glimpse of the Hudson's waters through the trees. One new historic marker on Washington Street, a half block south from my childhood home, notes the location where the steamboat *Swallow* shipwrecked in 1845.[16] Fourteen people drowned.

A half block north of my childhood home is another place with deep roots in slavery. The Van Loon house, built by Albertus, son of the village founder Jan Van Loon, is the oldest house in town. Its most ancient portion, some figure, had been built in 1709, with the main part of the house added in 1724. I had wanted to see inside since I was a little girl—it seemed so old, so full of ghosts. The house, covered with creeping ivy, abuts the cracked sidewalk and the busy road. Each time I walked by, I would lean down and try to peek inside the windows. Whether the house had settled in its three hundred years or whether the pavement of the road had gradually been built up, the squat building of brick and wood and wavy glass looked as if it would eventually sink all the way into the Hudson River just beyond its walls.

I finally got the chance to see inside when I connected with Carrie Feder, a New York City native who bought the house with her husband, Randall Evans. Feder invited me to visit on a sunny autumn day. Although the ceilings are low and the rooms compact, the place was flooded with light. On one end of the room, a deep brick fireplace was supported by an ancient horizontal beam. Some walls showed exposed brick and others cracked plaster, all held up by a ceiling supported by foot-wide hand-hewn beams. I had the feeling I was inside an impromptu museum, a home, and a curiosity shop.

When she and her husband bought the house more than twenty years ago, it had been a decrepit mess, littered with dead animals, mold, dirt, and dust. The couple had a business in architectural design and restoration, and Feder currently curates exhibitions that juxtapose historic artifacts with contemporary art. They had bought old homes in the past, loving the challenge of restoring and reclaiming history. This one was a far bigger project than either of them imagined. "We couldn't believe our luck when we were able to actually own it," she told me. "If you can own a house like this."

Feder and her husband knocked out plaster drywall and exposed the home's original fireplaces and beams. In the process, they started collecting items that had been tucked inside its walls and doorways: pottery shards, coins, combs, marbles, a rusted revolver, a doll's head, pipe stems, silver spoons, and a collection of child-size leather shoes that look like a family of elves had left in a hurry. She keeps the items on display in a glass-topped table. A cornerstone shows the letters AVL—for Albertus Van Loon, my seven times great-grandfather.

Feder pushed open a panel to reveal a hidden staircase, dark and narrow as a tomb. On one wall were several painted designs, relics of history. One was a multipointed X surrounded by a circle in light blue and pink paint. Feder told me she thought it was a Bakongo cosmogram—a spiritual symbol that had originated in the Congo. While she didn't know where Athens's enslaved people had originated, she liked the idea of a marking that she thought "illuminates the passage from the physical to the spiritual world." A cosmogram is also linked to water, which would tie in with the Hudson so close to the house, she said. We stared at the symbol. Was it painted by an enslaved woman or someone in the Van Loon family?

"Carrie, I can assure you that slaves lived here," I said. She knew, she told me, about New York's history with slavery, and she assumed that the house had been built with slave labor. Later, I gave her even more details about the house's links to a very dark past. Albertus's wife was Maria Hallenbeck—the daughter of Jacob Hallenbeck, the man whose two small children were murdered by the family slave.[17] Albert and Maria Van Loon didn't let the brutal murder of Maria's siblings dissuade them from owning at least two people—a man named Jak, who changed his name to Pieter when he was baptized at Zion, and a woman named Susanna. A plaque outside the house says, "A VAN LOON HOUSE. BUILT IN 1724 BY ALBERTUS VAN LOON. OCCUPIED AS RESIDENCE SINCE DATE OF ERECTION." I wondered where Pieter and Susanna spent their days and nights.

The only reference I found to slavery in Athens was just four words on an ancient map tucked away inside folders at Vedder Library in Coxsackie. It shows two tiny squares on the outskirts of the village, marked with the words "OLD SLAVE BURYING GROUND." I think of that every time I drive past on Leeds-Athens Road, but I haven't been able to work out whether it's on farmland or whether the burying ground rests inside an area that had been clear-cut for power lines. These bones are probably lost.

Seven miles north of Athens, I came back to the place that had been the source of so much of my research, situated on the property of the biggest enslaver in Greene County. The Bronck House in Coxsackie, built in 1663 by Pieter Bronck, was also home to Leonard Bronk (who anglicized the spelling of the family name) and generations of enslaved workers who worked, died, and were likely buried there.[18] It's one of the oldest existing homesteads in the state. By the time the American Revolution began, the family had been farming right here for 113 years.

The Bronck House acknowledges slavery, but in ways that are oddly detached and inaccurate. The property is also home to the Greene County Historical Society and its Vedder Research Library, named for the first county historian, Jessie Van Vechten Vedder. The squat modern brick building that faces the Bronck House, barns, and the Bronck museum holds hundreds of years of records: in addition to Bronck family papers that date to 1673, its multitudes include personal letters, legal documents, Revolutionary War correspondence, Civil War journals, newsletters, genealogical books, and newspapers that go back to 1792. Mixed in are occasional documents showing bills of sale for slaves, wills that bequeath "wenches" and "boys" to descendants, and the rare manumission paper. Most of the records pay scant attention to the Black families who, at times, made up close to 20 percent of the local population.

While I had spent many hours inside the library, straining my eyesight as I stared at faint handwriting or turned over newspaper pages thin as gossamer with letters that looked like tiny ants, I hadn't taken a tour of the Bronck House next door since I was a child. Eight generations of the Bronck family had lived on this land and in this house. Shelby Mattice, Bronck Museum curator, invited me into the oldest portion of the house, built in 1663.[19] Who had slept within these thick stone walls and walked on the wide panels of the wooden floors?

On this day, I was on the hunt for the enslavers. There he was. Judge Leonard Bronk, the scion of the fifth generation of Bronks to live in America, gazed out at me. His handsome portrait, which showed a man with piercing hazel eyes, an aquiline nose, and a bald head, sat over his writing desk. That desk, Mattice said, had also been used by his father. I imagined Leonard sitting here, planning his purchases of slaves and deciding how to allocate the farm's supply of butter during the lean Revolutionary War years. I wondered in which room Leonard's stepmother Susannah Bronk took her last breath, hoping she had been able to free Mary and Phillis and Tom.

In the next room I came upon the man I had wanted to see face to face ever since I read his 1741 will. Samuel Van Vechten left his enormous estate to the nephew he had raised. In its entirety, the will of my ancestor is a classic accumulation, marking wealth and self-satisfied comfort. To Thunis Van Vechten he bequeathed his lands, including "all the houses, out-houses, grist-mill, barns, barracks, orchard garden," plus household goods that included "furniture, utensils and implements." He went to the trouble of detailing them: "Beads, beading lining, woolen, iron, brass, puter, wooden-ware, waggons, slayes, ploughs, harrows, plate, cash, money and moneys worth in hand." Only then does Van Vechten get to "all my personal chattels as negro slaves, male and female, horses, cows, sheep, swine, poultry." The land, he wrote, should remain with his nephew and his heirs "to the end of the world."[20]

He was blind to the irony that as he was grouping his enslaved people with the swine and the cows, he could pivot to recommending his soul into the hands of "Almighty God who gave it" and seeking to "obtain full pardon and remission of all my sins and to inherit everlasting life." Did it ever occur to him that pardon of his sins had anything to do with holding humans in bondage? I suppose he also figured a painting would give him, if not everlasting life, then a few hundred years of immortality.

My seven times great-uncle had commissioned the painting during a trip to Holland in 1710. It's a creepy painting of an aging bachelor: his

Figure 18. Samuel Van Vechten had this portrait painted when he visited the Netherlands in 1710. The portrait is now on the walls of the Bronck House Museum in Coxsackie. Photo courtesy Greene County (NY) Historical Society.

skin has a sickly tone, and he stands, half smiling, with one hand slipped inside the waist of his vest, Napoleon style, as if he's scratching his belly button. Henry Brace, who wrote the chapter on Catskill in the *History of Greene County*, had a far more flattering interpretation. Van Vechten was wearing "the fashionable dress of the day, in a flowing brown wig, in a brown coat with large cuffs." He also "seems to have been a man of fine presence. His eyes are full of intelligence and a pleasing smile is about his mouth."²¹ Jessie Van Vechten Vedder, herself a descendant of the family, wrote in her book *Historic Catskill* that Samuel never married and "had little use for womankind apart from his mother."²²

Outside the house, the property of the Bronck family is far quieter today than in the years when it was a working farm. Benches and picnic tables are scattered across the grounds for visitors. At one end of the property is a barn that dates to 1790. Jonathan Palmer, the former archivist at Vedder Library, said this was the one place on the property where historians could be certain enslaved people spent their days.

I walked into the Bronck House Museum in front of the 1790 barn. I had just looked at the faces of my enslaving ancestors, but here was the first reference to slavery that visitors would see. One placard was devoted to the Bronk family's history with slavery. There was a copy of the Coxsackie Record of Free Born Slaves, with red dots next to Leonard Bronk's name, showing when his slaves gave birth. There was also the bill of sale from Leonard Bronk to his stepmother Susannah. This was the record of the purchase Susannah made to free the woman named Mary just days before Susannah's death.

Next to the documents were two circa 1860 tintypes of a Black man and woman, described as the "first 2 slaves freed on Bronk farm." They were not named. Underneath the tintypes were the words,

> From the very beginning, the colonie of New Netherland experienced severe labor shortages. By 1626 the practical Dutch began the importation of enslaved blacks to address this problem. For the next two centuries the institution of slavery would play a part in the commercial, political, and social history of New York. . . .. Like many of the earliest settlers the Bronk family acquired slaves to augment family labor. The family continued to own slaves until the abolition of slavery in NY. The freed Bronk slaves and their descendants continued to work for the family as paid farm labor until the late 1920s.

Figure 19. This 1860 tintype of an unidentified Black man at the Bronck House Museum in Coxsackie purportedly shows one of the first two freed slaves on the farm. Photo courtesy Greene County (New York) Historical Society.

Figure 20. An 1860 tintype of a young Black woman at the Bronck House Museum, described as a freed slave. Her white cap, gloves, and gold earrings mean she was likely a servant for the Bronk family. Photo courtesy Greene County (New York) Historical Society.

These words didn't shy away from slavery, but they deflected the sting. Readers are offered a justification—slavery was caused by a labor shortage—and a dismissal—if slavery had been so bad, people would not have stayed around. If only the Dutch hadn't been so practical. The museum's approach was like that of many historic sites. When they mentioned slavery at all, they smoothed its edges.

Partial, self-exculpatory information was the kind of equivocation that could cloud understanding and allow visitors to the Bronck Museum to feel better about the family's role in slavery. Showing tintypes of Black people but not putting them into proper context bothered me almost as much as the language. No one took the trouble to record their names. If they were the last freed slaves in 1860, they would have been at least sixty-one years old in the tintypes. This young couple might have been the offspring of those slaves, but they were not the freed slaves themselves. If the Bronck Museum used the term "slaves" the way the Coxsackie Register called them "free born slaves," then this couple might qualify. Either way, their names have disappeared with the erasure of time and apathy.

Who was the elegant young woman in a lace collar and gold hoop earrings, holding white gloves? She may have been born on the Bronk farm in the twilight period, one of those last "freeborn slaves." If she was Mary Ann, born to Leonard Bronk's enslaved woman named Maria in 1818, she would be forty-two in the tintype. Unless some future researcher uncovers a previously undiscovered slip of paper or diary, we may never know who she was. Interestingly, the museum also holds another related artifact: an enormous door knocker with the letters MVB. It's from Martin Van Bergen's house, the one pictured in the overmantel.

Maybe one more visit to the Bronk family cemetery would yield a hint at some of the mysteries. The cemetery doesn't show up on the maps. Visitors having a picnic lunch might notice a sign at the edge of the grounds, but most people would have no reason to wander back there.

On this day I was alone. It was early spring, and the birds were singing madly after a dull winter. As I stood near Leonard Bronk's grave, a giant crane swooped down to land on the creek that ran parallel to the tiny plot. He hesitated, then lifted off again when he saw me, once more the interloper.

I stared, trying to make out the names and dates on the headstones in the bright sunshine. Most of the graves are now indecipherable, worn by time and weather. I walked downhill and back, ten steps, twenty steps, almost to the spot where the land slopes back down into the creek. The Black section of the cemetery is marked by a solitary wooden post. Was it once part of a fence, separating the races for eternity?

Ezra Bronk's stone was easy to read, but most were triangles and jagged shards jutting out of the earth, looking more like accidents of frost upheaval than pieces of history. I was hoping for answers. I touched each stone jutting out, as if the stones might be able to transmit something to me. I wondered if the elegant woman in the lace collar was here. I counted fourteen stones standing out from the earth, and as I rested my hand on each one, I moved almost to the edge of the creek where bullfrogs croaked out a welcome or a warning. I found a few more: fifteen, sixteen, seventeen on the side of the hill wearing away into the water. I willed them to tell me who they were. Stones this old, representing people so long gone, would have much to say.

In telling this story, I've probably spent as much time poking around old cemeteries looking for my own ancestors and hoping for proof of Black communities as I have spent in libraries. I love to think about the stories hidden behind the words chiseled on the stone, like "Aunt Mary, FELL ASLEEP" in Coxsackie's Village Cemetery. It was easy to find the Conines, the Bronks, and the Van Dykes in that old cemetery. I just couldn't find the burial places of the people they enslaved. Some of that had to do with the "practical Dutch" who, in the seventeenth and eighteenth centuries, often cared less about marking grave sites than their New England neighbors. But of course, much of the reason had to do with the larger erasure of slavery in New York. Why be reminded that the enslaved lived, worked, died, and rested forever on this northern land?

The more I looked around, the more I realized that the Kingston burial ground was a rarity. Few towns or private property owners want to give permission for anyone to investigate whether people who were owned in life and disrespected after their death could be lying beneath their soil.

What happened in New Paltz, fourteen miles south of Kingston, is far more typical of how Black burial grounds are lost. New Paltz, like Kingston, was one of the centers of centuries-long enslavement in New York. It was also home to generations of my Huguenot ancestors. The Deyo family lived in New Paltz, enslaved humans, and then moved further north up the river to marry into the Dutch branches of my family.

No one knows for certain the location of its ancient cemetery for the enslaved and free Blacks. Historians tried to find the burials. Researchers had found a brief paragraph in an 1864 newspaper that mentioned the funeral of a Black woman named Susan Tinbrook.[23] She had been buried at a cemetery not far from Historic Huguenot Street, one of the best-preserved areas of intact eighteenth-century homes in the state. Although the city set up a study group to help pinpoint the exact location of the burial place, the site was never identified, in part because of resistance.[24] The owners of the property that archeologists suspected had been the burial ground refused to let anyone on their land to do ground-penetrating radar. Instead, the city put up a plaque near the site. It reads, "A burial ground used by Africans and their descendants is located near this marker. After the Civil War, when whites allowed African-American burials in a segregated portion of the New Paltz Rural Cemetery on Plains Road, this burial ground was no longer used and its existence nearly forgotten." Nearby is a stone bench set atop thick chains to symbolize slavery.

For years, New Paltz's history museum owned a human skull that had been dug up in 1900 by Abraham Deyo Brodhead, a descendant of the earliest Huguenots. The original house on the site had been built in 1692. First thought to have been a skull from a Native American man or woman, in 2011 archeologists determined that it instead belonged to a middle-aged Black man, one who had probably been enslaved by the Deyo family. The skull was reinterred in 2016 in Huguenot Street's French Reformed Church. Its stone is carved with a symbolic bird and the word "Sankofa," which means, "It is not wrong to go back for that which you have forgotten."[25]

I wondered if any of the enslaved people I'd tried to trace first touched land—after the horrific Middle Passage—on the arid island of Curaçao, the Dutch island with the deep port that served as the entrepôt for its slave trade in the Americas. Curaçao had been the major hub for New York's slave trade in the seventeenth century. How different it must have seemed from Africa's lushness. In the early days of my research I pored over the translations of the Curaçao Papers, written by the officious officers of the Dutch West India Company and translated over years by Albany's Charles Gehring. I wanted to see the island for myself. I wanted to look for the souls lost to slavery, and I wanted to find out if anyone on the island had honored them.

Petrus Stuyvesant, the last director-general of New Netherland, had initiated the idea of exporting enslaved people north from Curaçao to help fill the labor gap in the earliest days of New Netherland and New York. Is there a reckoning with that history, one that involved shipping thousands of enslaved men, women, and children to the North?

In the early days of my research, just as I was reading about the slave trade and Stuyvesant, I came upon an azure-colored glossy advertisement in the *New York Times Magazine*. A new all-inclusive resort, Sandals Royal Curaçao, would be a "dream getaway" on an island with "an exuberant mix of Latin, European, and African roots." Visitors, when they were ready to take a break from the resort's infinity pools and spa, could pop over to the capital city of Willemstad and check out the Museum Kura Hulanda, situated in a "former 19th-century merchant's house, featuring a sculpture garden and an unusual collection of art and artifacts from West Africa." When I looked more closely, I saw it was more than an "unusual collection." It was a museum about the slave trade. Maybe Curaçao was doing a better job at this reckoning than its counterparts in the North.

Convincing my husband that I needed to make a research trip to Curaçao took about three seconds. "On it," he said, and before I had a chance to warn him that I was thinking more of digging into a dark past than digging my toes into soft sand, he had booked plane tickets, found a hotel, and figured out how to navigate the COVID rules. This was in early 2022, and the pandemic meant that we hadn't been anywhere in two years.

When we got there, we saw that today's Curaçao is a charming island with a tropical Dutch ambience, eager for the same Caribbean tourists who were drawn to nearby Aruba. The waters of Willemstad's harbor port are choppy and Delft blue, lined with buildings that look like a child's drawing of houses: pink and blue and pale green facades with pointed red roofs. Most of the tourists were Dutch, escaping their gloomy northern climate.

We set out to see just what evidence remained of Curaçao's enslaving past. In Willemstad we walked across Saint Anna Bay, part of the city's harbor, on a pontoon floating bridge called the Queen Emma Bridge. There in the Otrobanda neighborhood was the museum we had come to see. At the entrance to the Kura Hulanda Museum is a statue of a heavy Black woman sitting placidly on a bench. Behind her on the wall beneath the sign for the museum is a series of words in large bold capital letters.

EVOLUTION, SLAVE TRADE/MIDDLE PASSAGE, WEST AFRICAN EMPIRES, KINGDOMS OF BENIN. What that meant was certainly not clear to us, and in fact gave a hint of the disorganized chaos within.

The museum turned out to be packed with words and artifacts and pictures but bereft of any context. Its fifteen buildings described slavery in a sweep from its earliest origins in Africa to its culmination in the Americas. A lower-level exhibit was even designed to resemble the claustrophobic berths of a slave ship, with low beds and dark wood. There were shackles used to hold the enslaved, model ships, and newspaper clippings. Other rooms were filled with African artifacts: masks, sculptures, drums, spears, all dusty items that our guide assured us were reproductions and not original treasures that may have been stolen from Africa. One room was dedicated to twentieth-century civil rights protests in America, lined with pictures of Malcolm X and Dr. Martin Luther King Jr.

Just one document on display made a specific reference to Curaçao's slave history by showing the 1863 manumission of Curaçao slaves. A small building on the grounds was described as a slave hut. The courtyard offered an enormous stone sculpture in the shape of the African continent and an ironworks display alongside the words "Emancipate yourself from mental slavery—Bob Marley." In all, the museum managed to find a bizarre incongruity, in which one was told things about slavery and its modern legacy without learning much of anything at all. Exactly why this museum was situated in Curaçao was another part of the mystery. If a tourist didn't know of Curaçao's role in the slave trade, he wouldn't learn it here.

The origins of the museum are murky. The museum's owner and creator, the late entrepreneur Jacob Gelt Dekker, purportedly had been inspired to create a museum about slavery when he learned that the people living on his property had no idea that they were descended from enslaved Africans.[26] If that were true, the museum might have tried to point that out. I wondered if Dekker instead began with a desire to display his impressive collection of African art and decided to create a smokescreen of hand-wringing over slavery to justify his ownership of the items.

Frustrated, we moved on to other historical sites in Willemstad. We decided to visit the Mikve Israel-Emanuel Synagogue, dating from the 1650s and said to be the oldest surviving synagogue in the Western Hemisphere. Jewish refugees from the Portuguese Inquisition had been living in Curaçao since the 1500s, and its synagogue tells their story.[27] Its floors are covered in sand, to symbolize the need Jews had to conduct services secretly in Portugal during the Inquisition. Sand-covered floors would muffle the sound of worship. Outside the synagogue, we found a history time line that offered new clues. There had been two eighteenth-century slave revolts in Curaçao. Slave revolts? The museum dedicated to slavery had no mention of moments in history that seemed rather important. One revolt, said the time line, took place in 1750 when, having endured "harsh treatment and inhumane living conditions on Curaçao," slaves at Hato Plantation "established an uprising against their masters." The uprising, which lasted just a day, was a failure, and thirty-four slaves were eventually executed, I later learned. The site of the Hato Plantation is today home to the island's international airport.

The time line had a second date: a slave revolt in 1795, Curaçao's "largest slave uprising," was a month-long battle at Kenepa Plantation, led by slaves Tula Rigaud, Louis Mercier, Bastiaan Karpata, and Pedro Wakao. After gunfights involving as many as a thousand slaves, the revolt was "suppressed," and the leaders of the revolt were tortured and executed. An important story that involved a thousand slaves and resulting executions was nowhere to be seen at the slavery museum. When a waitress at a local restaurant asked us why we were visiting Curaçao, we explained that we were investigating slavery. She remembered visiting a museum dedicated to the 1795 uprising when she was a child. It turned out she was right: the Museo Tula, situated at the other end of the island, was dedicated to that uprising.[28] But when we tried to call and arrange a visit, no one answered the phone. Later, we learned that the museum has been closed for years. The site is open for sustainable dive tourism, "where history merges with nature."[29] (The museum finally reopened in January 2024.)

We kept looking. We walked over to Fort Rif at the entrance to Willemstad's harbor. A plaque advertised a free history walking tour, noting Curaçao's role as a "slave transshipment center." "Here [slaves] remained in camps for two years where they were taught new skills," it said. We never learned what those skills might be or where exactly these "camps" were. We had once again stumbled across a random and unconnected fact that appeared nowhere else in our explorations.

We signed up for the history walking tour. That took us through Otrobanda, near the slavery museum. Walls were covered with a colorful array of street art celebrating racial justice and freedom. Toward the end of the tour we came across a large black wall covered with the words "Tula Taught Me." Our guide told us that Tula's failed revolt ended in his torture and dismemberment, with pieces of his body hanging in different places around the city. Gift shops sell T-shirts with those words: "Tula Taught Me." Of course, most tourists would have no idea who Tula was, or what he might have taught anyone.

At the end of 2021 the Dutch issued a formal apology for its role in slavery, an apology that some of its former colonies said was not enough. Curaçao, still a territory of the Netherlands with the freedom to form its own government, seemed to have a lukewarm reaction to that apology. Curaçao prime minister Gilmar Pisas, a Black man who had grown up in a poor family in a rural part of Curaçao, said he was optimistic that the apology was a first step and that it would lead to help with the country's future development.[30]

I decided to offer Bob a reprieve from this scattershot history. We booked an excursion to Klein Curaçao, or "little Curaçao," a tiny island southeast of the main island of Curaçao, for a day of snorkeling and sunning on the beach. Klein Curaçao turned out to be an arid island dotted with stunted bushes. Our snorkeling revealed murky water and the occasional lethargic fish, and the narrow beach was lined with stones and driftwood.

Bored, we started strolling and almost immediately came upon a plaque. It said,

> In the 17th century the West Indian Company (WIC) brought slaves from Africa to Curaçao. Before these slaves arrived in Curaçao, the sick ones were first put in quarantine on Klein Curaçao. The remains of this first quarantine building can still be found in the northwestern part of the island. Slaves and other passengers who did not survive the long, very harsh voyage or the quarantine were buried right here on Klein Curaçao. Some graves have been found in the southern part.

Wow. Beneath our feet was the first land that enslaved Africans touched after they had been stolen from Africa.

Here was one more piece of the puzzle, and here again, we had only stumbled upon it by chance. We set out to try to find some sign of their graves or the quarantine station. If we could do that, we could come full circle and pay our respects to those who made it so far across the ocean only to lose their lives on this barren island. Our search was futile. Paths ended and we tried to pick our way through scrub brush and shells. All we found were rusty hulks of shipwrecks and boats that had been stranded on rocky beaches.

Even so, without trying, we had found the place where sick and suffering Africans first touched ground after the horrors of the Middle Passage. In 1664 the slave ship *Gideon* had arrived in Curaçao with 348 enslaved Africans. The ship had left Guinea and Angola with 421 people, so seventy-three had already died.[31] The biggest cause of death on slaving ships in the Middle Passage was scurvy, caused by a lack of vitamin C. Its symptoms are fatigue, shortness of breath, and bleeding. Those who died before they made it to this tiny island were tossed into the sea.

We had happened upon a place that deserved reverence, hallowed ground like the Pine Street burial grounds. Again, I had the sense that I was being tapped on the shoulder. This uninhabited island had almost hidden its secrets. Almost despite Curaçao's chaotic and incomplete references to slavery, we had arrived at its origins. The footprints of those who survived the Middle Passage were long gone, but serendipity brought us to a sacred place.

13

REPAIR

When I started my research around 2019, I had a hard time finding any place in the Hudson Valley that I could say was truly reckoning with slavery. Now I struggle to keep track of all of them. I started this process as a reluctant archeologist, afraid to confirm what I knew was there. Now that I knew it was there, I wanted more and more: real, concrete *things* that acknowledged the enslaved and their lives—who they were, how they lived, what they dreamed of, and who they loved. William Carlos Williams said there was "no ideas but in things." Without the physical manifestation of a life, a world, all is lost.

Repair is coming, not just in academic books and articles, but in museum exhibits, monuments, online projects, and so many lectures and conversations that I've lost count. Some of the change is expansive, some is more subtle, and some is nothing more than a collection of well-intentioned plans.

A few places stand out. The most egregious whitewasher has engineered the biggest change. Philipsburg Manor, once the largest slave plantation in

Figure 21. Klein Curaçao, just off the coast of the main island, was the landing place and quarantine station for thousands of enslaved Africans transported to the West Indies. Photo by author.

the Hudson Valley, has repaired its history. I kept thinking about that sun-drenched 1972 film supposedly depicting life at the mill, the one in which Black people, the workers who forked the hay and ground the wheat, were played by well-fed white men.

No longer. Philipsburg Manor, run by the nonprofit Historic Hudson Valley, has been striving for close to twenty years to revisit and reinterpret its history. Today the site brings its gaze back to the people who ran the plantation in the first place. My husband and I visited the manor, just thirty miles north of New York City, on a warm summer day in June 2022. Even the language on the museum's website promised to tell a fuller story: "Cross the millpond bridge and enter the year 1750 when Philipsburg Manor was home to 23 enslaved individuals of African descent and a thriving milling and trading complex."[1] Also on its site online was one of the best summaries of New York's history of enslavement, called "People Not Property."

As we walked across the bridge and reached the mill, a docent handed us a piece of paper with a list: "Inventory of all and Singular the goods, Rights Chattels & Credits of the Estate of Mr. Adolph Philipse Deceased." Included in the list were the "Negros"—men, women, "Men not fitt for work," boys, and one girl, Betty, three years old. The docent portrayed Caesar, the enslaved man who ran the mill. No white people lived on the site. The manor house itself was a storage place for wheat and a place to process the milk from the farm, tasks that fell to female slaves.

On each stop of the tour—the mill, the manor house kitchen, the barn, the outdoor oven—docents described the daily work of the enslaved. Flip, Dimond, Caesar, Abigal, and Susan worked endlessly hard and, of course, never profited from the wealth accrued by the Philipse family. After the death of Adolphe Philipse, they were sold off, adding further to the family's prosperity. This was now a story of the enslaved and their lives.

Back in the 1970s, Philipsburg Manor hosted annual celebrations of Pinkster, the Christian holiday of Pentecost fifty days after Easter. The 1970s version was a spring festival of tulips and wooden shoes.[2] Today, the celebrations are closer to what they might have been: eighteenth-century parties that served as a once-a-year opportunity for the enslaved to feel some degree of freedom, meeting friends and family, drinking, and, at least for a few days, escaping the drudgery of work. It was also a time of resistance, in which an anointed "king" would mock people of all races and the social order was temporarily upset.

At the northern tip of the Hudson Valley, Albany's transformation is more subtle. Its favorite son, Philip Schuyler, faced his own reckoning. Schuyler and his wife, Catherine Van Rensselaer, were two of the state's biggest enslavers. Philip Schuyler—Revolutionary War major general, New York State senator, and father-in-law to Alexander Hamilton, the first secretary of the Treasury—was also long a source of hometown pride.

Since 1925, Schuyler's statue stood in the center of a traffic circle in the heart of downtown, with its back to Albany's Romanesque-style city hall. Wearing a tricorne hat, his head tilted down and he seemed to be lost in thought. His arms crossed over his torso, and a cape rested lightly on his shoulders. If he could have looked up, he would have faced the state capitol building, toward land that had once been a place of revelry during Pinkster celebrations and of horror as Gallows Hill, where slaves had been hung.

After the country's racial protests in 2020, Mayor Kathy Sheehan signed an executive order to remove the statue and place it in storage.[3] As late as June 2023—three years after the order—that move hadn't happened. Costs, indecision about where to put the statue, political sensitivities—all had been cited as reasons why the move was stuck. I decided to see Philip before he was tucked away. As I parked my car near city hall and made my way to the traffic circle, I realized that I couldn't easily approach Schuyler from the front without venturing into the fast-moving traffic whipping around the circle. I contented myself with staring at his back. He looked oddly anonymous, surrounded by grass and signs advertising Albany's tulip festival. This was no colossus but a forgotten man, resolutely ignoring the hubbub of the twenty-first century. In turn, his surroundings ignored him. I wondered what Schuyler would have made of the city's more recent Tulip Queens, crowned each May. The queen in 2022 was Sam Mills, a nonbinary comedian.[4] In 2023 a twenty-three-year-old Black math teacher named Olivia Owens won the honor.[5]

A Department of Public Works truck and worker were parked next to the traffic circle.

"Do you know when they are moving the statue?" I asked the man.

"I don't know nothing," he said. "And I like knowing nothing."

Finally, later in the summer of 2023, the statue, standing on the back of a flatbed truck, was finally rolled off. For now, he waits in storage. The city of Albany has asked a study group to suggest locations for the statue.

I decided to call on the Schuyler home. A mile or so south of the statue, Schuyler Mansion is a stately Georgian brick house built in the 1760s that today overlooks a poor but slowly gentrifying neighborhood. There's a romantic residue about the place. Ever since the blockbuster musical *Hamilton* hit the stage in 2015, visitors have packed the tours, wanting to see the room where Eliza, Schuyler's daughter, married Alexander Hamilton.

Schuyler lived here for forty years. The interior of the house is filled with signs of eighteenth-century wealth and privilege: luxurious curtains, painted murals, brocade wallpaper. The affluence of the family came, in part, from the wheat crops it generated on its eighty acres and then sold to the West Indies where it bolstered the slave trade. In the 1790 census Philip Schuyler listed thirteen enslaved workers.[6]

But inside the visitors' center, I found new interpretations of some of the people enslaved by the Schuyler family. It wasn't always that way. When it was first opened in 1993, the center offered no hint of the enslaved, even as scholars knew they had ample evidence: a thick folder filled with details about the enslaved. Site manager Heidi Hill told me that there wasn't enough time or money to expand the story for the public. That all changed when she attended a public history workshop sponsored by Yale's Gilder Lehrman Center for the Study of Slavery, Resistance, and Abolition in New Haven, Connecticut. "It was a game changer," she said. She came back to Albany, inspired with the goal of helping visitors "leave the place with a deeper thought process and . . . start thinking more deeply about these people's lives," she said. "Maybe have their idea of slavery turned around a bit."[7]

Today the visitors' center makes the stories of the enslaved hard to miss. An interactive video tells the story of Prince, the family's enslaved butler. He says: "I am always at the beck and call of the entire family." He also knows that no matter how much he might imagine he is like a member of the family, he must retain his deference. "It is not my place to treat guests with any familiarity," he says.

Another actress portrays Diana, a woman enslaved by the Schuyler family. Diana had escaped from the Schuyler Mansion in the chaos at the start of the Revolutionary War but had been recaptured. In the video Diana says, "I pray you won't betray my trust." She had worked in the kitchen and heard of others who had escaped, so she tried to run. After she was caught, she was put in jail. One button let me ask her, "What might be your fate?" Diana answers: "When a chance to escape comes again, I will be ready." The videos gave me a better sense of the real people who labored for the Schuyler family.

As I was about to leave the Schuyler Mansion, Heidi Hill started talking about Samuel Schuyler. I knew the name. He had been a Black Hudson River boat captain, but for years no one knew why his name was Schuyler. As with the legends that accompanied the Vanderzee name, some historians theorized that the boatmen had borrowed the name from the capital's most illustrious family. Nope. Using DNA matches, descendants discovered that Captain Sam Schuyler was the biological son of a white man named Dirck Schuyler of Albany, a third cousin of Philip Schuyler.[8] Dirck Schuyler was also the captain of a Hudson River sloop. Samuel's freedom was granted in 1805, and subsequent records described him as both a "free person of color" and as white. Samuel's sons were described as "mulatto." By the middle of the nineteenth century, the family was listed as white in records. As the Black Schuylers married both white and mixed-race partners, it looks as though the evidence of their Black ancestry was blanched out. In a family genealogical book that listed descendants, "you can see that something was ripped out," Hill said. Without the DNA connections, these Schuyler descendants today would not have realized they had a Black ancestor.

I told Eleanor about the solved mystery of the Black Schuylers. She was not surprised. "These are stories so long known in the Black community but denied in the white community," she emailed me. "I get the feeling that within the next ten years or so, a Black cousin will be a must at every cocktail party."

My Huguenot ancestors got me an invitation to join the Ulster County Truth and Reconciliation Commission. Formed a few years ago by Susan Stessin-Cohn and others, it gave itself a monumental task: to create a detailed interactive online map tracking every trace of slavery in Ulster County. Beginning with census records, wills, tax records, genealogies, and old maps, the database will let anyone click on a place—a house, land, a farm—and learn the names of the enslaved who lived and worked there. It will be a way to visualize what had been hidden from sight. "Now do one for Greene County," I told the group, only half joking.

The committee goes beyond simple fact-gathering. Albert Cook, a Black high school history teacher in New Paltz and a member of the group, told me that the goal was to reach out to the families of both enslavers and enslaved people still living in the area and start a symbolic reconciliation process. After that, there could be some form of reparation. It gave me a feeling of direction: after each of our monthly online meetings, I had this sense of people carefully placing tiny puzzle pieces into a vast landscape. When it's done, the picture will be vast and maybe even mind-blowing.

In Dutchess County a group called Celebrating the African Experience focuses on "the legacy of Africans and their descendants in Poughkeepsie, NY." Vassar College hosts the Mid-Hudson Anti-Slavery Project in order to develop a digital "freedom trail" that tracks slavery and freedom in the area. The Dutchess County Historical Society offers an African heritage site that pinpoints African American burial grounds, records of oral histories, and digitized documents about slavery. The Columbia County Historical Society and the African American Archive of Columbia County have teamed up to offer a series of in-person and virtual lectures on slavery in the Hudson Valley.[9]

In nearby Connecticut I found a fascinating response to the erasure of the enslaved in its Witness Stones Project.[10] They were inspired by Germany's Stolpersteine project, which inserts brass plaques with the names of Nazi victims in sidewalks to draw attention to and honor their lives. Witness Stones, similarly, is an educational mission that places stones to honor enslaved individuals "where they lived, worked, or worshipped." Since 2019 the project has placed 126 stones in Connecticut, New York, New Jersey, Massachusetts, and Rhode Island.

Only one place in Greene County is doing something significant on slavery. The Thomas Cole National Historic Site in Catskill is known for the founder of the Hudson River School of artists. The ancestral family of Cole's wife, Maria Bartow, a member of the Thomson family, has received less attention. The Thomson family had lived in Catskill long before Cole arrived in 1825. Their history is a dark one.

The Thomsons were enslavers both in Catskill and on a sugarcane plantation in the South American Dutch colony of Demerara, situated in what is today Guyana. Not only did Thomas Thomson live for ten years on his plantation there, but he also had a family with an enslaved woman. That history was uncovered in letters from his common-law wife, Priscilla Mary Thomson, as well as in other records. The couple had five children: George Washington, James Madison, John Adams, Thomas Jefferson, and Helen.[11] Priscilla may not have ever left South America, but her sons' names reflected her faith in America's founders.

In Catskill the Thomson family lived with enslaved people and free Black servants. A 2021 exhibition in the house, called "In Process: W/Hole History: The People Who Lived and Labored Here," presents what researchers have found, along with updated information on its website.[12]

I took a tour in May 2023 to see how those changes appeared after a year of updates. As we stood on the porch of the Cole house, called Cedar Grove, and looked out at a view of the Catskill Mountains that the painter had captured many times, our tour guide Bethany Wynne told us that the house had been built with the wealth accrued through the slave trade of Thomas Thomson in South America.

Inside, the rooms were dotted with small signs describing the workers in the house. One sign said, "On whom did Thomas rely to clean up his painting rags and spilled pigments?" next to blue silhouettes of people wearing nineteenth-century garb. One room displayed a document of the manumission of a man named Cesar and an explanation: "We have found four manumission documents in the Thomson family papers: for a woman named Chloe, a man named Cesar, a man named Bill, and a man named Josephus Thomson." I found hints in later research that William Thomson (also sometimes spelled Thompson), likely the son of Thomas Thomson, had a role in supporting the Underground Railroad, but I didn't find proof. I also knew he lived in Athens, and I wished I could find his home. Josephus Thomson, born of an enslaved woman named Abigail, was also probably the son of Thomas Thomson, researchers have reported.[13]

Athens still hides its secrets. Just up the street from my mother's house, directly in front of my Italian grandparents' home, is Zion Lutheran Church. On its façade is a bronze plaque: "Zion Lutheran Church had as its first pastor Justus Falkner 1703–1723. Ordained—Philadelphia, Nov. 24, 1703. His was the first ordination of a Protestant clergyman in America." Next to that plaque is a larger one in Latin and Greek, written by the pastor who succeeded him, Wilhelm Berkenmeyer. Another plaque gives the translation. It says, "The resting place of Berkenmeyer, prepared in a pious sense of his mortality." The rest of the plaque describes, in a muddle of words, "his itinerant ministry among the North Americans," ending with this confusing word salad: "Salvation prepared for all men, no matter how many they have been, are, or will be, to be obtained through faith in the God-Man alone the 1744th chosen in Christ before the creation of the universe for whom there is therefore no condemnation in Christ Jesus." Berkenmeyer may have proclaimed salvation for all men, but he was also the pastor who enslaved several people and was accused of fathering a child with Grit Christiaan, the free Black girl, an accusation that destroyed his legacy more than his status as an enslaver. The church that stands today was built in 1853 on the site of the old church.

Gethen Proper, the member of Zion who first directed me to the church records, told me her story. When she first opened early church records and discovered that its founding pastors and church members not only talked about slavery but owned slaves themselves, "It was really mind-boggling. I had no idea there was so much of it." Since that day, she had been trying to get the church council to add that part to their official narrative. "There's so much history missing. People need to know the history."[14]

She brought it up with the council. At first, members told her, "Oh, no. We don't want to get into this." She waited a month and at the next council meeting asked them, "Have you thought about this? Do you have any thoughts about what we should do?"

"Everybody just kind of sat on their hands," she told me. One radical idea, which she suggested to pastor Beth George, was to "take a marker and write their names on the walls inside the church, to make it visible for everybody to see. To let the people in the Black churches know that we were sorry for what happened."

I talked to Pastor Beth not long after that. "I'm all for doing something," she said. "Whether we can get the whole council to agree—that's my holdup." When she first talked to the council about discovering the names of the baptized enslaved in the church's eighteenth-century records, one member said that at least they could celebrate the fact that they had been baptized. "You are assuming they had a choice," she told them. "We would hope that the holy spirit moved them to become Christian, but it may not have been that way."[15]

Frustrated that nothing was happening collectively in her church, Gethen Proper found a Lenten devotional practice created by a group called the Repentance Project, a collection of people in churches, non-profit groups, and other Christian organizations. They asked, "How can Christians concretely recognize the awful legacy of 400 years of racial oppression in the United States, and recognize the ongoing effects in the black community?" It offered what it called a "journey through America's history of slavery, segregation, and racism" through Lent's forty days, with daily prayers, exercises, and meditations.[16] While the practice helped her think more deeply about white privilege, Proper told me she was still frustrated that she couldn't convince any of her religious friends to join in the devotional. "The whole thing just leaves me wondering where we are going," she told me. "Our divisions are too great." She's still a believer, though. "God is in this somewhere. He has to be."

As for Pastor Beth, she had some ideas after she talked to some local Black pastors. One idea was a worship service for healing and repentance.

In that service, the names of the 146 or so enslaved members of the church would be read out loud. She had a second idea: "Why can't we make a banner with all of their names? And hang that banner in the worship space somewhere." When she said that, a chill ran through me. It was perfect. I still wondered whether those ideas would remain ideas.

Gethen's devotional practice made me think more about what one individual can do. I've spent so much time looking at old stuff: Dutch houses, graveyards, miniature feathery handwriting, old portraits of colonial fathers, walls of stone older than the country. I've hoped for an epiphany. I wanted a voice from the grave to give me a message. Mumbet was silent. The river told me nothing. Samuel Van Vechten looked like a dyspeptic ghost who would have fit in at Disney's Haunted Mansion. Because I lucked into that earlier serendipitous connection with Eleanor, I had assumed that the universe was blessing this enterprise. Now I feel as if the forces are pushing back. Examining my internal bias in the style of Coming to the Table reminds me a bit of the feminist consciousness-raising group I joined when I first went away to college. It was both enlightening and discomforting. Maybe that was the point.

I wonder if writing an entire book on my enslaving ancestors is my incredibly elaborate way of avoiding that discomfort. Okay, I can't "repair," but I can tell a lot of stories, and maybe those stories are a form of repair. We do need more of these stories. Our history must be corrected and expanded, both in scholarly ways and with in-your-face gestures like New York's stealth sticker campaign of 2021. A group called Slavers of New York posted stickers on parking meters and walls around the city, such as one that said, "Peter Stuyvesant was a slave trader. Peter Stuyvesant trafficked 290 human beings in the first slave auction in Manhattan."[17] Genealogical societies can't whitewash the missing slaves out of the record. Cemeteries cannot be paved over because a deliberate and collective amnesia forgot humans were interred there. Museums cannot pretend that there were no enslaved people, or that the "servants" who worked there were happy to be there serving the war heroes in the dining rooms.

We must also acknowledge as a society that institutional racism created a chasm that has not yet been bridged. There is a connection between saying "it wasn't that bad" and redlining. There is a connection between forgetting to honor the buried dead and schools that don't teach kids to read. From that acknowledgment we must apologize. We, as a country, have to say we are sorry for chattel slavery.

Eleanor doesn't like it when I apologize for something, or when I thank her for reading a draft. "We're past that," she tells me. That is true of friendship, or friendship by our definition, but we have not gotten to that point in the United States. Zion Lutheran in Athens should read the names of its baptized enslaved aloud. It should create a banner honoring them, a banner that church members will be able to gaze at every Sunday.

Kitt Potter said that when someone asked her what she meant by reparations, she responded: "You don't have enough money." A Black writer told me, "It's a debt nobody wants to deal with." As I was struggling with these thoughts, I read a book, *Go Back and Get It*, by the writer Dionne Ford.[18] She was working her way through her own family history, one of both enslavers and enslaved, and a comment she made toward the end of the book struck me. She wrote, "Who is to blame is not the problem surrounding reparations for slavery. The real question is not from whom reparations should be extracted, but what we, the descendants of the enslaved, want—what would help make us feel whole." I can't answer that question. I can say that better, fuller histories—told in writing, art, museums, music, and film—is a good first step. A good second step is finding a way to offer financial reparations through universities that blocked Black students, through cities that redlined white neighborhoods, and through industries that poisoned Black neighborhoods, for starters. Those actions are also forms of apology.

Wendy Harris is a documentary filmmaker whose 2018 film, *Where Slavery Died Hard: The Forgotten History of Ulster County and the Shawangunk Mountain Region*,[19] dove deeply into the old houses, churches, cemeteries, and records of that remote area. As Harris showed me around the Shawangunk area one summer, we spent a lot of time talking about the role of white people in this large discovery. We must thread the needle: acknowledge and repair the harms, but also understand that maybe Black people are just tired of white people getting in their faces and apologizing. It's draining, and I've encountered more than one Black person who just doesn't care to extend the conversation.

This kind of repair also must contend with an entire line of thinking that believes that acknowledging the history of slavery is too "woke," and that students should not be made to feel uncomfortable in their history or ashamed of the United States. The anti-woke people miss the point. Discomfort comes from the cognitive dissonance that is part of education. Encountering beliefs that challenge one's values or reading about history that doesn't fit into a tidy upward sweep of progress—a World's Fair carousel that's always improving—is what makes our country great.

My own discomfort gave me a direction. I realized, finally, that in the years that Eleanor and I had worked together to investigate to the smallest nuances of the Vanderzees, the Van Bergens, the Egberts, the houses, the wars, the newspaper articles, we had danced around the subject of race.

"Were you suspicious of me when we first connected?" I asked her.[20]

"My biggest issue," she said, "was could I trust you?" She explained she had been burned in the past. She learned not to tell people she was Black at first. "They run away and then you lose that stream of information."

She grew up in an integrated neighborhood in coastal Massachusetts and had friends of all races. But even there she faced moments of racism: "You'd make friends, until the mother or father saw you. All of a sudden, they would say, 'My mother says I should play with this person and not you, and I can't invite you to my house.'" There was also a terrible falling out with her best friend, whose husband called her the N-word after the two of them had had an argument. "That was the last time I talked to either one of them." It changed her. "When your best friend does something like that, all bets are off."

I can't change history, but I can explain where I belong in this history. Having a genetic and ancestral link to America's original sin as well as the time and ability to tell the story makes it my responsibility. So far, I've counted twenty of my family names who were enslavers, from Bronk to Vosburgh. It feels almost biblical. The Bible says that God "visits the iniquity of the fathers on the children and the children's children, to the third and the fourth generation." When I sang those words in my chorus's performance of Mendelsohn's oratorio *Elijah*, I got chills. We are not humans who popped out of nowhere to live in this complicated America; we are people who have inherited the sins of our fathers and the traumas of our ancestors. They touch us as absolutely as I touched the shards of stone jutting from the earth in the Bronk cemetery.

It is not just my inheritance. I got into an argument not long ago with an acquaintance who believed that my family had been rich. Since hers was not, she seemed to want to keep any responsibility for reckoning with slavery at arm's length. Even though it was true that any white person who had a family history in this country that went back far enough was likely to find a story of enslavers, she had missed the point. The point was about complicity. To know the beauty of the Declaration of Independence and the Constitution is to accept that only some people have fully benefited from their promises. To deny that and to distance ourselves from that truth is to misunderstand how our country grew, prospered, and exists today.

I'm changed. I see now that my vision had been clouded with the blurry haze of simplistic history. My lens now makes it impossible for me to see my nation's story without the overlay of slavery. Now I look at every old house and think: where did the enslaved live? The older the house, the more I ask whether humans shivered in the basement or sweated in the attic, whether they rested in the room behind the stairs. I pick my way through the stones and paths of old cemeteries and think: Who took the trouble to mark the births and deaths of the enslaved people? Are they buried there in unmarked graves, or were they pushed to the far outskirts of a town? How many plows and backhoes have turned up bones that were quietly tossed to the side? How many people were deprived the honor of a headstone? At Curaçao I could look out at the sea and imagine the Africans who were about to set foot on sandy soil for the first time since they left Africa. Now I carry my conjuring to my home.

I've had to rethink my dual role as both an outsider and a native daughter. When I was growing up in my large family, I created space to breath by devouring chapter books and creating imaginary worlds in my backyard. I had a "fort" that I built out of a discarded wooden pallet, likely tossed there by the tides of the Hudson. I had my tree near the river that I climbed so I could stare at the river's changing colors. I was comfortable, mostly happy, but it was like living inside a quilted box, soft but muffled. I left for college, and the world expanded. When I came back to visit, I started seeing my beloved and boring Athens through the lens of an outsider.

On the wrenching day that my brother and I had to choose a casket for my father's burial, the funeral director asked me where I lived. I told him I lived in Washington, DC. "Well, look at YOU," he said. It was as if I were putting on airs, the automatic black mark against the person who left. But even though I felt like an outsider, I knew I still belonged there. There was the house where my father was born. There was the former convent where I babysat a sweet little boy named Gregory. There was the church where my 4-H club learned to "Suds Your Duds." I could never be a stranger here in this safe and claustrophobic place.

That sense of belonging began to shift when I started learning about slavery and filling in the missing blanks of the enslaved in Athens. The first moment of dissonance was so unreal that I could have convinced myself I was reading about Athens, Greece, or a fairy-tale place called Loonenburg. The comfortable ordinariness of Athens's streets and houses didn't line up with these facts of slavery or its aftermath.

When I started looking into the history of the twentieth century in my hometowns, I found a 1903 story of a near-lynching in New Baltimore. "Assaults by Negro Fiends" told of a nineteen-year-old Black man named James Little who asked some girls picking berries by the side of the road whether they had anything to eat. When one of them went to find her mother, Little allegedly assaulted eleven-year-old Emma Cole and tried to drag her into the woods. The girl's friend returned to the spot and the man ran off, but he was soon apprehended and confessed to the attack, said one report. "In the meantime news of the capture reached New Baltimore and a mob of 15 enraged farmers started for Coxsackie . . . all frankly avowing their intention to lynch the negro," the newspaper said.[21] They wanted vigilante justice.

A sheriff's deputy, "realizing that the coming of darkness would mean the breaking of the flimsy local lockup and the violent death of his prisoner, smuggled the negro out and took him down the river on the boat to Catskill, where there is a well built jail," another newspaper reported.[22] The next day, when Little was taken from Catskill and arraigned before a justice in New Baltimore, the mob reappeared. The girl's father "was in an excited state and as the boat docked drew a revolver."[23] His gun was taken away before he could shoot. Later that year, Little pled guilty and was sentenced to twenty years in Clinton prison, nearly two hundred miles north of New Baltimore.[24] We will never learn the true story of what happened that day. One report noted that the child "is seriously injured, but may recover," while a different newspaper said, "The favorable condition of the assaulted child has somewhat allayed the excitement." My grandmother, Edna Collier, was born in nearby Coxsackie just two years after that incident. Emma Cole could have been her cousin. My grandfather, Orrin Van Valkenburg, was a four-year-old boy when that happened. He could have been there that day. The story was a few steps closer to me now.

I came across a reference to a man named George Sylvester Nichols, who had owned a house on South Franklin Street in the village.[25] Franklin Street is one of the most elegant streets in Athens. My Italian grandmother called it Easy Street, and it's lined with enormous maple and oak trees as well as some of the larger homes in the village. Nichols had fought in the Battle of the Wilderness west of Fredericksburg, Virginia, during the Civil War. That fact caught my eye because that was the battle where James Dunbar Van Valkenburg, the Confederate officer, had captured an entire regiment of northern soldiers. Maybe, I thought, Nichols had been one of the captured Union troops, and I wondered if Nichols was one of the "mortified" officers so angry at Van Valkenburg's ruse.

Nichols's Athens home had been built in 1803 by a man named Seth Hamilton. Hamilton then sold it to Abraham Van Buskirk.[26] This stopped me a second time. Van Buskirk was the Athens man, a vestryman for Trinity Episcopal Church, who had advertised for a runaway slave named Jim in 1811.

I looked up the address. I knew the place. I jog by the house every time I visit Athens. On my next trip to Athens, I had to go see it again. There it sat on the corner of Franklin and Third Streets, on a hill that sloped down to the Hudson in front of it. This time, I stopped and stared for long enough that I'm surprised curious neighbors didn't come out and ask me what I was doing. What had been in my mind an old heap was now something different. Its layout is odd: the entrance door is on the second floor, accessed by a rickety narrow porch that looks as if it was added in more recent years. The lower level has its own entrance door, and I saw a light was on inside. I knocked; no one answered. Many of the lower windows were close to the ground. I pictured Abraham Van Buskirk and his family sitting around the fireplace on a winter's evening in the floor above as Jim, a lionskin coat wrapped around his body and his feet slipping out of too-large boots, snuck away on that freezing February night. Did he head north toward Coxsackie and eventual freedom in Canada? Or did

Figure 22. The home of Abraham Van Buskirk in Athens, N.Y., from which an enslaved man named Jim fled in February 1811, taking a lionskin coat. Photo by author.

he run south in the direction of Catskill, looking for family and work in New York City? Did he walk on the frozen Hudson? The Hudson River is a block away from the house; he could have marched off on the slippery ice. Van Buskirk died in 1826, a year before slavery ended in the state.[27] In the 1820 census he listed one slave and one free Black in his household. I haven't found his grave.

I spend a lot of time looking for the dead, asking to be haunted. Twice in the last few years when I've jogged up Washington Street past Zion Lutheran Church, I've tripped and executed a skidding fall, ripping skin on my elbows and knees. Some say that Berkenmeyer is buried beneath the church. Maybe that's the only haunting I'll get.

Maybe that haunting was from Pieter Christiaan, the Madagascar man and freed slave who married two German women in Loonenburg. His home was probably right there next to the river, like mine was. Did he miss the warm climate of Madagascar? He was a child when he was stolen from his land. He was braver than I've ever been: How could a former slave build a life, sitting on the church council and then finally upending the community in the 1740s by challenging the most powerful man in town? How could he laugh at him and essentially drive him away from his fiefdom?

Maybe my fall was a message from Pieter's daughter Catharine, the biracial woman who kept bearing babies she didn't want. Had she been raped? Life for a single woman with an infant meant a life of poverty and the shame of having one more bastard. She wouldn't have been able to keep working with a tiny baby. What happened on that winter day when she walked down the frozen Hudson with her newborn? What depths of despair would drive a new mother to kill a newborn? And how could Zion Church treat almost certain infanticide with a gentle admonition to "improve"? The community looked the other way. Pastor Berkenmeyer defended her, citing his Christian faith as a reason for forgiveness. But maybe he was defending the girl he impregnated.

I think often of Nancy Jackson, a woman as resilient as Mumbet Freeman and Sojourner Truth. She was sold off with her baby and toddler to an enslaver north of Coxsackie. Her children were sent away as indentured servants in front of her eyes. What happened to her son Jack, whose name was crossed off the Coxsackie Register? Did he go with her to the family of John LaGrange? What happened to her daughter Sarah, the one she was trying to get settled? Sojourner Truth's biographer said that if she had just stayed in Kingston, her name might have been lost to history.[28]

Was it a triumph for Molly Van Slyke, the New Baltimore girl who won the right to stay in there with her two little children? What did she do next? Where did they live? I found records of two Black men from New Baltimore—Sylvanus and Samuel Van Slyke—who served in the Colored Troops in the Civil War. They could have been her sons, born in the years after she returned to New Baltimore. I've put my hand on the sun-warmed stone of Sylvanus's headstone in Coxsackie's Riverside Cemetery.

I imagine Tone Van Bergen standing in the crowd at Catskill's water-front, straining to get a glimpse of the great Lafayette. I found a note describing his son, the child he named Marquis Lafayette Van Bergen, in a Van Bergen family history at Vedder Library. Lafayette the American was enormous. When he was asked to play the fiddle at the cornerstone-laying for Albany's state capitol building in 1871, he needed a proper outfit, so a local seamstress stayed up all night to make him a new pair of pants. He stood "6 feet 7 inches in his bare feet."[29] Other accounts said he was seven feet tall and played for local square dances.[30]

I can see Lon Van Valkenburg switching hats with his enslaver David Abeel and telling him *he* is now the slave. I imagine Alexander Coventry's man Cuff coming home drunk after his extra few days off around Easter and mouthing off about it.

Eleanor and I often muse about how wonderful it would have been to sit at the knee of Mary Vanderzee and hear her stories. She outlived much of her family and was honored and celebrated in her New Baltimore community. Would she have spoken with a Dutch accent, like Sojourner Truth? We think she may have had several other children who didn't survive. What did she think when her father bought her sexual freedom? Did she, like Sojourner Truth or Harriet Tubman, choose a new first name for herself? Would she have told us she had had a happy life?

Mark Twain said that his understanding of the Mississippi River changed once he learned how its currents were treacherous for navigation, when he could sense that the rippling eddies just below its surface were signs of navigational peril. When he became a pilot, "All the grace, the beauty, the poetry, had gone out of the majestic river!" he wrote.[31] To Twain, his Mississippi had been reduced to a challenge, a question of how well he could pilot the waters.

My understanding of my Hudson River, whose restless waters gently slap its muddy banks, is different too. The river changes by the hour as the tides move water up and down and the currents pass each other heading north and south, in a dance that caused the Native people to call it "the river that runs two ways."

Now I understand that of the many thousands of ways the river reflects the sky, the winds, the currents, and the demimonde of bald eagles, trout, geese, and cranes that draw their sustenance from it, many other people that I hadn't imagined have gazed at the same scenery. The setting sun hits the river reeds on the island that separates my portion of the river from its eastern banks, lighting them in a golden band as if someone had aimed a celestial spotlight just at that angle. Clouds light up the sky and become Hudson River School pink and peach, giddy colors that the waters reflect. In my eyes, it's always been a beauty that transcends time and place.

As I pass by what had been the Collier flats, this long, fertile region between the hills that roll down to the Hudson and the deep blue outline of the Catskills off in the distance, I wonder if any of Eleanor's ancestors, or mine, looked at the river and mountains the way I do: the ever-changing waters, one moment as still as glass, another moment choppy with whitecaps. The mountains one moment hidden behind a cloudy haze, another moment crisp and dark. Were these exquisite visions to them? Or did the river represent a chance at freedom, a place to murder a baby, a dangerous trap where they could be kidnapped? Did they see the mountains as the giver of sunsets, sustenance, life?

All my life, I had the feeling that the river I faced every day was heading south to my left and north to my right. I was wrong. I grew up on the west side of the Hudson. When I looked at the river sparkling in the morning light, north was to my left, south to my right. The direction I faced was east, toward Massachusetts, with the Catskill Mountains at my back.

I'm not sure why I never got that right. If I could imagine slaves fleeing north to Canada, I would have to think of them moving on the river from my right to my left. If I could imagine it at all.

My internal GPS, which has served me well in the narrow hutongs of Beijing and in the outer arrondissements of Paris, was somehow set wrong. When it came to my sense of the Hudson River, *my* Hudson River, I had no true north. Everything I thought was wrong.

AFTERWORD

Full Circle

By Eleanor C. Mire

WOW! This is them! That was my first thought when I opened the packet from Roberta. Roberta Neizer is the wife of Donald Neizer—a first cousin once removed—on my maternal grandmother's side of our family. Roberta had gotten into her family's genealogy and then worked on her husband's genealogy and found his maternal side, which is my maternal side. She was fascinated enough to take trips from her home in Delaware to New Baltimore, New York, to go through volumes of birth and death certificates as well as church records.

I had heard the name Vanderzee from my grandmother, Vera Washington. Her mother was Ella Vanderzee, and my grandmother said Ella's family was from New York and that we had Native American and Dutch ancestors. She also said firmly that there were not any enslaved people "on our side of the family," even though we all knew that this could not be true. She had been brought up in an era when enslavement was considered an embarrassment, and something better not discussed. Roberta had gathered a thick notebook of information with an overwhelming amount of detail. At the time I was working and raising a child. Though I was interested, I had to put the research aside.

After I retired in 2013, I had the time and inclination to get involved with finding more information. That involved frequent phone calls with Roberta, parsing inconsistencies from documents in the big black book Roberta had sent, and joining genealogical websites. That work added to my knowledge of my ancestors who were enslaved and also their enslavers. But as anyone in the genealogical world knows, data is elusive, and the more you learn, the more questions you have. Who were the people who "owned" my ancestors? How did they become free? What did they do after they had been freed? How had they fared while in New Baltimore? And what had happened to the rest of my very large family?

One day I received a message from another cousin, Teresa Vega. Teresa is from the New Jersey side of the family, but she knew of my struggles with my New York side. She suggested I check a Facebook page to which we belonged, "I've Traced My Enslaved Ancestors and Their Owners." There was a woman, Debra Bruno, looking for information about enslaved people in upstate New York.

With a bit of trepidation, I messaged Debra that my ancestors had been from New Baltimore. It is a sad fact that when dealing with the issue of enslaved ancestors, I had found that white people whose families may have been involved in enslavement did not want to get involved in any way with the issue. That was especially true if they are contacted by a Black person whose ancestors may have been enslaved by theirs. Routinely I was ignored, if not blocked, when I brought up the issue.

That did not happen this time. Debra wrote that her ancestors owned enslaved people and were from Coxsackie. I mentioned the Vanderzees and told her that our research showed that they were apparently enslaved by a family named Houghtaling. Debra responded that her family names included Houghtalings. Finding that they had once enslaved people was what brought her to the website. It took a few minutes for each of us to catch our breath.

This was a rare moment. I told Debra the story of my maternal great-great-great-grandmother Mary Egberts Van Bergen Vanderzee. The more I learned about Mary, the more she became the ancestor I held in my heart. Debra and I, separately and together, looked into the dynamics of the area in which the Vanderzees and Houghtalings lived. We became invested in finding out much more about Mary and the connections between our families.

Still, my guard was up. There are those who minimize the impact of enslavement in the North, arguing it was more benign than in the South. They ignore the reality of the people who lived through it and are not sensitive to the feelings about what enslavement actually meant. Since the North did not have big plantations and enslavement tended to involve only a few enslaved per household, many people believed it didn't involve much hardship and the enslaved were treated like members of the family. But they were members of a family that could buy and sell them and their children, and beat them with impunity. Everything that could happen to an enslaved person in the South could happen to an enslaved person in the North. The enslaved in the North lived with that knowledge.

Debra understood that. We talked, and with that talk came trust, and with that trust came friendship. In time I joined her on a few of the frequent trips she makes to Coxsackie. She drove me around New Baltimore where we discovered the places my ancestors lived, including the house of Mary Vanderzee and her family, which is still there and well cared for. To know Mary's story, which was a hard one, to know I was walking in the house where she sat until the end of her days—it was a feeling I cannot put into words.

In July 2022 Debra and I, along with my son and my sister Beverly, traveled to the Fenimore Art Museum in Cooperstown to view a painting, the Van Bergen Overmantel. I had never heard of it; Debra had found it for us. The painting, attributed to John Heaten, was painted between 1728 and 1738. Depicted are members of the Van Bergen family, Native Americans, and what could possibly be the first painted images of enslaved people in what would become the United States. The Van Bergen name is an ancestral one that Debra and I share. Seeing depictions of people who could possibly be the ancestors of both of us was again emotionally overwhelming.

When we first embarked on this journey, Debra was doing the hands-on research. I parsed information, read between the lines, and passed on family stories and information I collected about enslaved people in the North. We had excited phone calls when we uncovered tiny bits of information and especially when we had an "AHA!" moment, such as the time when I did a backwards count of the date on Mary's death certificate to

Figure 23. Debra Bruno, Eleanor Mire, and Beverly Mire stand at the grave site of matriarch Mary Vanderzee at Riverside Cemetery in Coxsackie.
Photo by Jonathan Palmer.

figure out her date of birth. Why, I asked myself, didn't I think of that earlier? Of course, that led to more questions about her parentage. It was never-ending.

When Debra asked me about cowriting a book, I said no. For me, it was too overwhelming to even consider. I know myself. I tend to leave everything until the last minute. The book would never have been finished. Debra is the opposite. She was born to write this book. Her research is impeccable, and she is very respectful of the lives of the people she writes about. People often ask how we could have formed such a tight friendship. She comes from a family that enslaved people, and I am the descendant of the enslaved. I believe we are only responsible for ourselves and what we do, not for our ancestors. Debra and I together try to tell the story of the real lives of real people, especially Mary's story and our shared legacy, so we can gain an understanding of what happened before us. Through that work, our families are coming together, full circle, in us.

Acknowledgments

This labor of love and attention would not have happened without the many people who encouraged me, read parts of chapters or the entire book, and helped me get this project going in the first place.

I begin my thanks with the writer Mary Kay Ricks, the historian who first suggested that if I had Dutch ancestors in New York, they were likely enslavers. I can still remember that sinking feeling when I learned she was spot-on correct. The encouragement of Zofia Smardz, formerly an editor with the *Washington Post Magazine*, meant that the idea took fruition and saw its first form there. The encouragement of former *Washington Post* editor Claudia Townsend, who also read a final draft of the book, kept me honest, especially in the chapter about the South.

Without the conversations, coffees, lunches, and silly texts from Rebecca Frankel, I would not have had the courage to begin this, or the absolute luck in finding an agent who immediately embraced the idea of the book and stuck with me through the process. Esmond Harmsworth, you are a treasure and a loyal man.

Finding Michael McGandy, formerly of Cornell's trade imprint Three Hills, made me realize that I had found my book's perfect home. My deepest thanks to Andrea Mosterman for suggesting him and for your steady encouragement. Michael's careful editing, attention to detail, and disciplined reading always kept me moving onward. I was also lucky in next inheriting a smart and responsive editor in Mahinder Kingra, Cornell's multitasking editor-in-chief and the most patient respondent to my twelfth email of the day. I'm deeply grateful to my peer reviewers, Myra B. Young Armstead and Andrea C. Mosterman, as well as to my all-seeing copyeditor, Lori Rider.

The deep-dive research part of this book, ongoing and never-ending, brought me to a brilliant archivist, historian, and all-around good guy in the Hudson Valley. Jonathan Palmer, you were not just along for the ride; you rode shotgun. Along with the other folks at the Vedder Research Library and the Greene County Historical Society—Heather Bizanos, Jean and Clesson Bush, Shelby Mattice, Bob and Ann Hallock, and David Dorpfeld (who wins extra points for traipsing around a snowy Riverside Cemetery with me)—thank you.

The New Netherland Institute and the incomparable Charles Gehring, along with Dennis Maika, Russell Shorto, and Deborah Hamer, helped me with a research grant, ideas on unpublished source material, the reading of chapters, and unwavering support. Nicole Mahoney at New-York Historical Society, thank you.

Thank you to the people in my hometowns of Athens, Coxsackie, and New Baltimore who helped make all of this real. Debra Sottolano welcomed us into her home, one of the last residences of Mary Vanderzee, and made us feel the presence of the Vanderzee matriarch. Gethen Proper knew she needed to do something about her church's history of slavery. Carrie Feder was an immediate friend showing me around the Van Loon house. In Macon, my thanks to Wayne Dobson, who was both courteous and welcoming. At Fenimore Art Museum, Paul D'Ambrosio, Ann Cannon, Cassidy Percoco, Todd Kenyon, and Kelli Huggins brought us to the Van Bergen Overmantel. Emelie Gevalt of the American Folk Art Museum talked to us for an exhibition about the Van Bergen Overmantel. I think we cried. Robin Young of NPR's *Here and Now* and Ari Shapiro of *All Things Considered* made us sound thoughtful and smart on the radio.

There have been so many people I call my angels: professional colleagues who many times became friends: Susan Stessin-Cohn, Wendy Harris, Michael Douma, Nicole Maskiell, Graham Russell Hodges, Travis Bowman, Joyce Goodfriend, Henry Wiencek, Michael Groth, Joan Devries Kelley, Wendy Hamand Venet, Anne Farrow, Mike Osterhout, Michael Lord, Heidi Hill, Rob Sweeney, Lydia Newcomb, and Taylor Bruck. At the Thomas Cole National Historic Site, my thanks to Heather Palmer, Sofia D'Amico, and Beth Wynne. Without the welcome from Cathy Roberts of Coming to the Table, I would not have found "I've Traced My Enslaved Ancestors." Sylvia Hasenkopf, you kept me honest with your attention to detail, your years of research, and your encouragement.

Bob Cullen, patiently and cheerfully, went through two rounds of photography with me when I decided the first version of a headshot made me look like a motivational speaker (and it was not his fault). Tom Langton, a lifelong friend, helped improve an ancient photo to make it clearer, as did the world's best son-in-law, Udi Falkson.

To the friends who have shared their publishing stories with me, listened to me talk, made suggestions, and were there for me when I needed help: Cornelia Read, who imagines lives far beyond what I can imagine; Mark Stein, Jim Johnston, Anne Rosen, Ruth Kassinger, Susan Price, Fabienne Spier, Micaela Massimino, Diane Fresquez, Martha Ertman, Laura Schenone, Bob Chaloner, and all of the WriterMoms: thank you for asking, thank you for listening. I am especially grateful to Josh Chin of the *Wall Street Journal*, who gave me one of the smartest edits of all, even when he really had no time for it.

Roberta Neizer, in her years of research, brought us to Mary Vanderzee. My Vanderzee kin—especially Kitt Potter, Angela Barnes, Bev Mire, Jake Mire, and always, first and foremost, Eleanor Mire—thank you. Without you, Eleanor, not one part of this could have happened. Thank you for taking the leap with me. Thank you for being a steady friend, and for saying yes. I can't wait to see what we do next, serendipitously.

My family has always had my back: Daniel and Joanna Davis, Udi Falkson, Mom, Lori, Claudia, Kim, and Lisa (thanks for the Van Valkenburg books!), Alanna Davis, and all the rest of the ravioli-worthy bunch. To my grandchildren, Lane and Casey Falkson, I hope you tell your own grandchildren this story. I love you all. And most of all, forever and ever, the world's best editor, who never wavered in his support and faith in me, and who has listened for years about the minutiae of Dutch names, archeology, Confederate heroes, and wills. Bob Davis, you are the best.

NOTES

Introduction

1. The National Association of the Van Valkenburg Family in America, "Lambert Jochemse van Valckenburch of Fort Orange," https://navvf.org/lambert-albany.html.

2. Isaac Collier (Isaac Collyer), will dated April 8, 1796, probated October 30, 1796, pp. 335–37, New York, U.S., Wills and Probate Records, 1659–1999. Ancestry.com.

3. 1790 United States Federal Census, Coxsackie, Albany, New York. Series M637, roll 6, p. 163, image 96, Family History Library Film 0568146. Ancestry.com.

4. [Possibly] John Schuneman, Coxsackie Declaration, Albany Institute of History and Art Library, 1775, ms-ov-79001, https://www.albanyinstitute.org/collection/details/coxsackie-declaration.

5. Herbert Furman Seversmith, *Colonial Families of Long Island, New York and Connecticut: being the ancestry & kindred of Herbert Furman Seversmith . . .* Washington [D.C.?], 1939–1958. Vol. 2, Colyer, 720. Ancestry.com.

6. Coming to the Table (website), accessed December 21, 2023, https://comingtothetable.org/.

7. Constance Ross Ulrich, "Mathys Coenradtsen Houghtaling of Coxsackie, New York, and His Descendants," *New York Genealogical and Biographical Record* 101, no. 4 (October 1970): 193–99.

1. Fifty Beaver Skins

1. "Ship Journey: 1636—*Rensselaerswyck*, bound for Rensselaerswyck—arrived 1637," Mapping Early New York, New Amsterdam History Center, https://encyclo pedia.nahc-mapping.org/shipjourney/1636-rensselaerswyck-bound-rensselaerswyck-arrived-1637.

2. Thomas E. Burke Jr., *Mohawk Frontier: The Dutch Community of Schenectady, New York, 1661–1710,* 2nd ed. (Albany: State University of New York Press, 1991), 43.

3. Burke, *Mohawk Frontier,* 8.

4. Linda M. Rupert, *Creolization and Contraband: Curaçao in the Early Modern Atlantic World* (Athens: University of Georgia Press, 2012), 89.

5. Rupert, *Creolization,* 107.

6. Charles T. Gehring, trans. and ed., *Curaçao Papers, 1640–1665* (Albany: The New Netherland Research Center and the New Netherland Institute, 2011), 28.

7. Gehring, *Curaçao Papers,* 41.

8. Gehring, *Curaçao Papers,* 105.

9. Dennis J. Maika, " 'To experiment with a parcel of negroes': Incentive, Collaboration, and Competition in New Amsterdam's Slave Trade," *Journal of Early American History* 10 (2020): 63.

10. Gehring, *Curaçao Papers,* 131.

11. Charles Z. Lincoln, A. Judd Northrup, and William H. Johnson, *The Colonial Laws of New York from the Year 1664 to the Revolution* (New York: J. B. Lyon, 1894), 157–59, 448–49, 484, 519–21, 533–34, 580–84, 588, 597–98, 631, 761–67.

12. *Passenger and Immigration Lists Index, 1500s–1900s,* Ancestry.com. Original data: P. William Filby, ed. New York, 1664, 60.

13. Albany County (N.Y.), *Early Records of the City and County of Albany,* Notarial Papers 1 and 2, 1660–1696, p. 537, https://www.google.com/books/edition/Early_Records_of_the_City_and_County_of/tfwLAAAAYAAJ?hl=en&gbpv=1&dq=Bill+of+sale+of+a+negr o+from+Amadoor+Vopie+to+Claes+van+Petten&pg=PA537&printsec=frontcover.

14. Dave Lucas, "Papscanee Island Nature Reserve Returned to Stockbridge-Munsee Community," WAMC Northeast Public Radio, May 14, 2021, https://www.wamc.org/capital-region-news/2021-05-14/papscanee-island-nature-preserve-returned-to-stockbridge-munsee-community.

15. A. J. F. Van Laer, trans. and ed., *Minutes of the Court of Fort Orange and Beverwyck 1657–1660,* vol. 2 (Albany: University of the State of New York, 1923); A. J. F. Van Laer, trans. and ed., *Minutes of the Court of Albany, Rensselaerswyck and Schenectady 1668–1673,* vol. 1 (Albany: University of the State of New York, 1926).

16. A. J. F. Van Laer, trans. and ed., *Van Rensselaer Bowier Manuscripts* (Albany: University of the State of New York, 1908), 805–46.

17. A. J. F. Van Laer, trans. and ed., *Minutes of the Court of Albany, Rensselaerswyck and Schenectady 1675–1680,* vol. 2 (Albany: University of the State of New York, 1929), 430–44. Although the trial was also described elsewhere, I relied on the minutes of the court, since this is the most detailed account.

18. Graham Russell Hodges, *Root and Branch: African Americans in New York and East Jersey, 1613–1863* (Chapel Hill: University of North Carolina Press, 1999), 53.

19. Burke, *Mohawk Frontier,* 104–8.

20. A. J. F. Van Laer, *Minutes of the Court of Albany, Rensselaerswyck and Schenectady 1680–1685,* vol. 3 (Albany: University of the State of New York, 1932), 277–78.

21. Van Laer, *Minutes of the Court of Albany, Rensselaerswyck and Schenectady 1680–1685,* 3:278.

22. Sylvia Hasenkopf, "The Hallenbecks of Greene County," *Porcupine Soup*, November 4, 2021, https://porcupinesoup.com/the-hallenbecks-of-greene-county.

23. Will for Casper Janse Hallenbeck, Record of Wills Recorded at Albany, New York, 1629–1802; Index 1629–1828. Ancestry.com.

24. Wills, Letters Testamentary, Letters of Administration, Etc., 1787–1902, s.v. Casper Janse Halenbeck (1723–1798), probate date October 5, 1798, Coxsackie, Albany, New York. Ancestry.com.

2. The Lost History

1. Historic Hudson Valley, *The Mill at Philipsburg Manor*, 1972, https://www.youtube.com/watch?v=7YwFW_TJr9w.

2. Joseph Reade, "Adolph Philipse Estate Records," New York Public Library, Manuscripts and Archives Division, MssCol2412.

3. Michael Lord, phone interview, January 14, 2022.

4. Annette Wynne, "Indian Children," in *Treasure Things* (New York: P. F. Volland, 1922).

5. *The Heritage of New Baltimore* (New York: New Baltimore Bicentennial Committee, 1976), 17–18.

6. Washington Irving, *The Legend of Sleepy Hollow* (Rockville, MD: Wildside, 2004).

7. Washington Irving, "The Devil and Tom Walker," in *Tales of a Traveller*, 1824, Project Gutenberg, 2004, https://www.gutenberg.org/files/13514/13514-h/13514-h.htm#chap24.

8. Brian Jay Jones, *Washington Irving: An American Original* (New York: Arcade, 2008), 301.

9. Alan Taylor, *William Cooper's Town: Power and Persuasion on the Frontier of the Early American Republic* (New York: Vintage, 1995), 299–300.

10. James D. Wallace, "Cooper and Slavery," presented at the Cooper Panel of the May 1992 conference of the American Literature Association in San Diego. https://jfcooper-society.org/content/04-crit/articles/ala/1992ala-wallace.htm?Highlight=Cooper%20and%20Slavery.

11. "Fenimore Cooper's Defense of Slave-Owning America," *American Historical Review* 35, no. 3 (April 1930): 575–82. https://www.jstor.org/stable/1838423.

12. James Fenimore Cooper, *Satanstoe; or, the Littlepage Manuscripts. A Tale of the Colony* (New York: Burgess, Stringer, 1845), 39.

13. Anne Grant, *Memoirs of an American Lady: With Sketches of Manners and Scenery in America, As They Existed Previous to the Revolution* (Carlisle, MA: Applewood, 2007), 15, 85.

14. Grant, *Memoirs*, 16.

15. Grant, *Memoirs*, 16.

16. Lucy Dillon, *Memoirs of Madame de la Tour Du Pin* (London: Century, 1969), 251.

17. Dillon, *Memoirs*, 253.

18. Dillon, *Memoirs*, 282.

19. "The Abolition of Slavery," *New York Times*, January 19, 1859, 4.

20. "Abolition of Slavery," 4. Italics in original.

21. Leslie M. Harris, professor of history at Northwestern University, phone interview, January 8, 2020.

22. Marc Ross, professor emeritus of political science at Bryn Mawr, phone interview, October 10, 2019.

23. Joanne Pope Melish, *Disowning Slavery: Gradual Emancipation and "Race" in New England, 1780–1860* (Ithaca, NY: Cornell University Press, 2000), 225.

24. Joe Heim, "Teaching America's Truth," *Washington Post*, August 28, 2019, https://www.washingtonpost.com/education/2019/08/28/teaching-slavery-schools/.

25. Dunkin H. Sill, "A Notable Example of Longevity," *New York Genealogical and Biographical Record* 56, no. 1 (January 1925): 65.

26. Allison Bennett, "Old Caesar—A Slave's Story," *Spotlight*, November 12, 1970, 1–2.

27. Debra Bruno, "History Lessons," *Washington Post Magazine*, July 22, 2020, https://www.washingtonpost.com/magazine/2020/07/22/after-i-discovered-that-my-ancestors-had-enslaved-people-i-connected-with-descendant-those-who-were-enslaved/.

28. "Toni Morrison's 'Good' Ghosts," interview by Renee Montagne, *Morning Edition*, National Public Radio, September 20, 2004, https://www.npr.org/2004/09/20/3912464/toni-morrisons-good-ghosts.

3. "They Are Calling to Us"

1. Sylvia Hasenkopf, *Tracing Your Roots in Greene County: The First Fifty Articles* (North River Research, 2012).

2. Anonymous, phone interview, March 3, 2019.

3. Sylvia Hasenkopf, email to author, June 2019.

4. Cheryl Rollins, email to author, July 25, 2020.

4. "A Vile Slander"

1. U.S., *Dutch Reformed Church Records in Selected States, 1639–1989* (Holland Society of New York), New York City Lutheran, vol. 1, book 85, s.v. Isaac Kalior baptism, January 1, 1726. Ancestry.com.

2. *Dutch Reformed Church Records*, s.v. Hannes Christian.

3. *Dutch Reformed Church Records*, s.v. Jannetje.

4. *Dutch Reformed Church Records*, s.v. Elizabeth.

5. *Dutch Reformed Church Records*, s.v. Pieter Christian.

6. Zion Lutheran Church, baptismal records, 1712–1800, sent to author.

7. William S. Pelletreau, "Athens," in *History of Greene County, New York: With Biographical Sketches of Its Prominent Men* (New York: J. B. Beers, 1884), 164.

8. Attrib. to John Heaten, Van Bergen Overmantel, c. 1733, Fenimore Art Museum, Cooperstown, New York, Museum purchase NO366.1954.

9. Kristin Lunde Gibbons, "The Van Bergen Overmantel: A Thesis," Master's thesis, State University of New York College at Oneonta, 1966.

10. Henry Brace, "Old Catskill," in *History of Greene County*, 96.

11. Jessie Van Vechten Vedder, *Historic Catskill* (Fawcett, 1922), 11.

12. Vedder, *Historic Catskill*, 11.

13. Sylvia Hasenkopf, "The Long Road to Freedom for Slaves in North America," *Porcupine Soup*, February 11, 2022, https://porcupinesoup.com/the-long-road-to-freedom-for-slaves-in-north-america.

14. 1790 United States Federal Census, Coxsackie, Albany, New York. Series M637, roll 6, p. 163, image 96, Family History Library Film 0568146. Ancestry.com.

15. 1790 United States Federal Census, Coxsackie, Albany, New York. Series M637, 12 rolls. Ancestry.com.

16. "Slavery in Brooklyn," Lefferts Family Papers at Brooklyn Historical Society, https://lefferts.brooklynhistory.org/slavery-in-brooklyn/.

17. Julius F. Sachse, *Justus Falckner: Mystic and Scholar* (Philadelphia, 1903), 106.

18. Wilhelm Christoph Berkenmeyer, *The Albany Protocol: Wilhelm Christoph Berkenmeyer's Chronicle of Lutheran Affairs in New York Colony, 1731–1750*, available at New York State Library, Albany, 25, 50.

19. John P. Dern, introduction to Berkenmeyer, *Albany Protocol*, xlii.

20. Berkenmeyer, *Albany Protocol*, 37.

21. Berkenmeyer, *Albany Protocol*, 221.

22. Zion Lutheran Church baptismal records.

23. Berkenmeyer, *Albany Protocol*, 185.

24. Berkenmeyer, *Albany Protocol*, 195.

25. Berkenmeyer, *Albany Protocol*, 262.

26. Berkenmeyer, *Albany Protocol*, 284.

27. Berkenmeyer, *Albany Protocol*, 284.

28. Berkenmeyer, *Albany Protocol*, 320.

29. Berkenmeyer, *Albany Protocol*, 334–35.

30. Berkenmeyer, *Albany Protocol*, 337.

31. Berkenmeyer, *Albany Protocol*, 343.

32. Berkenmeyer, *Albany Protocol*, 345.

33. Berkenmeyer, *Albany Protocol*, 351.

34. Berkenmeyer, *Albany Protocol*, 376.

35. Gethen Proper, phone interview with author, March 25, 2021.

36. Graham Russell Hodges, "The Pastor and the Prostitute," in *Sex, Love, Race: Crossing Boundaries in North American History* (New York: New York University Press, 1999), 60–71.

37. New York Genealogical and Biographical Society, "Baptismal Records of Zion Lutheran Church, Loonenburg, now Athens, Greene County, New York," *New York Genealogical and Biographical Record* 82, no. 1 (January 1951): 15.

38. Joshua Taylor, president of New York Genealogical and Biographical Society, phone interview with author, June 13, 2022.

39. Remsen Varick Messler, *A History or Genealogical Record of the Messler (or Metselaer) Family*, North American Family Histories, 1500–2000. Ancestry.com.

40. Will for Elsie Van Loon, in New York, U.S., Wills and Probate Records, 1659–1999, Record of Wills Recorded at Albany, New York, 1629–1802; Index 1629–1828. Ancestry.com.

41. David N. Gellman, *Emancipating New York: The Politics of Slavery and Freedom, 1777–1827* (Baton Rouge: Louisiana State University Press, 2006), 17.

42. Peter Van Vechten Jr., *The Genealogical Records of the Van Vechten's from 1638 to 1896* (Milwaukee, WI: Radke Bros. & Kortsch, 1896), 10–13.

43. Will of Gerrit Van Bergen, July 5, 1758, in New York, U.S., Wills and Probate Records, 1659–1999, Record of Wills Recorded at New York, New York, 1629–1802; Index 1629–1828 *Wills, Vol 021, 1758–1760*. Ancestry.com.

44. Abstracts of Wills on File in the Surrogate's Office, City of New York, vol. 7, June 6, 1766–November 29, 1771 (New York: New-York Historical Society, 1898), 319–24.

45. Will of Martin Van Bergen, July 10, 1770, in New York, U.S., Wills and Probate Records, 1659–1999, Record of Wills Recorded at New York, New York, 1629–1802; Index 1629–1828 *Wills and Administrations, Vol 0024–0027, 1763–1771*. Ancestry.com.

5. "We May Be Van Bergens after All"

1. Raymond Beecher, "A Van Bergen Legacy," *Greene County Historical Journal* 12, no. 4 (Winter 1988): 31–38.

2. War Department, Adjutant General's Office, 3/4/1907–9/18/1947, Van Bergen, Anthony—New York—Van Bergen's Regiment (Albany County Militia). Retrieved from the Digital Public Library of America, http://catalog.archives.gov/id/141295320.

3. Beecher, "Van Bergen Legacy."

4. S. V. Talcott, *Genealogical Notes of New York and New England Families* (Albany, N.Y.: Weed, Parsons, 1883), 301, https://archive.org/details/genealogicalnote00talc.

5. William S. Pelletreau, "Coxsackie," in *History of Greene County*, 244.

6. Pelletreau, "Coxsackie," 244.

7. 1790 U.S. Census, New York, https://www2.census.gov/prod2/decennial/documents/1790m-02.pdf.

8. 1790 U.S. Census, Coxsackie, Albany County, New York. Ancestry.com.

9. 1800 U.S. Census, Coxsackie, Greene County, New York. Ancestry.com.

10. Shane White, *Somewhat More Independent: The End of Slavery in New York City, 1770–1810* (Athens: University of Georgia Press, 1991), 21.

11. Alexander Coventry, *Memoirs of an Emigrant: The Journal of Alexander Coventry, M.D.; in Scotland, the United States and Canada during the Period 1783–1831* (The Institute, 1978), New York State Library and Manuscripts and Special Collections, 145.

12. Coventry, *Memoirs*, 145.

13. 1790 U.S. Federal Census, s.v. Thomas Houghtalen (1731–1824). Ancestry.com.

14. Grant, *Memoirs of an American Lady*, 172.

15. William Strickland, *Journal of a Tour in the United States of America, 1794–1795* (New York: New-York Historical Society, 1971), 74.

16. Strickland, *Journal*, 163.

17. Coventry, *Memoirs*, 145.

18. Cuyler Reynolds, ed., *Hudson-Mohawk Genealogical and Family Memoirs* (New York: Lewis Historical Publishing Company, 1911), Schenectady Digital History Archive, https://www.schenectadyhistory.org/families/hmgfm/schuyler-1.html.

19. Cadwallader Colden, *The Letters and Papers of Cadwallader Colden . . . 1711–[1775]* (New York: New-York Historical Society, 1918), 39.

20. Gellman, *Emancipating New York*, 62.

21. Grant, *Memoirs of an American Lady*, 86.

22. Henry Wiencek, *An Imperfect God: George Washington, His Slaves, and the Creation of America* (New York: Farrar, Straus & Giroux, 2003), 131–32.

23. Leonard Van Buren to Leonard Bronk, June 15, 1787, Bronk manuscripts, Vedder Research Library, Greene County Historical Society, Coxsackie, NY.

24. Coventry, *Memoirs*, 172.

25. 1790 U.S. Federal Census, s.v. Peter Anthony Van Bergen (1763–1804). Ancestry.com.

26. *Reformed Church Coxsackie, N.Y. Baptismal Records, 1738–1899*, 39.

27. *Reformed Church Coxsackie*, 104.

28. Malcolm X, "Make It Plain," *The American Experience*, PBS, 1994. Transcript of interview at https://www.pbs.org/wgbh/americanexperience/films/malcolmx/#transcript.

29. Coxsackie Town Record of Freeborn Slaves, 1800, Franklin D. Roosevelt Historical Manuscript Collection, 1636–1935, FDR Library, Hyde Park, NY.

30. Eleanor Mire, email to author, July 13, 2019.

31. Adam Grimes, "A Local Vision: Land, Landscape, and Labor in the Van Bergen Overmantel," master's thesis, University of Delaware, Spring 2020.

32. John Macomb receipt to Van Bergen, June 28, 1762, Van Bergen Family Papers 1670–1823, box 1, folder 5, New York State Library, Albany, New York.

33. Kristin L. Gibbons, "The Van Bergen Overmantel," master's thesis, State University of New York College at Oneonta, 1966.

34. Quotations in this paragraph and the next are attributed to Mabel Parker Smith, unpublished paper on the Van Bergen Overmantel in the author's possession.

35. *History of Greene County*, 95.

6. Resistance and Running

1. Nicole Saffold Maskiell, *Bound by Bondage: Slavery and the Creation of a Northern Gentry* (Ithaca, NY: Cornell University Press, 2022), 121.

2. Susan Stessin-Cohn and Ashley Hurlbut-Biagini, *In Defiance: Runaways from Slavery in New York's Hudson River Valley, 1735–1831*, 2nd ed. (Chatham, NY: Black Dome, 2023), 336.

3. Facebook group "Van Valkenburg to Vollick," for "descendants of Isaac Van Valkenburg, aka Vollick, Loyalist who left York for Canada during the American Revolution": https://www.facebook.com/groups/Vollick/.

4. Pelletreau, "Coxsackie," in *History of Greene County*, 238.

5. James Oliver Horton and Lois E. Horton, *In Hope of Liberty: Culture, Community and Protest among Northern Free Blacks, 1700–1860* (New York: Oxford University Press, 1997), 60.

6. Maya Jasanoff, *Liberty's Exiles: American Loyalists in the Revolutionary World* (New York: Knopf, 2011), 49.

7. Simon Schama, *Rough Crossings: The Slaves, the British, and the American Revolution* (New York: HarperCollins, 2005), 9.

8. Schama, *Rough Crossings*, 7.

9. David Murdoch, *The Dutch Dominie of the Catskills* (New York: Derby & Jackson), 1861.

10. Brace, "Old Catskill," in *History of Greene County*, 100.

11. Brace, "Old Catskill," 99.

12. Possibly John Schuneman, Coxsackie Declaration, 1775, Albany Institute of History and Art Library, https://www.albanyinstitute.org/collection/details/coxsackie-declaration

13. This account is taken from Brace, "Old Catskill," 103–5.

14. Brace, "Old Catskill," 103.

15. Vedder, *Historic Catskill*, 47.

16. Brace, "Old Catskill," 105.

17. 1790 U.S. Federal Census, s.v. David Abeel (1727–1813), Catskill, Albany, New York, series M637, roll 6, p. 175, image 102, Family History Library Film 0568146, Ancestry.com; 1800 U.S. Federal Census, s.v. David Abeel. Catskill, Greene, New York, series M32, roll 22, p. 1057, image 420, Family History Library Film 193710, Ancestry.com; 1810 U.S. Federal Census, s.v. David Abeel, Catskill, Greene, New York, roll 27, p. 199. image 00119, Family History Library Film 0181381, Ancestry.com.

18. Will of David Abeel, Surrogate's Court (Greene County) New York, U.S. Wills and Probate Records, 1659–1999, Ancestry.com.

19. John B. Dumond, October 22, 1780, "Taken Up in the Woods," Anderson Collection 23.5A, Vedder Research Library, Coxsackie, NY.

20. Catharine Maria Sedgwick, "Slavery in New England," *Bentley's Miscellany*, 1853, 417–24.

21. Pieter Hogenboom, s.v. Will, February 23, 1758, Albany County, New York, US, Wills and Probate Records, 1659–1999, Ancestry.com.

22. Catherine Tryntje Hogeboom, birth of child Johannes, May 30, 1740, with husband Philip Conyne, in *U.S. Dutch Reformed Church Records in Selected States, 1639–1986* (Holland Society of New York), Coxsackie, book 10, Ancestry.com.

23. Coventry, *Memoirs*, 156.

24. Susan Stessin-Cohn and Ashley Hurlburt-Biagini, *In Defiance: Runaways from Slavery in New York's Hudson River Valley, 1735–1831* (Delmar, NY: Black Dome Press, 2016), 84, 92.

25. Coventry, *Memoirs*, 116.

26. Coventry, *Memoirs*, 134.

27. Coventry, *Memoirs*, 209.

28. Coventry, *Memoirs*, 211.

29. Andrea C. Mosterman, *Spaces of Enslavement: A History of Slavery and Resistance in Dutch New York* (Ithaca, NY: Cornell University Press, 2021), 67–77.

30. Advertisement of Aaron W. Slingerland of Cobleskill, *Albany Gazette*, June 29, 1815.

31. Coventry, *Memoirs*, 464, 522.

32. Coventry, *Memoirs*, 1220, 1554.

33. Coventry, *Memoirs*, 1567.

34. Coventry, *Memoirs*, 1577.

35. Paul Grondahl, "Re-examining the Albany Fire of 1793 and Three Slaves Hanged for It," *Albany Times Union*, February 19, 2014.

36. Don R. Gerlach, "Black Arson in Albany, New York: November 1793," *Journal of Black Studies* 7, no. 3 (March 1977): 303.

37. "Articles of agreement, bounty hunters," June 7, 1811, Elting, Roelof J. and Ezekiel, Family Papers (1703–1928), Historic Huguenot Street, https://nyheritage.contentdm.oclc.org/digital/collection/p16694coll153/id/4497/rec/1.

38. Stessin-Cohn and Hurlburt-Biagini, *In Defiance*, 130.

39. Coxsackie Town Record of Freeborn Slaves, 1800.

40. Raymond Beecher, "Honoré Chaurand's Friendship's Asylum," *Greene County Historical Journal* 10, no. 3 (Fall 1986): 26–29.

41. Michael E. Groth, *Slavery and Freedom in the Mid-Hudson Valley* (Albany: State University of New York Press, 2017), Kindle ed., loc. 1382.

42. Stessin-Cohn and Hurlburt-Biagini, *In Defiance*, 136.

43. Stessin-Cohn and Hurlburt-Biagini, *In Defiance*, 204.

44. Stessin-Cohn and Hurlburt-Biagini, *In Defiance*, 220.

45. Thomas Williams, "One Cent Reward," *Catskill Recorder, and Greene County Republican*, May 7, 1829, 3.

7. Casper and Nancy in the Twilight

1. Gellman, *Emancipating New York*, 29.

2. Hudson Friends Meeting, "Quakers in Hudson Yesterday and Today," https://www.quakercloud.org/cloud/hudson-friends-meeting/pages/quakers-hudson-yesterday-and-today.

3. Richard Brookhiser, *Gentleman Revolutionary: Gouverneur Morris, the Rake Who Wrote the Constitution* (New York: Free Press, 2003), 3, quotation on 85.

4. Shane White, *Somewhat More Independent: The End of Slavery in New York City, 1770–1810* (Athens: University of Georgia Press, 1991), 20.

5. Daniel Littlefield, "John Jay, the Revolutionary Generation, and Slavery," *New York History* 81, no. 1 (2000): 98, https://www.jstor.org/stable/23181809.

6. Henry Brace, "Old Catskill," in *History of Greene County*, 114.

7. "An Act for the gradual abolition of slavery," New York State Archives, New York Department of State, Bureau of Miscellaneous Records, Enrolled Acts of the State Legislature, series 13036–78, laws of 1799, chapter 62, https://digitalcollections.archives.nysed.gov/index.php/Detail/objects/10815.

8. "County Census 1811," transcribed by Sylvia Hasenkopf from the *Catskill Recorder*, January 9, 1811, https://sites.rootsweb.com/~nygreen2/county_census_1811.htm.

9. Baptism, s.v. Casparus Kaljer, January 8, 1769, Coxsackie, Greene, New York. *Holland Society of New York*; Coxsackie, book 10, Ancestry.com.

10. Isaac Collier (Isaac Collyer), will dated April 8, 1796, probated October 30, 1796, pp. 335–37, New York, U.S., Wills and Probate Records, 1659–1999. Ancestry.com.

11. 1800 US Federal Census, s.v. Casper Colier, Coxsackie, Greene, New York; series M32, roll 22, p. 1106, image 467, Family History Library, film 193710. Ancestry.com.

12. 1790 United States Federal Census, s.v. Philip Bronk, Coxsackie, Albany, New York; series M637, roll 6, p. 163, image 96, Family History Library, film 0568146. Ancestry.com.

13. Mosterman, *Spaces of Enslavement*, 119.

14. 1810 US Federal Census, s.v. Casper Colyer, Coxsackie, Greene, New York; roll 27, p. 292, image 00169, Family History Library, film 081381. Ancestry.com.

15. Sylvia Hasenkopf, "The Long Road to Freedom for Slaves in New York," *Porcupine Soup*, February 19, 2022, https://porcupinesoup.com/the-long-road-to-freedom-for-slaves-part-ii.

16. Indenture of Gin to Henry Demarest, October 16, 1807, Greene County New York Archives.

17. James Bennet, town clerk, notice in *Catskill Recorder*, February 23, 1808, 2, https://nyshistoricnewspapers.org/lccn/sn83031455/1808-02-23/ed-1/seq-2/.

18. Alexander Flick to Franklin Delano Roosevelt, March 30, 1931, Franklin D. Roosevelt Historical Manuscript Collection, 1636–1935, FDR Library, Hyde Park, NY.

19. Judy Jackson obituary, Digital Collection, African American Presence in the Hudson Valley, Historic Huguenot Street, New Paltz, New York. Part of the online exhibit "The Missing Chapter: Untold Stories of the African American Presence in the Mid-Hudson Valley," https://omeka.hrvh.org/exhibits/show/missing-chapter/people/j-jackson.

20. Coxsackie Town Record of Freeborn Slaves, 1800.

21. Indenture of Molly through Overseers of the Poor to John H. Cuyler, August 24, 1810, New Baltimore records, Vedder Research Library, Greene County Historical Society, Coxsackie, NY.

22. Sales receipt for Tom, Vedder Research Library, Greene County Historical Society, Coxsackie, NY. 63.3.195.

23. Indenture for Nan Bronk, September 14, 1816, Vedder Research Library, Greene County Historical Society, Coxsackie, NY.

24. Jonathan Daniel Wells, *The Kidnapping Club: Wall Street, Slavery, and Resistance on the Eve of the Civil War* (New York: Bold Type, 2020).

25. Nell Irvin Painter, *Sojourner Truth: A Life, A Symbol* (New York: Norton, 1996), 32–35.

26. Painter, *Sojourner Truth*, 23.

27. Coxsackie Town Record of Freeborn Slaves, 1800.

28. Collier family manuscripts, Vedder Research Library, Greene County Historical Society, Coxsackie, NY.

29. 1800 US Federal Census, s.v. John LaGrange, Bethlehem, Albany, New York; series M32, roll 22, p. 105, image 111, Family History Library, film 193710, Ancestry.com; 1810 US Federal Census, s.v. John C. Legrange [*sic*], Bethlehem, Albany, New York; roll 26, p. 101, image Nym 252_26–0053, Family History Library, roll 0181380, Ancestry.com.

30. Michael Groth, email to author, August 30, 2018.

31. Painter, *Sojourner Truth*, 66–68.

32. Advertisement, *Albany Gazette*, December 22, 1820, 4.

33. Vivienne L. Kruger, "Born to Run: The Slave Family in Early New York, 1626 to 1827." PhD diss., Columbia University, 1985, esp. chapter 13. Reproduced at http://newyorkslavery.blogspot.com/.

8. The Last Enslavers

1. *The Heritage of New Baltimore* (New York: New Baltimore Bicentennial Committee, 1976), 114.

2. Sylvia Hasenkopf, "The Long Road to Freedom for Slaves in North America," *Porcupine Soup*, February 11, 2022, https://porcupinesoup.com/the-long-road-to-freedom-for-slaves-in-north-america.

3. "An Act relative to slaves and servants," New York State Archives, New York Department of State, Bureau of Miscellaneous Records, Enrolled Acts of the State Legislature, series 13036–78, Laws of 1817, chapter 137, section 4, https://digitalcollections.archives.nysed. gov/index.php/Detail/objects/10817.

4. "Society of negroes unsettled," September 5, 1810, Elting, Roelof J. and Ezekiel, Family Papers (1703–1928), Historic Huguenot Street, https://cdm16694.contentdm.oclc.org/digital/collection/hhs/id/480.

5. Stessin-Cohn and Hurlburt-Biagini, *In Defiance*, 250.

6. 1820 US Federal Census, s.v. Abraham Van Buskirk, Athens, Greene, New York, p. 60, NARA roll M33_64, image 71. Ancestry.com.

7. Benjamin Joseph Klebaner, "American Manumission Laws and the Responsibility for Supporting Slaves," *Virginia Magazine of History and Biography* 63, no. 4 (1955): 443–53. https://www.jstor.org/stable/4246165.

8. Manumission records for Greene County, including Catskill, Coxsackie, and New Baltimore: Greene County Records, Catskill; Vedder Research Library, Coxsackie; New Baltimore town records, https://sites.rootsweb.com/~nygreen2/new_baltimore_town_records.htm.

9. Groth, *Slavery and Freedom*, chap. 3, "The Ordeal of Emancipation," Kindle loc. 1510.

10. Matthew Kirk and Hartgen Archeological Associates, "Elizabeth Ten Broeck," Albany County Historical Association newsletter, May 2017.

11. Greene County manumission records, Tracing Your Roots in Greene County website, https://www.tracingyourrootsgcny.com/early_greene_county_records.htm.

12. New York, U.S., Wills and Probate Records, 1659–1999; s.v. John G. Voogd, probate date: July 26, 1802, Greene, New York. Ancestry.com.

13. New York, U.S., Wills and Probate Records, 1659–1999; s.v. Hannah G. Voogd, probate date: September 15, 1806, Greene, New York. Ancestry.com.

14. Raymond Beecher, "Three Wills and Susannah Bronck," *Quarterly Journal, a Publication of the Greene County Historical Society* 1, no. 3 (Fall 1977): 1, 3, 10.

15. 1790 US Federal Census; s.v. Leonard Bronk, Coxsackie, Albany, New York; series M637, roll 6, p. 163, image 96, Family History Library, film 0568146. Ancestry.com.

16. Sale of Phillis to Susannah Bronk, Bronk Manuscripts, Vedder Research Library, Coxsackie, NY.

17. 1806 will of Susannah Bronk, Vedder Research Library.

18. Both documents, Bronck Family Manuscripts, Vedder Research Library.

19. Bronck Family Manuscripts, Vedder Research Library, BM 1815.12.

20. Lewis Lampman, "Leonard Bronk: First Judge of the Court of Common Pleas, Greene County, N.Y." Paper prepared at the request of the Greene County Bar Association, and read at their annual banquet in 1911. Vedder Research Library.

21. Sylvia Hasenkopf, "The Curious Roots of Cuff Smith," *Porcupine Soup*, July 18, 2022, https://porcupinesoup.com/the-curious-roots-of-cuff-smith.

22. Chandler B. Saint, *Venture Smith* (Torrington, CT: Beecher House Center for the Study of Equal Rights, 2018), 88.

23. "Official list of families living in Catskill village in 1817," transcribed from *Coxsackie Union News*, November 11, 1904, available on Tracing Your Roots in Greene County website, https://tracingyourrootsgcny.com/catskill_1817.htm.

24. Greene County manumission records.

25. Oral history, transcribed in Vanderzee file, Vedder Research Library.

26. Manumission records, Vedder Research Library.

27. 1820 US Federal Census, s.v. Coenrad T. Houghtaling, New Baltimore, Greene, New York, p. 69, NARA roll M33_64, image 80. Ancestry.com.

28. New Baltimore emancipation records, *Tracing Your Roots in Greene County* website, https://www.tracingyourrootsgcny.com/new_baltimore_town_records.htm.

29. *Reformed Church Coxsackie, N.Y. Baptismal Records, 1738–1899.*

30. William S. Pelletreau, "Coxsackie," *History of Greene County*, 248.

31. First Reformed Church of Coxsackie, "Church History," website, http://firstreformedcoxsackie.com/church_history.

32. Philip H. Smith, *General History of Dutchess County, 1609 to 1876* (Pawling, NY, 1877), 358–60.

33. Vedder, *Historic Catskill*, 80.

34. Jonathan Palmer, "Greene History Notes for Oct. 27, 2022," *Columbia-Greene Media*, last updated November 4, 2022, https://www.hudsonvalley360.com/opinion/columnists/greene-history-notes-for-oct-27-2022/article_a1d04282-d975-5e4f-88b2-5c686e1be63a.html.

35. Russell Shorto, *Revolution Song: A Story of American Freedom* (New York: Norton, 2018), 430.

36. Ilyon Woo, *Master Slave Husband Wife: An Epic Journey from Slavery to Freedom* (New York: Simon & Schuster, 2023), 206.

37. Frank A. Gallt, *Dear Old Greene County; Embracing Facts and Figures. Portraits and Sketches of Leading Men Who Will Live in Her History, Those at the Front To-day and Others Who Made Good in the Past* (Catskill, NY, 1915).

9. "Roots of Poison and Bitterness"

1. "Propriety of Conduct," *Freedom's Journal*, July 13, 1827, 71.

2. *Greene County Republican*, July 4, 1827, 1, available at New York State Historic Newspapers, https://nyshistoricnewspapers.org/lccn/sn83031457/1827-07-04/ed-1/seq-1/.

3. "The Brooklyn Celebration," *Freedom's Journal*, July 18, 1828, 134.

4. "Propriety of Conduct," *Freedom's Journal*, July 13, 1827, 71.

5. *Documents of the Assembly of the State of New York. Eighty-eighth Session—1865.* Vol. 6, nos. 100–112 (Albany: C. Wendell, 1865), 195.

6. "Record of Inmates, Greene County Poorhouse," Hannah Brandow, #348, Vedder Research Library, Greene County files 244–407, 1880–1884.

7. "School for Colored Children," quoted from *Catskill Recorder* in *Liberator* 2, no. 22, June 2, 1832, 88.

8. Jim Planck, "1833: Colonization vs. Abolition in Catskill; Barbers Robert Jackson and Martin Cross Lead Black Voice against Liberia," *Greene County History* 46 (Spring 2022): 3–5, 10–12.

9. Arnold Buffum, letter on travels for *Liberator*, October 5, 1833, 2.

10. Robert Jackson, letter to *Liberator*, November 2, 1833, 3.

11. P. Gabrielle Foreman, Sarah Patterson, and Jim Casey, Colored Conventions Project, introduction at https://coloredconventions.org/introduction-movement/.

12. Planck, "1833," 4.

13. Frederick Douglass to Sydney H. Gay, October 4, 1847, Frederick Douglass Papers, 256–59, available at https://www.google.com/books/edition/The_Frederick_Douglass_Papers/iD07x9v-CiEC?q=&gbpv=1&bsq=Douglass%20to%20Gay,%20Albany,%20October%201847.

14. "Proceedings of the State Convention of Colored People: held at Albany, New-York, on the 22nd, 23d and 24th of July 1851." In *The Proceedings of the Black State Conventions, 1840–1865*, vol. 1, ed. Philip S. Foner and George E. Walker (Albany, NY: Charles Van Benthuysen, 1979). Online at Colored Conventions Project: https://omeka.coloredconventions.org/items/show/235.

15. "Colored Men's State Convention of New York, September 4, 1855." Transcript in Foner and Walker, *Proceedings of the Black State Conventions*, vol. 1. Online at Colored Conventions Project: https://omeka.coloredconventions.org/items/show/238.

16. Martin Bruegel, *Farm, Shop, Landing: The Rise of a Market Society in the Hudson Valley, 1780–1860* (Durham, NC: Duke University Press, 2002), 211.

17. Fergus Bordewich, email to author, October 26, 2020.

18. Tom Calarco, *The Underground Railroad Conductor* (Schenectady, NY: Travels thru History, 2003), 35.

19. William J. Switala, *Underground Railroad in New York and New Jersey* (Mechanicsburg, PA: Stackpole, 2006), 99.

20. Paul Stewart, email to author, March 22, 2023.

21. *Heritage of New Baltimore*, 115–16.

22. Mark Lawrence Schrad, "The Forgotten History of Black Prohibitionism," Politico, February 6, 2021, https://www.politico.com/news/magazine/2021/02/06/forgotten-black-history-prohibition-temperance-movement-461215.

23. "The Colored Temperance Celebration," *New-York Tribune*, July 11, 1843.

24. "Temperance," *New-York Tribune*, November 25, 1843, 2.

25. "Delavan Temperance Celebration at Hudson, July 8th," *Poughkeepsie (NY) Journal*, July 12, 1845.

26. "Temperance Celebration of July 7th," *Poughkeepsie (NY) Journal*, July 11, 1846.

27. John L. Myers, "The Beginning of Anti-Slavery Agencies in New York State, 1833–1836," *New York History* 43, no. 2 (April 1962): 149–81.

28. P. Gould, "For the Friend of Man," *Friend of Man*, December 19, 1838, https://fom.library.cornell.edu/?a=d&d=TFOM18381219.1.2&e=-------en-20--1--txt-txIN-March+1838------.

29. Letters to *Friend of Man*, June 26, 1839, https://fom.library.cornell.edu/?a=d&d=TFOM18390626.2.13&e=-------en-20--1--txt-txIN-March+1838------.

30. Manisha Sinha, "Black Abolitionism," in *Slavery in New York*, ed. Ira Berlin and Leslie Harris (New York: New Press, 2005), 252–53.

31. Amy Godine, *The Black Woods: Pursuing Racial Justice on the Adirondack Frontier* (Ithaca, NY: Three Hills, 2023), 93.

32. Allynne Lange, "Hudson River Cargoes and Carriers," originally published in the *Pilot Log*, 1999, and transcribed for the Hudson River Maritime Museum blog, February 17, 2023, https://www.hrmm.org/history-blog/hudson-river-cargoes-and-carriers.

33. "Running Off with a Vessel," *Brooklyn Daily Eagle*, August 3, 1859, 3.

34. "Running Off with a Vessel," 3.

35. "Stealing a Sloop," *New-York Daily Tribune*, August 5, 1859, 7.

36. John Field, "The Exciting Pursuit on the North River," *New York Express*, November 15, 1859.

37. "Civil War Diary of Isaac Van Loan," in *Athens: Its People and Industry, 1776–1976* (Athens, NY: Athens Bicentennial Committee, 1976). All quotations in this passage are from this document.

38. Monroe Henry Van Valkenburgh, s.v., New York, U.S., Civil War Muster Roll Abstracts of New York State Volunteers, United States Sharpshooters, and United States Colored Troops, ca. 1861–1900, box 1207, New York State Archives, Albany, NY. Ancestry.com.

39. Monroe Henry Van Valkenburgh photograph, Tracing Your Roots in Greene County website, http://tracingyourrootsgcny.com/wpe510.jpg.

40. "Colored Soldiers from Coxsackie Who Fought in the Civil War," New Horizons Genealogical Services, https://www.newhorizonsgenealogicalservices.com/ny-genealogy/greene-county/greene_county_ny_colored_soldiers.htm.

41. Samuel Van Slyke, s.v., New York, U.S., Civil War Muster Roll Abstracts of New York State Volunteers, United States Sharpshooters, and United States Colored Troops, ca. 1861–1900, box 378, New York State Archives, Albany, NY. Ancestry.com.

42. Cato Vanderzee, 8th U.S. Colored Infantry, *Compiled Service Records of Volunteer Union Soldiers Who Served with the United States Colored Troops: Infantry Organizations, 8th through 13th, including the 11th (new), microfilm serial M1821, roll 18*, NARA, Washington, DC. Ancestry.com.

43. Ezra Bronk, 8th U.S. Colored Infantry, *Compiled Service Records of Volunteer Union Soldiers Who Served with the United States Colored Troops: Infantry Organizations, 8th through 13th, including the 11th (new), microfilm serial M1821, roll 2*, NARA, Washington, DC. Ancestry.com.

44. Sylvia Hasenkopf, "Martin B. Cross, Catskill Resident and Soldier in the 54th Massachusetts Infantry Regiment," *Porcupine Soup*, August 11, 2021, https://www.porcupinesoup.com/greene-countys-african-american-civil-war-soldiers.

45. Henry Bronk (1823–1864), s.v., 20th U.S. Colored Troops, New York, U.S., Civil War Muster Roll Abstracts of New York State Volunteers, United States Sharpshooters, and United States Colored Troops, ca. 1861–1900, box 376, New York State Archives, Albany, NY. Ancestry.com.

10. Confederates in the Family

1. LTJG Van Valkenburg, "Civil War Soldier—James Dunbar Van Valkenburg," *News Notes*, National Association of Van Valkenburg Family, Spring 2016, 2–4. All quotations in this passage come from this account.

2. SFC A. M. Drake, "Does anyone have any family members that served in the Civil War? Whats your history?" Rally Point, May 14, 2014, https://www.rallypoint.com/answers/does-anyone-have-any-family-members-that-served-in-the-civil-war-whats-your-history.

3. "On the Altar of the Confederacy," *Howling Dawg*, August 2018, http://nebula.wsimg.com/d078a0a832bb3205b898616da7a6c8e4?AccessKeyId=41F9E8FA858C01EDA184&disposition=0&alloworigin=1.

4. Emails between Wayne Dobson and author, June 22, 2022.

5. Sam Richards, *Sam Richards's Civil War Diary: A Chronicle of the Atlanta Home Front*, ed. Wendy Hamand Venet (Athens: University of Georgia Press, 2009), 11.

6. John A. Eisterhold, "Commercial, Financial, and Industrial Macon, Georgia, during the 1840's," *Georgia Historical Quarterly* 53, no. 4 (December 1969): 424–41, https://www.jstor.org/stable/40579013.

7. Sarah V. Richards Diary, vol. 1, April 1852–October 1853, box 4, folder 4, Richards Family Papers, ahc.MSS176, Kenan Research Center at the Atlanta History Center. All quotations in Sarah's account come from this document.

8. Richards, *Sam Richards's Civil War Diary*, 109.

9. Richards, *Sam Richards's Civil War Diary*, 19.

10. Sarah V. Richards Diary, vol. 1.

11. Richards, *Sam Richards's Civil War Diary*, 202.

12. 1860 US Federal Census—Slave Schedules, Mary E. Van Valkenburg, s.v., Eighth Census of the United States, series M653, Records of the Bureau of the Census, RG 29, NARA, Washington, DC. Ancestry.com.

13. 1860 US Federal Census—Slave Schedules, James Van Valkenburg, s.v., Eighth Census of the United States, series M653, Records of the Bureau of the Census, RG 29, NARA, Washington, DC. Ancestry.com.

14. Woo, *Master Slave Husband Wife.*

15. Richards, *Sam Richards's Civil War Diary*, 30.

16. 1850 U.S. Federal Census—Slave Schedules, Bryant Bradley, s.v., Seventh Census of the United States, series M432, Records of the Bureau of the Census, RG 29, NARA, Washington, DC. Ancestry.com.

17. Author visit to Monocacy National Battlefield Archives, Frederick, Maryland, April 2, 2022.

18. Gresham, *War Outside My Window*, 173, 222–23.

19. Micah Johnston and Caleb Slinkard, "Crews Begin Moving Two Confederate Monuments in Macon after Years of Legal Battles," Georgia Public Broadcasting, June 22, 2022, https://www.gpb.org/news/2022/06/22/crews-begin-moving-two-confederate-monuments-in-macon-after-years-of-legal-battles.

20. Email from Dobson, May 29, 2023.

21. G. W. Nichols, *A Soldier's Story of His Regiment (61st Georgia)* (CreateSpace Independent Publishing Platform, 2012), 171.

22. "A Gallant Achievement," copy of a letter from James D. Van Valkenburgh to his wife, *Macon Telegraph*, June 1, 1864, 2.

23. Nichols, *Soldier's Story*, 144.

24. Glenn H. Worthington, *Fighting for Time: The Battle of Monocacy* (Baltimore: Day Printing, 1932; 2nd ed. rev. Brian C. Pohanka, Shippensburg, PA: White Mane, 1985), 132.

25. Nichols, *Soldier's Story*, 171.

26. Venet, *Sam Richards's Civil War Diary*, 176–77, 30.

27. Venet, *Sam Richards's Civil War Diary*, 23, quotations on 267, 269.

28. Monroe H. Van Valkenburgh (1835–1861), Eightieth Infantry, New York, U.S., Registers of Officers and Enlisted Men Mustered into Federal Service, 1861–1865, New York State Archives, Albany, New York, series A0389, vol. 6 (Volunteers Who Have Died While in Service). Ancestry.com.

29. US Soldiers' and Airmen's Home National Cemetery, on Arlington National Cemetery website: https://www.arlingtoncemetery.mil/Explore/Soldiers-and-Airmens-Home-National-Cemetery.

30. Ernest B. Furgurson, *Ashes of Glory: Richmond at War* (New York: Knopf, 1997), 338.

31. Nichols, *Soldier's Story*, 28.

11. Vanderzee by Vanderzee, Filling in the Puzzle

1. Cato Vanderzee, "Colored Boatman," 13 Dominick, Trow's New York City Directory, 1867–68, U.S. City Directories, 1822–1995. Ancestry.com.

2. Cato Vanderzee, Cypress Hills National Cemetery, Brooklyn, NY, US National Cemetery Interment Control Forms, 1928–1962. Ancestry.com.

3. New York State Census 1855, Jonas Collier, s.v., Coxsackie, Greene, New York, New York State Archives, Albany, New York. Ancestry.com.

4. US Federal Census, Casper J. Collier, s.v., Coxsackie, Greene, New York, roll M593_940, page 185A, Family History Library, film 552439. Ancestry.com.

5. Sandy VanDerzee, email to author, June 1, 2021.

6. Cynthia Brott Biasca, *Descendants of Albert and Arent Andriessen Bradt* (Wolfe City, TX: Henington, 1990).

7. *Heritage of New Baltimore*, 17–18.

8. Clesson S. Bush, *Episodes from a Hudson River Town: New Baltimore, New York* (Albany: State University of New York Press, 2011), 99.

9. "New Baltimore's Centenarian," *Coeymans Herald*, June 4, 1902.

10. "Last will and testament of John Vanderzee of the town of New Baltimore, County of Greene and State of New York," Vanderzee family archives, Vedder Research Library, Coxsackie, NY.

11. 1850 US Federal Census, Cesar Van Bergen, s.v., New Baltimore, Greene, New York, series M432, roll 509, p. 191a, Records of the Bureau of the Census, RG 29, NARA, Washington, DC; New York State Census 1855, Cesar Vanderzee, s.v., New Baltimore, Greene, New York, New York State Archives, Albany, New York. Both on Ancestry.com.

12. Coxsackie Reformed Church, baptismal records.

13. We haven't found the marriage records of Sarah and Thomas Van Allen, but John Vanderzee mentions "my daughter Sarah Van Allen" in his 1860 will.

14. Peter Hess, "The Albany Museum: Curiosities, Circus, and Performing Arts," *New York Almanack*, July 4, 2022, https://www.newyorkalmanack.com/2022/07/albany-museum/.

15. "Extraordinary," reprint from the *Coxsackie Standard* in *Albany Argus*, June 9, 1837, 3.

16. "An Albino at the Museum," *Albany Argus*, June 23, 1837, 2.

17. "The Coxsackie Albino," *United States Gazette* (Philadelphia), July 1, 1837, 1.

18. "A Negro Blonde," *Albany Argus*, June 23, 1837, 1

19. 1860 U.S. Federal Census, Sylvanus v Allen, s.v., Coxsackie, Greene, New York, series M653, roll M653_758, p. 497, Family History Library, film 803758, Records of the Bureau of the Census, RG 29, NARA, Washington DC. Ancestry.com.

20. *Hudson Evening Register*, January 31, 1874.

21. *Hudson New York Evening Register*, November 30, 1877.

22. *Catskill Recorder*, February 3, 1893, 3.

23. "Sudden Death," *Kingston Daily Freeman*, September 1, 1874, 1.

24. "Van Der Zee Clan Reunion Held," *Kingston Daily Freeman*, Sept. 7, 1937.

25. "'Round About the County," *Catskill Recorder*, October 6, 1911.

26. "Van Der Zee Family Had Picnic Labor Day," *Kingston Daily Freeman*, September 9, 1948.

27. Jim Haskins, *James Van Derzee: The Picture Takin' Man* (Trenton, NJ: Africa World Press, 1991).

28. Paula J. Massoud, *Making a Promised Land: Harlem in 20th-Century Photography and Film* (New Brunswick, NJ: Rutgers University Press, 2013), 39.

29. Haskins, *James Van Derzee*, 245.

30. Kate Abbott, "Jane Louise Van Der Zee: One of the First Black Women Filmmakers in the Country," *Berkshire Eagle*, March 29, 2019, https://www.berkshireeagle.com/history/jane-louise-van-der-zee-one-of-the-first-black-woman-filmmakers-in-the-country/article_730ca680-cb2a-52c7-8896-b1b5c8940112.html.

31. "We Are Doing Our Bit," Massachusetts Historical Society Collections Online, https://www.masshist.org/database/viewer.php?item_id=3050&pid=3.

32. Visit by author, August 13, 2021.

33. Haskins, *James Van Derzee*, 21.

34. "New Baltimore," *Coeymans Herald*, February 13, 1895, 2.

35. *Heritage of New Baltimore*, 115.

36. Cornelia Read, email to author, July 23, 2020. All quotations from Cornelia in this passage are from this email.

37. "Adams-Douglass-Vanderzee-McWilliams Families," Nebraska State Historical Society Finding Aid RG5440 AM, https://history.nebraska.gov/collection_section/adams-douglass-vanderzee-mcwilliams-families-rg5440-am/.

38. Cheryl Rollins, conversation with author, August 17, 2020.

39. "Historically Black," *Washington Post*, June 17, 2016, https://historicallyblack.tumblr.com/post/146071243636/van-der-zee-family-wedding-rings-kingston-new.

40. Kitt Potter, email to author, May 24, 2021.

12. What Remains

1. Joseph E. Diamond. "Owned in Life, Owned in Death: The Pine Street African and African-American Burial Ground in Kingston, New York," *Northeast Historical Archaeology* 35, no. 1, article 22 (2006), http://digitalcommons.buffalostate.edu/neha/vol35/iss1/22. All quotations from Diamond are from this article.

2. "African-American History Project," Old Dutch Church.

3. Kitt Potter, interview with author, March 14, 2022.

4. Elsworth Potter, s.v., New York, U.S., Civil War Muster Roll Abstracts, 1861–1900, New York State Archives, Albany, New York; Civil War Muster Roll Abstracts of New York State Volunteers, United States Sharpshooters, and United States Colored Troops, box 378. Ancestry.com.

5. Paul Kirby, "Descendants of Slaves, Slave Owner to Meet in Kingston," *Kingston Daily Freeman*, March 12, 2022, https://www.dailyfreeman.com/2022/03/12/descendants-of-slave-slave-owner-to-meet-in-kingston/.

6. "Uncovering History—DeWitt Family Historical Society," video posted on Facebook, January 7, 2021, https://www.facebook.com/watch/?v=761266418081404.

7. "Re-Dedication Ceremony of the Mt. Zion African-American Burial Ground in Kingston, NY in June 2011," Kingstoncitizens.org, May 2011, https://www.kingstoncitizens.org/2011/05/re-dedication-ceremony-of-the-mt-zion-african-american-burial-ground-in-kingston-ny-in-june-2011/.

8. William G. Pomeroy Foundation historic marker, "AME Mount Zion Cemetery," https://www.wgpfoundation.org/historic-markers/ame-mount-zion-cemetery/.

9. Robert Sweeney, interview with author, August 5, 2022.

10. Taylor Bruck, email to author, April 6, 2022.

11. "Balthus," Matthewis Persen House Phase 2 Downstairs, Ulster County Archives, accessed January 2, 2024, https://clerk.ulstercountyny.gov/archives/persen-house/phase2down.

12. Video from Old Dutch Church, August 11, 2022, Facebook, https://www.facebook.com/watch/live/?ref=watch_permalink&v=813893709980180.

13. John Camera, "Once Forgotten, Remains of Enslaved People Reburied in Kingston," *Spectrum News*, August 9, 2023, https://spectrumlocalnews.com/nys/hudson-valley/human-interest/2023/08/09/kingston-african-burial-ground-reburial-ceremony.

14. Patricia R. Doxsey, "New State Park in Kingston, Town of Ulster Named after Sojourner Truth," *Kingston Daily Freeman*, February 28, 2022, https://www.dailyfreeman.com/2022/02/28/new-state-park-in-kingston-town-of-ulster-named-after-sojourner-truth.

15. Historical Marker Database, "Sojourner Truth, 1797–1883," at Martinus Schryver's tavern, https://www.hmdb.org/m.asp?m=127589.

16. William G. Pomeroy Foundation, "Steamboat Disaster," https://www.wgpfounda tion.org/historic-markers/22621-2/.

17. Sylvia Hasenkopf, "The Hallenbecks of Greene County," *Porcupine Soup*, November 4, 2021, https://porcupinesoup.com/the-hallenbecks-of-greene-county.

18. The Bronck House and Barns, Greene County Historical Society, https://www.gchis tory.org/bronck-houses-barns.

19. Tour with Shelby Mattice, September 14, 2022.

20. Peter Van Vechten. *The Genealogical Records of the Van Vechten's From 1638 to 1896*. Milwaukee, WI.: Radtke Bros & Kortsch, 1896. 10–13.

21. Brace, "Catskill," *History of Greene County*, 91–92.

22. Vedder, *Historic Catskill*, 42.

23. *New Paltz (NY) Times*, May 6, 1864, 16.

24. Jesse Nason, "New Paltz Considers Proposal to Rediscover Its Black Cemetery," *Poughkeepsie (NY) Journal*, August 22, 1999, B1.

25. Frances Marion Platt, "Long-closed New Paltz Burial Ground Welcomes Remains of a Huguenot Street Slave," *Hudson Valley One*, April 1, 2016, https://hudsonvalleyone. com/2013/11/15/long-closed-new-paltz-burial-ground-welcomes-remains-of-a-huguenot- street-slave/.

26. Meg Pier, "Jacob Gelt Dekker on the Kura Hulanda Museum Curaçao," *People Are Culture* (blog), last updated October 13, 2023, https://www.peoplearuculture.com/blog/ jacob-gelt-dekker/.

27. Mikve Israel-Emanuel Synagogue website, https://snoa.com/about-us/.

28. Museo Tula, Facebook page, https://www.facebook.com/profile.php?id=100066949 670470.

29. Dive Curaçao, "The Kenepa Plantation—Where History Merges with Nature," https:// www.divecuracao.info/blog/sustainable-dive-tourism-in-curacao/the-kenepa-plantation- where-history-merges-with-nature/.

30. "Prime Minister Curaçao: Dutch Apology for Slavery Past Must Focus on Shared Future within the Kingdom," *Curaçao Chronicle*, November 7, 2022, https://www.curacao chronicle.com/post/local/prime-minister-curacao-dutch-apology-for-slavery-past-must-focus- on-shared-future-within-the-kingdom/.

31. Andrea Mosterman, "The Slave Ship Gideon and the African Captives It Transported to New Netherland," New Netherland Institute, https://www.newnetherlandinstitute.org/ research/new-stories-from-new-research-on-new-netherland-and-the-dutch-atlantic/the-slave- ship-gideon-and-the-african-captives-it-transported-to-new-netherland-by-andrea-mosterman/.

13. Repair

1. Historic Hudson Valley, Philipsburg Manor, Sleepy Hollow, New York, https://hud sonvalley.org/historic-sites/philipsburg-manor/.

2. Phone interview with Michael Lord, January 14, 2022.

3. Steve Hughes, "Sheehan Orders Albany City Hall's Schuyler Statue Removed," *Times Union* (Albany, NY), June 11, 2020, https://www.timesunion.com/news/article/Sheehan- orders-Schuyler-statue-removed-15333701.php.

4. Shaniece Holmes-Brown, "First Nonbinary Tulip Queen Crowned at Annual Albany festival," *Times Union*, May 7, 2022, https://www.timesunion.com/news/article/Sam-Mills- crowned-2022-Tulip-Queen-17156466.php.

5. WRGB, "Olivia Owens Is Crowned 2023 Tulip Queen," https://cbs6albany.com/ news/local/olivia-owens-is-crowned-2023-tulip-queen.

6. Stefan Bielinski, "Philip Schuyler," exhibitions, New York State Museum, https://exhibitions.nysm.nysed.gov/albany/bios/s/phschuyler1750.html.

7. Heidi Hill, phone interview with author, May 3, 2023; in-person interview with author, May 14, 2023.

8. Pamela D. Jenkins, "New DNA Evidence Reveals the Origin of Captain Samuel Schuyler's Surname," Friends of Schuyler Mansion newsletter, Winter 2022.

9. Celebrating the African Spirit website, https://celebratingtheafricanspirit.org/; Mid-Hudson Anti-Slavery Project (blog), https://pages.vassar.edu/mhantislaveryhistoryproject/; African Heritage Studies Dutchess County Historical Society website, https://dchsny.org/topics-african-heritage/; African American Archive of Columbia County website, https://www.afamarchivecc.org/.

10. Witness Stones Project website, https://witnessstonesproject.org/.

11. Thomas Cole National Historical Site, "2023 Cole Fellows Research Presentation," April 16, 2023, available at https://www.youtube.com/watch?v=uZwN-vOy0kw.

12. Thomas Cole National Historical Site, "Enslavement History of the Property," https://thomascole.org/enslavement/.

13. Sofia Thieu D'Amico, "To Obscure and to Equalize: Josephus Thomson, Black Life and Unacknowledged Labor in the Hudson Valley," courtesy of Thomas Cole National Historic Site, Cole Fellow Report, May 27, 2023, 26.

14. Gethen Proper, phone interview with author, March 25, 2021. All quotations from Gethen are from this conversation.

15. Beth George, phone interview with author, May 31, 2023. All quotations from Beth are from this conversation.

16. Repentance Project, "An American Lent Devotional," https://www.repentanceproject.org.

17. Julianne McShane, "The Stealth Sticker Campaign to Expose New York's History of Slavery," New York Times, May 7, 2021, https://www.nytimes.com/2021/05/07/nyregion/slavery-nyc.html.

18. Dionne Ford, Go Back and Get It: A Memoir of Race, Inheritance, and Intergenerational Healing (New York: Bold Type, 2023), 133.

19. Cragsmoor Historical Society, Where Slavery Died Hard: The Forgotten History of Ulster County and the Shawangunk Mountain Region, documentary by Wendy Harris, 2022, available at https://www.cragsmoorhistoricalsociety.com/slavery-film.

20. Eleanor Mire, conversation with author, May 15, 2023. All quotations in this passage are from this conversation.

21. "Assaults by Negro Fiends," Buffalo (NY) Times, July 15, 1903, 10.

22. "Deputy Sheriff Stole Prisoner Away from Mob," Buffalo (NY) News, July 15, 1903, 7.

23. "Father of the Child Drew a Revolver When Boat Arrived with the Prisoner," Buffalo (NY) Times, July 15, 1903, 10.

24. "Catskill Negro Gets Twenty Years," Post-Star (Glens Falls, NY), November 13, 1903. 5.

25. Pelletreau, "Athens," History of Greene County, 193–94; Bicentennial Walking Tour of Athens, 2003, https://sites.rootsweb.com/~nygreen2/bicentennial_walking_tour_of_athesn_2003.htm.

26. Pelletreau, "Athens," 194.

27. Abraham Vanbuskirk, s.v., Record of Wills, 1665–1916; Index to Wills, 116–1923 (New York County); Surrogates Court, New York, New York. Probated February 15, 1826. Ancestry.com.

28. Painter, Sojourner Truth, 24.

29. Delber W. Clark, "History and Genealogy Notes, C1700–1938 Greene County, NY Volume II, M–Z," unpublished book from notes 1932–38, transcribed by Charles E. Coner, 1989–90, Vedder Research Library, Coxsackie, NY, 886. These notes were taken from a "variety of Greene County newspapers," Clark wrote.

30. *Coxsackie Union*, March 19, 1920.

31. Mark Twain, *Life on the Mississippi*, from chap. 9, "Continued Perplexities," ebook available at Project Gutenberg, https://www.gutenberg.org/files/245/245-h/245-h.htm.

BIBLIOGRAPHY

Primary Sources

Colden, Cadwallader. *The Letters and Papers of Cadwallader Colden . . . 1711–[1775]*. New York: New-York Historical Society, 1918.

Coventry, Alexander, 1766–1831. *Memoirs of an Emigrant: The Journal of Alexander Coventry, M.D.; in Scotland, the United States and Canada during the Period 1783–1831*. The Institute, 1978. New York State Library and Manuscripts and Special Collections.

Coxsackie Town Record of Free Born Slaves, 1800. Franklin D. Roosevelt Historical Manuscript Collection, 1636–1935, FDR Library, Hyde Park, NY.

Dillon, Lucy. *Memoirs of Madame de la Tour Du Pin*. London: Century, 1969.

Donnan, Elizabeth, and Carnegie Institution of Washington Department of Archaeology. *Documents Illustrative of the History of the Slave Trade to America*. Washington, DC: Carnegie Institution of Washington, 1930.

Douglass, Frederick. *The Frederick Douglass Papers*. Edited by John W. Blassingame and John R. McKivigan. New Haven, CT: Yale University Press, 1985.

——. *My Bondage and My Freedom*. 1855. Project Gutenberg, 2023. http://public.ebookcentral.proquest.com/choice/publicfullrecord.aspx?p=3314416.

Gehring, Charles T., trans. and ed. *Curacao Papers, 1640–1665*. Albany: The New Netherland Research Center and the New Netherland Institute, 2011.

Gordon, John. *Reminiscences of the Civil War*. First Rate Publishers, 2022.

Grant, Anne. *Memoirs of an American Lady: With Sketches of Manners and Scenery in America, As They Existed Previous to the Revolution*. Carlisle, MA: Applewood, 2007.

Gresham, Leroy Wiley. *The War Outside My Window: The Civil War Diary of LeRoy Wiley Gresham, 1860–1865*. Edited by Janet Elizabeth Croon. El Dorado Hills, CA: Savas Beatie LLC, 2018.

Lincoln, Charles Z., A. Judd Northrup, and William H. Johnson. *The Colonial Laws of New York from the Year 1664 to the Revolution*. New York: J. B. Lyon, 1894.

Nicols, Private G. W. *A Soldier's Story of His Regiment (61st Georgia)*. CreateSpace Independent Publishing Platform, 2012.

Reformed Church Coxsackie, N.Y. Baptismal Records, 1738–1899. Transcribed and indexed by Arthur C. M. Kelly, 1976, Vedder Research Library, Coxsackie, NY.

Richards, Sarah V. Diary. Vol. 1, April 1852–October 1853, box 4, folder 4. Richards Family Papers, ahc.MSS176. Kenan Research Center at the Atlanta History Center. https://dlg.galileo.usg.edu/turningpoint/ahc/cw/pdfs/ahc0176-004-004.pdf.

Smith, Philip H. *General History of Duchess County, 1609 to 1876*. Pawling, NY, 1877.

Strickland, William. *Journal of a Tour in the United States of America, 1794–1795*. New York: New-York Historical Society, 1971.

Van Laer, A. J. F., trans. and ed. *Minutes of the Court of Albany, Rensselaerswyck and Schenectady 1668–1673*. Vol. 1. Albany: University of the State of New York, 1926.

——, trans. and ed. *Minutes of the Court of Albany, Rensselaerswyck and Schenectady 1675–1680*. Vol. 2. Albany: University of the State of New York, 1928.

——, trans. and ed. *Minutes of the Court of Albany, Rensselaerswyck and Schenectady 1680–1685*. Vol. 3. Albany: University of the State of New York, 1932.

——, trans. and ed. *Minutes of the Court of Fort Orange and Beverwyck 1657–1660*. Vol. 2. Albany: University of the State of New York, 1923.

——, trans. and ed. *Van Rensselaer Bowier Manuscripts*. Albany: University of the State of New York, 1908.

Venet, Wendy Hamand, ed. *Sam Richards's Civil War Diary: A Chronicle of the Atlanta Home Front*. Athens: University of Georgia Press, 2009.

Wheeler, Peter. *Chains and Freedom, or The Life and Adventures of Peter Wheeler*. Tuscaloosa: University of Alabama Press, 2009.

Secondary Sources

Alcott, Louisa May. *Little Women*. Melbourne: Penguin Books, 1953.

Athens: Its People and Industry, 1776–1976. Athens, NY: Athens Bicentennial Committee, 1976.

Ball, Edward. *Slaves in the Family*. New York: Farrar, Straus & Giroux, 1998.

Beecher, Raymond. "Honoré Chaurand's Friendship's Asylum." *Greene County Historical Journal* 10, no. 3 (Fall 1986): 26–29.

——. *Under Three Flags: A Hudson River History*. Hensonville, NY: Black Dome Press, 1991.

——. "Three Wills and Susannah Bronck." *Quarterly Journal, a Publication of the Greene County Historical Society* 1, no. 3 (Fall 1977): 1, 3, 10.

——. "A Van Bergen Legacy." *Greene County Historical Journal* 12, no. 4 (Winter 1988): 38–40.

Berkenmeyer, Wilhelm Christoph. *The Albany Protocol: Wilhelm Christoph Berkenmeyer's Chronicle of Lutheran Affairs in New York Colony, 1731–1750*. With an introduction by John P. Dern. Available at New York State Library, Albany.

Berlin, Ira. *Many Thousands Gone: The First Two Centuries of Slavery in North America*. Cambridge, MA: Belknap Press of Harvard University Press, 1998.

Berlin, Ira, and Leslie Harris, eds. *Slavery in New York*. New York: New Press, 2005.

Berry, Wendell. *The Hidden Wound*. San Francisco: North Point, 1989.

Biasca, Cynthia Brott. *Descendants of Albert and Arent Andriessen Bradt*. Wolfe City, TX: Henington, 1990.

Blight, David W. *Race and Reunion: The Civil War in American Memory*. Cambridge, MA: Belknap Press of Harvard University Press, 2001.

——. *A Slave No More: Two Men Who Escaped to Freedom*. Orlando: Harcourt, 2007.

Boles, James M. *When There Were Poor Houses: Early Care in Rural New York, 1808–1950*. Buffalo, NY: Museum of Disability History, 2012.

Brooke, John L. *Columbia Rising: Civil Life on the Upper Hudson from the Revolution to the Age of Jackson*. Chapel Hill: University of North Carolina Press, 2010.

Brookhiser, Richard. *Gentleman Revolutionary: Gouverneur Morris—The Rake Who Wrote the Constitution*. New York: Free Press, 2003.

Bruegel, Martin. *Farm, Shop, Landing: The Rise of a Market Society in the Hudson Valley, 1780–1860*. Durham, NC: Duke University Press, 2002.

Burke, Thomas E., Jr. *Mohawk Frontier: The Dutch Community of Schenectady, New York, 1661–1710*. 2nd ed. Albany: State University of New York Press, 1991.

Bush, Clesson S. *Episodes from a Hudson River Town: New Baltimore, New York*. Albany: State University of New York Press, 2011.

Calarco, Tom. *The Search for the Underground Railroad in Upstate New York*. Charleston, SC: History Press, 2014.

——. *The Underground Railroad Conductor*. Schenectady, NY: Travels thru History, 2003.

Collier, Edward Augustus. *A History of Old Kinderhook from Aboriginal Days to the Present Time*. New York: G. P. Putnam's Sons, 1914.

Cooper, James Fenimore. *Satanstoe; or, the Littlepage Manuscripts. A Tale of the Colony*. New York: Burgess, Stringer, 1845.

Davis, David Brion. *The Problem of Slavery in the Age of Revolution, 1770–1823*. New York: Oxford University Press, 1999.

DeWolf, Thomas Norman. *Inheriting the Trade: A Northern Family Confronts Its Legacy as the Largest Slave-Trading Dynasty in U.S. History*. Boston: Beacon, 2008.

Dewulf, Jeroen. *The Pinkster King and the King of Kongo: The Forgotten History of America's Dutch-owned Slaves*. Jackson: University Press of Mississippi, 2017.

Dray, Philip. *A Lynching at Port Jervis: Race and Reckoning in the Gilded Age*. New York: Farrar, Straus & Giroux, 2022.

Edmonds, Walter D. *Drums along the Mohawk*. New York: Random House, 1936.

Egerton, Douglas R. *Death or Liberty: African Americans and Revolutionary America*. Oxford: Oxford University Press, 2009.

Farrow, Anne. *The Logbooks: Connecticut's Slave Ships and Human Memory*. Middletown, CT: Wesleyan University Press, 2014.

Farrow, Anne, Joel Lang, and Jenifer Frank. *Complicity: How the North Promoted, Prolonged, and Profited from Slavery*. New York: Ballantine, 2006.

"Fenimore Cooper's Defense of Slave-Owning America." *American Historical Review* 35, no. 3 (April 1930): 575–82. https://www.jstor.org/stable/1838423.

Fischer, David Hackett. *Albion's Seed: Four British Folkways in America*. New York: Oxford University Press, 1989.

Foner, Eric. *Gateway to Freedom: The Hidden History of the Underground Railroad*. New York: Norton, 2015.

——. *The Story of American Freedom*. New York: Norton, 1998.

Ford, Dionne. *Go Back and Get It: A Memoir of Race, Inheritance, and Intergenerational Healing*. New York: Bold Type, 2023.

Furgurson, Ernest B. *Ashes of Glory: Richmond at War*. New York: Knopf, 1997.

Gallt, Frank A. *Dear Old Greene County; Embracing Facts and Figures. Portraits and Sketches of Leading Men Who Will Live in Her History, Those at the Front To-day and Others Who Made Good in the Past*. Catskill, NY, 1915. https://www.loc.gov/item/74172884/.

Gebhard, Elizabeth L. *The Parsonage between Two Manors: Annals of Clover-Reach*. Hudson, NY: Bryan Printing Company, 1910.

Gellman, David N. *Emancipating New York: The Politics of Slavery and Freedom, 1777–1827*. Baton Rouge: Louisiana State University Press, 2006.

——. *Liberty's Chain: Slavery, Abolition, and the Jay Family of New York*. Ithaca, NY: Three Hills, 2022.

Gerlach, Don R. "Black Arson in Albany, New York: November 1793." *Journal of Black Studies* 7, no. 3 (March 1977).

Gibbons, Kristin Lunde. "The Van Bergen Overmantel: A Thesis." Master's thesis, State University of New York College at Oneonta, 1966.

Godine, Amy. *The Black Woods: Pursuing Racial Justice on the Adirondack Frontier*. Ithaca, NY: Three Hills, 2023.

Goodfriend, Joyce D. *Before the Melting Pot: Society and Culture in Colonial New York City, 1664–1730*. Princeton, NJ: Princeton University Press, 1992.

——. *Who Should Rule at Home? Confronting the Elite in British New York City*. Ithaca, NY: Cornell University Press, 2017.

Gordon-Reed, Annette. *The Hemingses of Monticello: An American Family*. New York: Norton, 2008.

Grimes, Adam. "A Local Vision: Land, Landscape, and Labor in the Van Bergen Overmantel." Master's thesis, University of Delaware, Spring 2020.

Groth, Michael E. *Slavery and Freedom in the Mid-Hudson Valley*. Albany: State University of New York Press, 2017. Kindle ed.

Haley, Alex. *Roots: The Saga of an American Family*. New York: Doubleday, 1976.

Harris, John. *The Last Slave Ships: New York and the End of the Middle Passage*. New Haven, CT: Yale University Press, 2020.

Hasenkopf, Sylvia. *Tracing Your Roots in Greene County: The First Fifty Articles*. North River Research, 2012.

——. *Tracing Your Roots in Greene County.* Vol. 2. North River Research, 2014.

Haskins, Jim. *James Van Derzee: The Picture Takin' Man.* Trenton, NJ: Africa World Press, 1991.

The Heritage of New Baltimore. New York: New Baltimore Bicentennial Committee, 1976.

History of Greene County, New York: With Biographical Sketches of Its Prominent Men. New York: J. B. Beers, 1884.

Hodges, Graham Russell. "The Pastor and the Prostitute." In *Sex, Love, Race: Crossing Boundaries in North American History,* edited by Martha Hodes, 60–71. New York: New York University Press, 1999.

——. *Root and Branch: African Americans in New York and East Jersey, 1613–1863.* Chapel Hill: University of North Carolina Press, 1999.

Hondius, Dienke, Nancy Jouwe, Dineke Stam, and Jennifer Tosch. *Dutch New York Histories: Connecting African, Native American and Slavery Heritage.* Volendam, Netherlands: LM Publishers, 2017.

Horton, James Oliver, and Lois E. Horton. *In Hope of Liberty: Culture, Community and Protest among Northern Free Blacks, 1700–1860.* New York: Oxford University Press, 1997.

Humphreys, Mary Gay. *Catherine Schuyler.* New York: Charles Scribner's Sons, 1897.

Irving, Washington. *The Legend of Sleepy Hollow.* Rockville, MD: Wildside, 2004.

——. *Tales of a Traveler.* 1824. Project Gutenberg, 2004. https://www.gutenberg.org/files/13514/13514-h/13514-h.htm#chap24.

Jasanoff, Maya. *Liberty's Exiles: American Loyalists in the Revolutionary World.* New York: Knopf, 2011.

Johnston, James H. *From Slave Ship to Harvard: Yarrow Mamout and the History of an African American Family.* New York: Fordham University Press, 2012.

Jones, Brian Jay. *Washington Irving: An American Original.* New York: Arcade, 2008.

Jones-Rogers, Stephanie E. *They Were Her Property: White Women as Slave Owners in the American South.* New Haven, CT: Yale University Press, 2019.

Kaminski, John P. *A Necessary Evil? Slavery and the Debate over the Constitution.* Madison, WI: Madison House, 1995.

Kirk, Matthew, and Hartgen Archeological Associates. "Elizabeth Ten Broeck." Albany County Historical Association newsletter, May 2017.

Klebaner, Benjamin Joseph. "American Manumission Laws and the Responsibility for Supporting Slaves." *Virginia Magazine of History and Biography* 63, no. 4 (1955): 443–53. https://www.jstor.org/stable/4246165.

Kruger, Vivienne L. "Born to Run: The Slave Family in Early New York, 1626 to 1827." PhD diss., Columbia University, 1985. Reproduced at http://newyorkslavery.blogspot.com/.

Lampman, Rev. Lewis. "Leonard Bronk: First Judge of the Court of Common Pleas, Greene County, N.Y." Paper prepared at the request of the Greene County Bar Association, and read at their annual banquet in 1911. Vedder Research Library, Coxsackie, NY.

Lanning, Michael Lee. *African Americans in the Revolutionary War.* New York: Citadel, 2000.

Lepore, Jill. *New York Burning: Liberty, Slavery, and Conspiracy in Eighteenth-Century Manhattan*. New York: Vintage, 2006.

Lewis, Tom. *The Hudson: A History*. New Haven, CT: Yale University Press, 2005.

Littlefield, Daniel. "John Jay, the Revolutionary Generation, and Slavery." *New York History* 81, no. 1 (2000): 98. https://www.jstor.org/stable/23181809.

Maika, Dennis J. " 'To experiment with a parcel of negroes': Incentive, Collaboration, and Competition in New Amsterdam's Slave Trade." *Journal of Early American History* 10 (2020): 33–69.

Maskiell, Nicole Safford. *Bound by Bondage: Slavery and the Creation of a Northern Gentry*. Ithaca, NY: Cornell University Press, 2022.

Massood, Paula J. *Making a Promised Land: Harlem in 20th-Century Photography and Film*. New Brunswick, NJ: Rutgers University Press, 2013.

McDaniel, Donna, and Vanessa Julye. *Fit for Freedom, Not for Friendship: Quakers, African Americans, and the Myth of Racial Justice*. Philadelphia: Quaker Press of Friends General Conference, 2009.

McManus, Edgar J. *A History of Negro Slavery in New York*. Syracuse, NY: Syracuse University Press, 1966.

Melish, Joanne Pope. *Disowning Slavery: Gradual Emancipation and "Race" in New England, 1780–1860*. Ithaca, NY: Cornell University Press, 2000.

Merwick, Donna. *Death of a Notary: Conquest and Change in Colonial New York*. Ithaca, NY: Cornell University Press, 1999.

Morrison, Toni. *A Mercy*. New York: Knopf, 2008.

Mosterman, Andrea. "The Slave Ship Gideon and the African Captives It Transported to New Netherland." New Netherland Institute. https://www.newnetherlandinstitute. org/research/new-stories-from-new-research-on-new-netherland-and-the-dutch-atlan tic/the-slave-ship-gideon-and-the-african-captives-it-transported-to-new-netherland-by-andrea-mosterman/.

——. *Spaces of Enslavement: A History of Slavery and Resistance in Dutch New York*. Ithaca, NY: Cornell University Press, 2021.

Murdoch, David. *The Dutch Dominie of the Catskills; or the Times of the "Bloody Brandt."* New York: Derby & Jackson, 1861. Kindle ed., Miami: HardPress Publishing, 2014.

Myers, John L. "The Beginning of Anti-Slavery Agencies in New York State, 1833–1836." *New York History* 43, no. 2 (April 1962): 149–81.

New York Genealogical and Biographical Society. "Baptismal Records of Zion Lutheran Church, Loonenburg, now Athens, Greene County, New York." *New York Genealogical and Biographical Record* 82, no. 1 (January 1951): 15.

Painter, Nell Irvin. *Sojourner Truth: A Life, a Symbol*. New York: Norton, 1996.

Panetta, Roger, ed. *Dutch New York: The Roots of Hudson Valley Culture*. New York: Fordham University Press, 2010.

Planck, Jim. "1833: Colonization vs. Abolition in Catskill; Barbers Robert Jackson and Martin Cross Lead Black Voice against Liberia." *Greene County History* 46 (Spring 2022).

Richardson, Judith. *Possessions: The History and Uses of Haunting*. Cambridge, MA: Harvard University Press, 2003.

Ricks, Thomas E. *First Principles: What America's Founders Learned from the Greeks and Romans and How That Shaped Our Country*. New York: HarperCollins, 2020.

Rink, Oliver A. *Holland on the Hudson: An Economic and Social History of Dutch New York*. Ithaca, NY: Cornell University Press, 1986.

Rose, Ben Z. *Mother of Freedom: Mumbet and the Roots of Abolition*. Lincoln, MA: TreeLine Press, 2020.

Ross, Marc Howard. *Slavery in the North: Forgetting History and Recovering Memory*. Philadelphia: University of Pennsylvania Press, 2018.

Rothman, Joshua D. *The Ledger and the Chain: How Domestic Slave Traders Shaped America*. New York: Basic Books, 2021.

Rupert, Linda M. *Creolization and Contraband: Curaçao in the Early Modern Atlantic World*. Athens: University of Georgia Press, 2012.

Sachse, Julius F. *Justus Falckner: Mystic and Scholar*. Philadelphia, 1903.

Saint, Chandler B. *Venture Smith*. Torrington, CT: Beecher House Center for the Study of Equal Rights, 2018.

Schama, Simon. *Rough Crossings: The Slaves, the British, and the American Revolution*. New York: HarperCollins, 2005.

Sedgwick, Catharine Maria. "Slavery in New England." Originally appeared in *Bentley's Miscellany*, 1853. Available at http://loki.stockton.edu/~kinsellt/projects/sedgwick/storyReader$16.html (last updated June 7, 2006).

Seidule, Ty. *Robert E. Lee and Me: A Southerner's Reckoning with the Myth of the Lost Cause*. New York: St. Martin's, 2021.

Shorto, Russell. *The Island at the Center of the World*. New York: Doubleday, 2004.

——. *Revolution Song: A Story of American Freedom*. New York: Norton, 2018.

Sill, Dunkin H. "A Notable Example of Longevity." *New York Genealogical and Biographical Record* 56, no. 1 (January 1925): 65.

Smith, Clint. *How the Word Is Passed: A Reckoning with the History of Slavery across America*. New York: Little, Brown, 2021.

Stessin-Cohn, Susan, and Ashley Hurlburt-Biagini. *In Defiance: Runaways from Slavery in New York's Hudson River Valley, 1735–1831*. Delmar, NY: Black Dome Press, 2016.

Stewart, L. Lloyd. *A Far Cry from Freedom: Gradual Abolition (1799–1827)*. Bloomington, IN: AuthorHouse, 2005.

——. *The Mysterious Black Migration: 1800–1820*. Bloomington, IN: Xlibris, 2013.

Switala, William J. *Underground Railroad in New York and New Jersey*. Mechanicsburg, PA: Stackpole, 2006.

Taylor, Alan. *William Cooper's Town: Power and Persuasion on the Frontier of the Early American Republic*. New York: Vintage, 1995.

Thoreau, Henry David. *Walden; and, Civil Disobedience: Complete Texts with Introduction, Historical Contexts, Critical Essays*. Edited by Paul Lauter. Boston: Houghton Mifflin, 2000.

Twain, Mark. *Life on the Mississippi*. 1883. Project Gutenberg, 2018. https://www.gutenberg.org/files/245/245-h/245-h.htm.

Van der Donck, Adriaen. *A Description of New Netherland (the Iroquoians and Their World)*. Edited by Charles T. Gehring and William A. Starna. Lincoln: University of Nebraska Press, 2008.

Van der zee, Henri, and Barbara Van der zee. *A Sweet and Alien Land: The Story of Dutch New York*. New York: Viking, 1978.

Van Vechten, Peter, Jr. *The Genealogical Records of the Van Vechten's from 1638 to 1896*. Milwaukee, WI: Radtke Bros. & Kortsch, 1896.

Vedder, Jessie Van Vechten. *Historic Catskill*. Fawcett, 1922.

Venema, Janny. *Beverwijck: A Dutch Village on the American Frontier, 1652–1664*. Albany: State University of New York Press, 2003.

Washington, Margaret. *Sojourner Truth's America*. Urbana: University of Illinois Press, 2009.

Wells, Jonathan Daniel. *The Kidnapping Club: Wall Street, Slavery, and Resistance on the Eve of the Civil War*. New York: Bold Type, 2020.

Wermuth, Thomas S. *Rip Van Winkle's Neighbors: The Transformation of Rural Society in the Hudson River Valley, 1720–1850*. Albany: State University of New York Press, 2001.

White, Shane. *Somewhat More Independent: The End of Slavery in New York City, 1770–1810*. Athens: University of Georgia Press, 1991.

Wiencek, Henry. *The Hairstons: An American Family in Black and White*. New York: St. Martin's Griffin, 1999.

——. *An Imperfect God: George Washington, His Slaves, and the Creation of America*. New York: Farrar, Straus & Giroux, 2003.

Wilds, Mary. *Mumbet: The Life and Times of Elizabeth Freeman*. Greensboro, NC: Avisson, 1999.

Wilkerson, Isabel. *Caste: The Origins of Our Discontents*. New York: Random House, 2020.

Williams-Myers, A. J. *Long Hammering: Essays on the Forging of an African American Presence in the Hudson River Valley to the Early Twentieth Century*. Trenton, NJ: Africa World Press, 1994.

——. *On the Morning Tide: African Americans, History and Methodology in the Historical Ebb and Flow of the Hudson River Society*. Trenton, NJ: Africa World Press, 2003.

Woo, Ilyon. *Master Slave Husband Wife: An Epic Journey from Slavery to Freedom*. New York: Simon & Schuster, 2023.

Worthington, Glenn H. *Fighting for Time: The Battle of Monocacy*. Baltimore: Day Printing, 1932. Second edition revised by Brian C. Pohanka, 1985. Shippensburg, Pa: White Mane, 132.

Wynne, Annette. "Indian Children." In *Treasure Things*. New York: P. F. Volland, 1922.

Zilversmit, Arthur. *The First Emancipation: The Abolition of Slavery in the North*. Chicago: University of Chicago Press, 1967.

INDEX